Towards Inclusive Organizations

Diversity arising from the mixing of peoples from different cultural backgrounds has long been an issue in nations such as the United States and Australia, and, in recent decades, European nations have reached unprecedented levels of cultural diversity due to increased migration. This phenomenon of increasing cultural diversity at the national level sets the context for current social science research on the consequences of diversity for social integration, institutional functioning, and interpersonal relationships.

This book reviews theory and research in social and organizational psychology on the management of diversity in work organizations. The book shows how diversity management takes place across multiple levels: at a national level, at an organizational level, between workgroups and teams, in interpersonal relations, and at the level of individual experiences. Each chapter summarizes relevant empirical research and considers how the dynamics of workgroup relations are likely to be affected by cultural differences among group members. The contributors also describe the variables that organizational leadership should be sensitive to in designing and implementing policies and practices for inclusive organizations.

Towards Inclusive Organizations will be essential reading for researchers and advanced students in social and organizational psychology.

Sabine Otten is Professor at the University of Groningen, The Netherlands. Her research focuses upon social identity, group identification, intergroup biases, social integration, and (cultural) diversity.

Karen van der Zee is Dean of the Faculty of Social Sciences at VU University Amsterdam, The Netherlands, where she holds a chair in Intercultural Competence. She is also Professor of Organizational Psychology, Cultural Diversity, and Integration at the University of Groningen, The Netherlands. Her research focuses upon diversity management in organizations, integration issues in culturally diverse societies, and the measurement and development of intercultural competencies.

Marilynn B. Brewer was previously Professor at Ohio State University, USA before moving to the University of New South Wales, Australia in 2009. Her primary areas of research are the study of social identity, collective decision making, and intergroup relations and she is the author of numerous research articles and books in these areas.

Current Issues in Work and Organizational Psychology
Series Editor: Arnold B. Bakker

Current Issues in Work and Organizational Psychology is a series of edited books that reflect the state-of-the-art areas of current and emerging interest in the psychological study of employees, workplaces and organizations.

Each volume is tightly focused on a particular topic and consists of seven to ten chapters contributed by international experts. The editors of individual volumes are leading figures in their areas and provide an introductory overview.

Example topics include: digital media at work, work and the family, workaholism, modern job design, positive occupational health and individualised deals.

A Day in the Life of a Happy Worker
Edited by Arnold B. Bakker and Kevin Daniels

The Psychology of Digital Media at Work
Edited by Daantje Derks and Arnold B. Bakker

New Frontiers in Work and Family Research
Edited by Joseph G. Grzywacz and Evangelia Demerouti

Time and Work, Volume 1: How time impacts individuals
Edited by Abbie J. Shipp and Yitzhak Fried

Time and Work, Volume 2: How time impacts groups, organizations and methodological choices
Edited by Abbie J. Shipp and Yitzhak Fried

Burnout at Work: A psychological perspective
Edited by Michael P. Leiter, Arnold B. Bakker, and Christina Maslach

Towards Inclusive Organizations: Determinants of successful diversity management at work
Edited by Sabine Otten, Karen van der Zee, and Marilynn B. Brewer

Towards Inclusive Organizations
Determinants of successful diversity management at work

**Edited by Sabine Otten,
Karen van der Zee, and
Marilynn B. Brewer**

Ψ Psychology Press
Taylor & Francis Group

LONDON AND NEW YORK

First published 2015
by Psychology Press
27 Church Road, Hove, East Sussex BN3 2FA

and by Psychology Press
711 Third Avenue, New York, NY 10017

*Psychology Press is an imprint of the Taylor & Francis Group,
an informa business*

British Library Cataloguing in Publication Data
A catalogue record for this book is available from the British Library

Library of Congress Cataloging in Publication Data
Towards inclusive organizations : determinants of successful diversity
management at work / edited by Sabine Otten, Karen van der Zee,
Marilynn B. Brewer. – 1 Edition.
pages cm
Includes bibliographical references and index.
1. Diversity in the workplace. 2. Intercultural communication.
3. Personnel management. 4. Social psychology. I. Otten, Sabine,
editor of compilation. II. Zee, Karen van der, 1966– editor of
compilation. III. Brewer, Marilynn B., 1942– editor of compilation.
  HF5549.5.M5T693 2014 2015
   658.3008–dc23
                                                    2014006396

ISBN: 978-1-84872-189-0 (hbk)
ISBN: 978-1-84872-190-6 (pbk)
ISBN: 978-1-315-84938-6 (ebk)

Typeset in Times
by Graphicraft Limited, Hong Kong

Printed and bound in the United States of America by Publishers Graphics,
LLC on sustainably sourced paper.

Contents

Illustrations

Figures

Tables

Contributors

Christopher T. Begeny, University of California, Los Angeles, USA

Kevin R. Binning, University of Pittsburgh, USA

Marilynn B. Brewer, University of New South Wales, Australia

S. Alexander Haslam, The University of Queensland, Australia

Astrid C. Homan, University of Amsterdam, The Netherlands

Yuen J. Huo, University of California, Los Angeles, USA

Wiebren S. Jansen, University of Groningen, The Netherlands

Daan van Knippenberg, Rotterdam School of Management, The Netherlands

Sabine Otten, University of Groningen, The Netherlands

Paul B. Paulus, University of Texas at Arlington, USA

Kim Peters, University of Exeter, UK

Jan Pieter van Oudenhoven, University of Groningen, The Netherlands

Michelle K. Ryan, University of Exeter, UK

Niklas K. Steffens, The University of Queensland, Australia

Maykel Verkuyten, University of Utrecht/ERCOMER, The Netherlands

Thomas de Vroome, University of Leuven, Belgium

Karen van der Zee, VU University Amsterdam and University of Groningen, The Netherlands

1 Towards inclusive organizations

Introduction

*Marilynn B. Brewer, Sabine Otten, and
Karen van der Zee*

It is by now something of a truism to acknowledge that modern societies are both complex and diverse. Within modern nation-states, diversity is manifest along many dimensions, including demographic, economic, and ideological differences. Of the many sources of population diversity, however, the dimension that receives the most political (and often emotional) attention is that of *cultural diversity*.

Broadly defined, culture is a system of shared meanings and understandings, together with a set of practices that enact and reinforce the shared worldviews (Triandis, 1972). A critical element in this definition is that culture involves *shared* understandings among people who see themselves as part of a meaningful collective with some sense of shared identity, temporal continuity, and social interdependence. Cultures provide group members with answers to fundamental questions, including questions of self and identity (Who am I?, or Who are we?), questions about how the physical and social world works and how things are interrelated (beliefs), and questions about how things should be and what is the right course of behavior (values) (Brewer & Chen, 2007). Seen from this perspective, cultural systems (and cultural differences) can arise from any meaningful social groupings, including gender, age cohorts, professions, trades, and other occupational groupings and social institutions. But, in both public discourse and the social science literature, culture is associated primarily with national and ethnic identities and heritage groups, and it is this source of cultural diversity that will be the focus of the present volume.

Diversity arising from the mixing of peoples from different ethnic/national cultural backgrounds has long been an issue for historically "immigrant nations," such as the United States and Australia. In recent decades, European nations have also reached unprecedented levels of cultural diversity as a consequence of patterns of migration. In 2010, 47.3 million people living in the European Union (EU), or 9.4 percent of the total population, had been born outside their resident country. Of these, 31.4 million (6.3 percent) had been born outside the EU, with the largest absolute numbers of people born outside the EU in Germany (6.4 million), France (5.1 million), the United Kingdom (4.7 million), Spain (4.1 million), Italy (3.2 million), and the Netherlands (1.4 million) (Vasileva, 2011). In many countries, the presence of a majority subculture is gradually giving way to demographic changes whereby no single cultural group constitutes a numerical majority. In the US, for example, recent waves of immigration from Asian and Latin American countries, combined with existing cultural minorities (African-Americans, Native Americans), are projected to equal or outnumber the population of white European-Americans by 2040. This phenomenon of increasing cultural diversity at the national level sets the context for current social science research on the consequences and effective management of diversity.

Diversity in the workplace

Cultural diversity at the national level inevitably leads to increasing cultural diversity among employees of large business organizations, educational institutions, government agencies, and other workplace environments. Again, workplace diversity can be defined along many different dimensions—gender, age and tenure, educational background, etc.—but diversity in cultural background has proven to be the most salient and challenging form of diversity for managers, policy makers, and social scientists. Given that ethnic segregation of residential neighbourhoods is still common, even in highly diverse communities, work provides the context in which individuals are most likely to come into close contact with other individuals from different cultural backgrounds. The workplace is thus the crucible in which intercultural relations in diverse societies are being tested. Effective management of diversity in work organizations has direct implications for both economic productivity and intergroup relationships in the society at large.

Within the social science literature, there are two overarching perspectives on the study of consequences of cultural diversity in the workplace. One is commonly referred to as the value-in-diversity perspective (e.g. Van Knippenberg & Haslam, 2003) which represents the upside of diversity in terms of potential benefits for both individuals and organizations. The basic idea is that differences in cultural traditions imply differences in how issues are conceptualized, what perspectives are brought to problem-solving and goal pursuit, and how solutions are generated and evaluated. Thus, communication across cultural lines increases the range of ideas and cognitive resources that can be brought to bear for purposes of problem-solving, innovation, and planning, as well as benefits for working with diverse clientele. At the individual level, extended contact with other cultures has been found to enhance cognitive flexibility and creativity (Leung et al., 2008). At the group level, diversity is assumed to enhance elaboration of task-relevant information and perspectives within the group, which has a beneficial effect on team functioning (e.g. Kooij-de Bode et al., 2008). Consequently, and because people with different backgrounds and experiences bring unique perspectives to a problem, one might expect demographically diverse teams to be more innovative (e.g. Egan, 2005; Holtzman & Anderberg, 2011; Lubart, 2010).

The second perspective on the study of the consequences of cultural diversity derives from social psychological research and theory on social categorization and social identity, and reflects the potential downside of diversity. Social categorization is implicit in the conceptualization of diversity. According to the social identity theory perspective (Tajfel, 1978), all social categorizations involve a further distinction between ingroups (categories to which the perceiver belongs) and outgroups (categories to which the perceiver does not belong). Social categories, in effect, create we–they, us–them distinctions. When such categorizations also have emotional significance for an individual's self-concept (ingroup identification), the motivational components of ingroup–outgroup distinctions are engaged. These include ingroup loyalties and favoritism, implicit intergroup rivalries, and negative stereotypes and distrust of outgroup members (Brewer, 1979; Tajfel, 1978). When cultural identities are salient in workgroup contexts, these intergroup processes conspire to impede coordination among members of diverse work teams, reduce effective performance, and lead to a failure to take advantage of the potential benefits of diverse perspectives.

These two perspectives on the consequences of diversity are not competing theories but rather represent two sides of the same coin. There is an inevitable tension between the value of airing differences for the sake of innovation and the risk of activating ingroup–outgroup differentiation. On the one hand, intercultural contact carries the potential for increasing cognitive resources, innovation, and effective problem-solving. On the other hand, confronting differences in worldviews, values, and normative practices challenges individuals' tolerance for uncertainty and cognitive flexibility and may be seen as threatening to the self and the cultural ingroup. For members of the dominant majority cultural group, threat arises from change in traditional ways of doing things and potential loss of cultural hegemony and privilege. Minority group members face both threat of discrimination from the majority and loss of own cultural identity from pressures to accommodate the dominant culture. Perceived threat in turn elicits resistance, derogation, and hostility toward outgroup members, and/or alienation from the organization. The challenge for diversity management, then, is to recognize the dual-edged nature of diversity effects and to implement policies and practices that will minimize ingroup–outgroup processes and capitalize on the benefits of difference.

The present volume: an overview

This volume represents a collective effort to bring theory, empirical findings, and insights from social and organizational psychology research to bear on the challenges of cultural diversity in the workplace. The contributors share a view that successful diversity management lies in creation of inclusive organizations wherein employees from both majority *and* minority cultural backgrounds feel safely included and appreciated and, accordingly, function equally well. While our focus is on work organizations, we recognize that diversity management takes place across multiple levels—at the societal or national level, at the level of the organization as a whole or of intraorganizational work groups and teams, or interpersonal relations within the workgroup, and at the level of individual experiences. Furthermore, we recognize that there are mutual causal relationships influencing the effectiveness of policies and practices across levels. Shared understandings and multicultural policies at the national level constrain and shape the demands that organizations face in creating and implementing effective management, and also influence the attitudes toward diversity that individuals bring with them to the workplace. Official policies and cultural climate at the organizational level impact working relationships at the level of the workgroup and team, which most directly determine the nature of experiences with diversity at the individual level. The experienced consequences of participating in a diverse workplace shape the attitudes and beliefs that individual members of majority and minority cultural groups bring to the national discourse on multiculturalism and thus feed back into national politics and policies.

In recognition of the multi-level structure of diversity management, the organization of the present volume reflects a progression from societal, to organizational, to work team, to individual levels of analysis. In Chapter 2, De Vroome and Verkuyten set the stage by highlighting the importance of economic integration (education and employment) as a determinant of national identification on the part of members of immigrant groups. For many cultural minorities, participation in the workplace is their primary point of contact with the national culture, and experiences in the workplace shape their feelings of national belonging and acceptance. Unemployment or underemployment are associated with alienation from the national identity, while successful participation in education and employment settings promotes positive identification with the nation. The authors point out, however, that there is a dual-edged nature to the consequences of work participation—what they refer to as the "integration paradox." On the one hand, high education and employment status is associated with social integration, which is positively correlated with national identification. On the other hand, high education and employment status increases exposure to discriminatory practices and outcomes resulting in feelings of relative deprivation that lead to negative attitudes and cynicism toward the host nation.

This insight regarding the integration paradox underscores the critical role that work organizations play in the success of multiculturalism at the national level. Effective integration of minority cultural identities and cultural perspectives in the workplace is essential to overcoming the integration paradox. The four chapters that follow de Vroome and Verkuyten review factors at the level of organizational policies, procedures, and climate that influence whether the workplace provides an inclusive environment and associated effects of cultural diversity for both majority and minority group members.

In Chapter 3, Van der Zee and Otten review alternative perspectives on diversity at the organizational level. Analyses of diversity policies often begin with a distinction between so-called "colorblind" ideology, which advocates evaluation and treatment of employees based solely on individual merit, and multicultural (or "colorful") ideology, which explicitly acknowledges and values cultural differences. Van der Zee and Otten expand upon this overly simplified distinction, recognizing more subtle variations in orientations toward diversity and diversity policies across organizations. Building from Ely and Thomas's (2001) differentiation among three types of diversity orientations, Van der Zee and Otten distinguish five different perspectives that vary in terms of underlying philosophy, evaluation of diversity, and the determinants of fit between the individual and the organization. They point out that preferences among these alternative models may differ between members of majority and minority cultural groups. Ultimately they advocate for an approach that can be regarded as an extension of the integration-and-learning perspective by Ely and Thomas (2001), which may avoid negative responses among both majority and minority members in that it departs from a definition of diversity limited to cultural background and includes other dimensions such as competencies, age, or gender. This extended integration-and-learning perspective goes beyond a focus on fair treatment, to openly acknowledge and encourage differences, in order to achieve added value and mutual learning from diversity.

As a complement to the focus on organizational policies in Chapter 3, the succeeding chapter by Huo, Binning, and Begeny calls attention to procedures and practices in an organization that convey *respect* for individual employees and their significant group memberships. Respect is defined as feelings of being valued by other group members and by the group as a collective. Huo and colleagues discuss three manifestations of experienced respect that might be particularly relevant to the culturally diverse workplace—personal respect (feelings of being valued by the organization as an individual group member), subgroup respect (perceived valuing of one's important membership groups, such as ethnic group, *within* the organization), and intragroup respect (feelings of being valued by other members of one's own ethnic subgroup in the workplace environment). The authors review results of empirical research assessing the role played by all three types of felt respect in contributing to institutional commitment and personal well being among members of majority and minority ethnic groups. Findings indicate that felt personal respect is an important determinant of feelings of belonging and commitment to the organization on the part of both majorities and minorities, but subgroup respect and intragroup respect are uniquely important to members of minority cultural groups. The authors conclude by suggesting that treatment by institutional authorities in the form of procedural fairness and the way in which multicultural policies are conveyed and implemented are critical to meeting employees' needs for respect at all three levels.

In Chapter 5, Otten and Jansen continue the theme of felt respect and value as important components of the experience of *inclusion* in an organization. The authors emphasize that creating an inclusive organization involves more than reducing or eliminating discrimination or exclusion of minority groups. They develop a two-dimensional conceptualization of inclusion that contends that the subjective experience of inclusion requires both a sense of belonging *and* of individual authenticity. If achieving a sense of belonging comes at the perceived expense of expressing one's idiosyncratic personality, opinions, or skills in the workplace, the failure of the organization to acknowledge and value authenticity means that it does not meet the definition of full inclusion. From this perspective, creating an inclusive environment requires organizational policies and practices that provide employees with both social identity (organizational belonging) and personal identity within the work context. Like Van der Zee and Otten, this chapter points out that diversity policy orientations may have different implications for minority and majority cultural group members with respect to these two needs. A strictly color blind ideology may convey valuing of individual authenticity but reduces perceived belonging for cultural minorities who do not fully fit the normative expectations represented by the dominant culture. On the other hand, multicultural approaches that explicitly value cultural difference may enhance feelings of belonging for cultural minorities but at the same time *reduce* experienced inclusion for majority group members (Plaut et al., 2011). Successful diversity management thus rests on finding a fine balance between fulfilling the inclusion needs of both minority and majority groups.

A programmatic approach to achieving a successful balance between valuing difference and creating a shared organizational identity is described in the next chapter by Peters, Haslam, Ryan, and Steffens. Starting from a social identity theory perspective, the authors note that successful integration within a diverse organization requires nurturing dual identification, i.e. simultaneous identification with the organization as a superordinate group identity and with one's important subgroup(s) within that organization. For dual identification to be successful, individuals must perceive that the values and goals of the organization are aligned with those of their valued subgroups. The authors' ASPIRe model for organizational leadership prescribes a process for building a shared organizational identity through consultation with and collaboration among component organizational subgroups. Although the ASPIRe program is not specific to cultural subgroups, the participatory, "bottom-up" strategy for developing organizational goals and policies is consistent with the ideas presented in the preceding chapters for creating inclusive organizations that can harness the benefits of cultural diversity.

Organizational policy statements and practices set the tone for working relationships within the diverse organization, but it is at the level of the work group or team that individual employees experience the effects of diversity most directly. How policies of inclusion and integration are implemented "on the ground" ultimately determine whether members of different cultural subgroups feel the belonging and respect that are essential to inclusion. It is also at this level that the benefits of diversity of perspectives and resources are most likely to be realized, if at all.

The value-added perspective on diversity is particularly relevant to the performance of work teams charged with creative innovation and problem-solving. Interacting teams provide the setting in which diverse perspectives can be expressed and shared. In Chapter 7, Paulus and Van der Zee review the research literature on team creativity to explore the conditions under which diverse teams will, indeed, be more creative than homogeneous work groups. Although the link between diversity and creativity is a positive one in theory, its realization in practice depends on whether team members actually do express diverging ideas and whether diverse ideas are elaborated on and accepted in the group process. Research on the effects of cultural diversity on team performance has shown mixed results, due in part to negative social reactions that can be associated with this form of diversity in face-to-face groups. Paulus and Van der Zee outline the major processes involved in creative performance and some key moderators of the impact of diversity on these processes and on actual creative outcomes in teams.

Importantly, they point out, whether culturally diverse groups produce more novel ideas than culturally homogeneous groups will depend on whether differences in cultural experiences and perspectives are relevant to the task at hand. This issue of match between diversity and task is largely neglected in the literature on the value of diversity. But, even if novel ideas are produced and aired in the idea-generation stage of team process, social and motivational factors determine whether and to what extent these ideas are attended to, elaborated, and ultimately accepted by the team as a whole. Among the potential moderators of creative outcomes, Paulus and Van der Zee highlight three that appear to be particularly important for multicultural teams. One of these is the extent of shared experience as a team, with experience likely to be associated with group cohesion and shared understandings that allow the group to bond along the dimensions they have in common while accepting differences in other dimensions. A second factor is whether group members have a positive attitude toward working in diverse groups and believe in the value of diversity as a contributor to performance. Finally, a third critical factor is elements of group climate that foster psychological safety in groups—the extent to which group or team members feel free to express their ideas without concern for negative consequences. Conditions that promote shared identification with the team, shared goals, and interpersonal trust are essential to overcoming resistance to differences and capitalizing on the positive potential of diversity.

In Chapter 8, Homan and Van Knippenberg discuss one of the social factors that may inhibit successful exchange and integration of information in culturally diverse teams. This is the spectre of ingroup–outgroup differentiation that arises when social category distinctions are salient in the work group context. Category salience is enhanced when the group compositional structure is characterized by "diversity fault lines," where different dimensions of diversity are aligned or convergent (Lau & Murnighan, 1998). Diversity fault lines have negative effects on team functioning to the degree that they lead team members to split up into homogeneous subgroups, with potential distrust and negativity between subgroups reducing cohesion, communication, and the development of shared understandings.

Although carefully composing work teams to avoid potential fault lines is one approach to this problem, Homan and Van Knippenberg point out that dormant fault lines (potential fault lines that exist based on objectively measured demographic characteristics) do not necessarily have to become active in the form of subgroup differentiation. If team members do not experience the fault line, it will also not affect their attitudes, cognitions, and behaviors. Homan and Van Knippenberg suggest a number of factors that may serve to "de-activate" dormant faultlines, including the presence of strong shared goals and superordinate identity, clarity of shared objectives and task interdependence, leadership styles that promote individual and relational orientations, and positive attitudes toward diversity. Thus, many of the characteristics of organizational and team climate that have been highlighted in preceding chapters are also implicated in avoiding the negative effects of ingroup–outgroup categorization within teams.

The final chapter of this volume turns attention to the interface between organizational diversity and individual characteristics. Strategies for creating an inclusive organizational climate have to take into account the fact that individuals differ in their degree of preparation for and openness to intercultural experience. In Chapter 9, Van Oudenhoven, Van der Zee, and Paulus review individual differences in personality and dispositions that relate to intercultural competence. Drawing from the research literature on cross-national intercultural experience, the authors identify individual level variables that might be particularly relevant to intercultural effectiveness in the workplace. Three types of individual difference variables are highlighted– intercultural personality traits (specifically, cultural empathy, social initiative, emotional stability, flexibility, and open-mindedness), attachment style (particularly the role of secure attachment in promoting integration and acculturation), and attitudes toward workplace diversity. Together, these characteristics help predict whether individuals will be open to or threatened by intercultural exchange, whether they will seek out intercultural experiences, and how much they will benefit from exposure to different ideas and perspectives.

Although personality dispositions are generally considered something an individual brings with him/herself to the workplace context, workplace policies and organizational climate can be more or less sensitive to these individual characteristics. Managing a culturally diverse institution may be relatively easy with a workforce characterized by secure attachment style, high openness to experience, emotional stability, and positive attitudes toward the value of diversity. The challenge of diversity management is that of reaching and engaging employees (from both majority and minority cultural groups) whose background experiences, personality dispositions, and attitudes make them more likely to be threatened by or antagonistic to a multicultural workplace. Again, the factors associated with creating an inclusive organization— shared identity, secure belonging with room for authenticity, individual and subgroup respect, diversity values, and psychological safety in workgroups— may all be critical to overcoming personality-based resistance to intercultural effectiveness.

This final chapter brings us full circle in linking individual, interpersonal, organizational, and societal levels of analysis. Creating inclusive organizations where cultural diversity is successfully mobilized requires integration across all four levels. Both top-down and bottom-up strategies must be engaged to ensure that values, goals, and practices that promote effective multiculturalism are aligned across the levels of organizational leadership and policies, workgroup climate and procedures, and individual experience.

Some concluding perspectives

The contents of this volume represent a sampling of the current state-of-the-art research and theory in social and organizational psychology related to cultural diversity in the workplace. This is an evolving area in our understanding of human social relations, and as a consequence there are many yet unresolved issues and many questions yet to be raised, let alone answered. Nevertheless there are some interesting points of convergence among the recommendations presented in the various chapters in this volume. Whether focusing on organizational policies, work team processes, or individual attitudes and experiences, the message is clear that achieving an inclusive organizational environment is critical to engendering commitment to the organization, adherence to organizational norms, and personal wellbeing of employees from both majority and minority cultural groups. Importantly, all chapters acknowledge the inevitable tensions between different goals, motives, and psychological needs involved in this endeavor. Successful diversity management requires finding an appropriate balance between meeting needs for belonging and for individual recognition, between the goals of achieving a shared identity and acknowledging and valuing group differences, between leadership and participatory processes, and between the ideals represented in colorblind and multicultural values.

The complexity of these issues makes the translation from theory to practice a challenging one. However, as this volume illustrates, social and organizational psychology research can provide insights on the potential consequences of various approaches to cultural diversity in the workplace, how the dynamics of workgroup relations are likely to be affected by cultural differences among group members, and what variables organizational leadership should be sensitive to in designing and implementing policies and practices. These insights, we hope, will be helpful for organizations that are striving to become more inclusive. Ultimately we need more systematic research evaluating the outcomes of specific diversity management practices in situ to link theories of inclusiveness to managerial best practices.

Acknowledgement

The plan for this book was inspired by a large-scale research program on cultural diversity at the workplace. The program was driven by the question under what conditions cultural diversity at the work place may contribute to the integration of cultural minorities in society. Part of the research outcomes are reported in chapters 2, 3, 5 and 9 of this volume. The research program was made possible by a grant from "Instituut Gak," awarded to Karen van der Zee and Sabine Otten. "Instituut Gak" is a Dutch non-profit organization that supports projects and research focusing on social security and labor market issues in the Netherlands.

References

Brewer, M. B. (1979). In-group bias in the minimal intergroup situation: A cognitive-motivational analysis. *Psychological Bulletin, 86,* 307–324.

Brewer, M. B. & Chen, Y. (2007). Where (who) are collectives in collectivism: Toward a conceptual clarification of individualism and collectivism. *Psychological Review, 114,* 133–151.

Egan, T. M. (2005). Creativity in the context of team diversity: Team leader perspectives. *Advances in Developing Human Resources, 7*(2), 207–225.

Ely, R. J. & Thomas, D. A. (2001). Cultural diversity at work: The effects of diversity perspectives on work group processes and outcomes. *Administrative Science Quarterly, 46,* 229–273.

Holtzman, Y. & Anderberg, J. (2011). Diversify your teams and collaborate: Because great minds don't think alike. *Journal of Management Development, 30*(1), 75–92.

Kooij-de Bode, H. J., Van Knippenberg, D., & Van Ginkel, W. P. (2008). Ethnic diversity and distributed information in group decision making: The importance of information elaboration. *Group Dynamics: Theory, Research, and Practice, 12*(4), 307.

Lau, D. C. & Murnighan, J. K. (1998). Demographic diversity and faultlines: The compositional dynamics of organizational groups. *Academy of Management Review, 23*(2), 325–340.

Leung, K. Y., Maddux, W. M., Galinsky, A. D., & Chiu, C. Y. (2008). Multicultural experience enhances creativity: The when and how. *American Psychologist, 63,* 169–181.

Lubart, T. (2010). Cross-cultural perspectives on creativity. In J. C. Kaufman & R. J. Sternberg (Eds.), *The Cambridge handbook of creativity* (pp. 265–278). New York: Cambridge University Press.

Plaut, V. C., Garnett, F. G., Buffardi, L. E., & Sanchez-Burks, J. (2011). "What about me?" Perceptions of exclusion and whites' reactions to multiculturalism. *Journal of Personality and Social Psychology, 101*(2), 337–353. doi:10.1037/a0022832.

Tajfel, H. (1978). The psychological structure of intergroup relations. In: H. Tajfel (Ed.), *Differentiation between social groups: Studies in the social psychology of intergroup relations*. London: Academic Press.

Triandis, H. C. (1972). *The analysis of subjective culture*. New York: Wiley.

Van Knippenberg, D. & Haslam, S. A. (2003). Realizing the diversity divided: Exploring the subtle interplay between identity, ideology and reality. In: S. A. Haslam, D. Van Knippenberg, M. Platow, & N. Ellemers (Eds.), *Social identity at work: Developing theory for organizational practice*. New York: Taylor & Francis.

Vasileva, K. (2011). Population and social conditions. *eurostat, 34/2011*; http://epp.eurostat.ec.europa.eu/cache/ITY_OFFPUB/KS-SF-11-034/EN/KS-SF-11-034-EN.PDF.

2 Labour market participation and immigrants' acculturation

Thomas de Vroome and Maykel Verkuyten

Cultural diversity is a fact of modern life and a challenge for organizations and institutions. Diversity can lead to a lack of commitment and feelings of belonging together, which are prerequisites for the successful functioning of organizations and institutions. There is evidence that higher cultural diversity is related to reduced social cohesion and more conflict in work groups, and to lower organizational commitment (e.g. Milliken & Martins, 1996; Watson *et al.*, 1998). Yet, there also is evidence that diversity has positive outcomes on productivity, creativity, innovation and learning potential of work groups in the workplace (Ely & Thomas, 2001). The different chapters in this book extensively discuss the various determinants of successful diversity management at work and the conditions for inclusive organizations.

An additional question relates to the relevance of being part of the workforce for feeling appreciated and included in society. Cultural diversity is not only a challenge for organizations but also for the cohesion and unity of societies. Politicians and the media often claim that many immigrants have divided loyalties and a lack of attachment to the host society and therefore undermine a cohesive national identity. In European countries, there is a renewed societal emphasis on traditional national values and scrutinizing immigrants for their assimilation to a set of 'core values' and their loyalty to the host nation (see Kundnani, 2007; Vasta, 2007). Leading politicians have argued that a shared sense of nationhood would be (part of) the solution to the lack of social cohesion and stability (see Kundnani, 2007; Uberoi, 2008).

Proponents of multiculturalism argue that a society cannot ignore the demands of cultural diversity because minority group members need and deserve cultural recognition and affirmation (Taylor, 1992). Ignoring these demands would provoke resistance, create suspicions and threaten the very unity that assimilationists seek (Modood, 2007; Parekh, 2000). At the same time these proponents argue that unity and a shared national identity is equally important. A well-functioning society needs a sense of commitment and common belonging, making it important to foster a spirit of shared identity.

A prevalent and widely shared assumption is that structural integration (participation and achievement in the education system and in the labour market) is a key factor for developing a sense of national belonging among

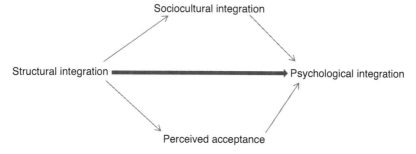

Figure 2.1 Overview of the relations discussed in this chapter.

immigrants. Through education and work immigrants would feel accepted and develop social contacts with majority group members which, in turn, contribute to a sense of belonging. This assumption is in line with classic assimilation theories in sociology which assume that structural integration drives cultural and social integration, with immigrants' identification with the host society forming the last step in the integration process (e.g. Gordon, 1964). In these theories the terms 'integration' and 'assimilation' are used for the process of economic and sociocultural incorporation in the country of settlement and do not specify a particular acculturation position as in Berry's (1997) acculturation model.

In this chapter we discuss the importance of structural integration for immigrants'[1] sense of host national belonging (psychological integration) and we consider the mediating roles of social integration and perceived acceptance (see Figure 2.1). For this we use empirical research on samples of immigrants that differ in educational level, employment and occupational status. Specifically, we focus on large-scale survey research among migrant groups, particularly in the Netherlands.

Integration processes

There are many studies that examine cultural diversity in organizations and institutions and in relation to productivity, creativity, innovation, team relations and organizational commitment (see, for overviews, Paulus and Van der Zee, Chapter 7 this volume; Homan and Van Knippenberg, Chapter 8 this volume). There is also quite some social psychological research on the impact of diversity ideologies like multiculturalism, colour-blindness and assimilation on intergroup relations (see Deaux & Verkuyten, 2013; Rattan & Ambady, 2013). This literature focuses on the normative and identity-supporting or -threatening implications that these ideologies have.

The focus in the sociological migration and integration literature is different. The early research used an assimilation perspective by arguing that immigrant integration is a gradual, long-term process of generational change (Gordon, 1964; Park, 1950). The assimilation perspective lost much of its popularity after the 1960s but in more recent years social scientists have argued that it is necessary to seriously rethink and rehabilitate assimilation theory as an alternative to multiculturalism (e.g. Alba & Nee, 1997; Brubaker, 2001; Gans, 2007). These scholars argue that integration implies a set of interrelated processes of incorporation in different domains. According to Esser (2003), for example, immigrants' adaptation to the host society consists of integration in four domains: the structural, cultural, social and psychological domain. Structural integration involves educational achievements and participation in the labour market. The process of cultural integration concerns the learning of cultural codes, customs and language that enable meaningful interaction with others in society. Social integration refers to the establishment of social contacts and relationships across ethnic boundaries, and with majority members in particular. Psychological integration is defined as the development of an emotional relationship with the host society, including national identification and feelings of loyalty and trust.

Most researchers agree that these domains do not necessarily represent stages that follow each other in a fixed order (Alba & Nee, 1997; Brubaker, 2001; Esser, 2003). For example, having a job can contribute to learning the host language, but learning the language can also contribute to finding a job. And having a job can lead to developing social contacts with majority members, while these contacts also contribute to immigrants' economic success (Kanas & Van Tubergen, 2009). Yet, most agree that structural integration is an important first step in the integration process. This comes from the idea that improving economic conditions is a central motive for migrating to a new country in the first place. Indeed, a main explanation of immigrants' settlement intentions revolves around economic incentives, based on the difference between economic opportunities in the origin country and the host society (Constant & Massey, 2003; Dustmann & Weiss, 2007). Following human capital theory, it is argued that migrants try to maximize the returns to their individual skills by moving from one country to another, taking migration costs into account (Constant & Massey, 2003; Jensen & Pedersen, 2007). The material benefits of structural integration subsequently provide the motivation to stay in the host country and to invest in cultural, social and psychological integration. Furthermore, education and employment in the host country facilitate immigrants' contact opportunities and the development of inter-ethnic relationships. In turn, these relationships can lead to a stronger sense of belonging to the national category (see Figure 2.1).

Structural integration can also be an important determinant of feeling included in society because of the contributions that one makes. There is a research tradition that relates unemployment and poverty to reduced social integration and mental well-being (Bohnke, 2008; Strandh, 2000). Being economically unsuccessful makes people feel 'left out' and leads to disengagement from society (Heath & Roberts, 2006). In contrast, people who participate economically and are more successful on the labour market will have a feeling that they contribute to society, and will more easily be accepted because they are perceived as making a contribution. As a result they can feel that they belong and 'fit in'. Especially among immigrants, having a job and educational achievements confirm that one is a valued member who makes a useful contribution (Hagendoorn *et al.*, 2003). This means that immigrants' structural integration in the host country can lead to feelings of belonging.

Most researchers examining domains of integration argue that psychological integration is the most demanding and not likely to develop before considerable advances have been made in structural, cultural and social integration. Psychological integration would occur later and would be more difficult than integration in the other domains (e.g. Snauwaert *et al.*, 2003). Finding a job, learning the language or establishing relations with majority members is something different than developing a sense of belonging and feeling emotionally connected to the host society. Learning new customs, norms and values calls on different skills and needs than establishing social relations and changing your sense of group belonging (see Van Oudenhoven *et al.*, Chapter 9). It is probably easier to find a job, develop bicultural competences and form ethnically mixed networks, than to really feel emotionally connected with a new community.

Immigrants' national and ethnic identification

Cross-national research shows that in almost all countries immigrants have lower host national identification than majority group members (e.g. Elkins & Sides, 2007; Staerklé *et al.*, 2010). In addition, immigrants' identification with their ethnic group tends to be considerably stronger than their host national identification (e.g. De Vroome, Verkuyten, *et al.*, 2014). This is in agreement with the social identity perspective (Tajfel & Turner, 1986) that argues that members of minority groups value the distinctiveness of their ethnic identity.

It is not clear how the difference in national identification between immigrants and majority members should be explained. Research has shown that legal, structural, political and social factors play a role in immigrants' national identification. For example, having citizenship, being of a later generation, length of stay in the country, higher host language proficiency and more social contacts with majority members have all been found to be associated with stronger host national identification (e.g. Heath & Roberts, 2006; Walters *et al.*, 2007; Zimmermann *et al.*, 2007). Yet, research that takes these kinds of factors into account shows diverse patterns of national identification of immigrant groups. For example, in our study among Turkish and Moroccan migrants we found that the former but not the latter had lower national identification than Dutch natives (De Vroome, Verkuyten, *et al.*, 2014). Research in other countries has also shown that some groups (e.g. African Americans, and Black Caribbeans in the UK) have lower national identification than the majority, while other immigrant groups (e.g. Mexican Americans, and Indians in the UK) do not (Heath & Roberts, 2006; Sidanius *et al.*, 1997).

Furthermore, the relatively high ethnic identification of immigrants does not necessarily mean that it contradicts a sense of national belonging. Indeed, the mean national identity scores for migrant groups are typically above the neutral midpoint of the scale, indicating a moderate sense of belonging (e.g. Elkins & Sides, 2007). A strong ethnic identification can form the backdrop against which a moderate level of national identification acquires self-relevance. In addition, in our study it turned out that ethnic and national identification were unrelated. This indicates that immigrants can value and take pride in their ethnic identity without this necessarily being associated with lower levels of national commitment (De Vroome, Verkuyten, *et al.*, 2014; but see Verkuyten & Yildiz, 2007). This finding is in line with international studies which show that ethnic identification and national identification are two relatively independent aspects of minorities' identity (Staerklé *et al.*, 2010). Moreover, results from another study among Turkish and Moroccan migrants in the Netherlands show that both national identification and ethnic identification are positively and independently associated with levels of life satisfaction (De Vroome & Hooghe, 2013). These findings suggest that not only ethnic belongingness but also feelings of national belonging are important for minorities' subjective well-being.

Structural integration and host national belonging

Relatively few studies have examined the relation between immigrants' structural integration and their feelings of belonging to the host society. Furthermore, the findings of these studies are not consistent, with some demonstrating no association (Walters *et al.*, 2007; Zimmermann *et al.*, 2007) and others finding that structural integration contributes to psychological integration (Heath & Roberts, 2006; Nesdale, 2002). This mixed evidence is partly due to the different operationalizations of national identification as well as the different national contexts and the minority groups considered.

Our research in the Netherlands provides clear support for the assumption that structural integration is positively related to immigrants' psychological integration. For host national identification, a large-scale study among first- and second-generation Turkish and Moroccan immigrants showed that being employed is positively associated with national identification. This was found for both immigrant groups and also for the comparison group of native Dutch (De Vroome, Verkuyten, *et al.*, 2014). Furthermore, occupational status was positively related to national identification for immigrants but not for natives. A second study among refugee groups in the Netherlands also showed that structural integration fosters national identification (De Vroome *et al.*, 2011).

Researchers have argued that a sense of national belonging has a civic dimension consisting of feelings of solidarity towards others in society and trust in the democratic and political institutions of society (Esser, 2003; Heath & Roberts, 2006). The importance of economic integration is substantiated when we look at levels of social and institutional trust. For example, a research among Turkish and Moroccan immigrants and Dutch natives indicates that for all three groups education level, occupational status and financial security are positively associated with generalized social trust and trust in political institutions of the host society (De Vroome *et al.*, 2013). This is in line with previous research that shows that socio-economic attainment is positively related to trust in others in society (Alesina & La Ferrara, 2002; Delhey & Newton, 2003).

It is also interesting to investigate whether structural integration in society is associated with feelings of subjective well-being, such as life satisfaction. In general, research shows that there is a positive but relatively weak association between income and life satisfaction (Headey *et al.*, 2004; Moghaddam, 2008). Yet, when measures are used that assess people's perceived sense of economic well-being and financial security, a stronger relation between (perceived) economic position and life satisfaction is found (Headey *et al.*, 2004; Moghaddam, 2008). Moreover, recent research suggests that the impact of one's economic position on life satisfaction is greater for immigrants than for natives (Bartram, 2011; Olgiati *et al.*, in press). In a study among people of Turkish and Moroccan background in the Netherlands, we found that labour market integration and higher occupational status are associated with higher life satisfaction in the host society (De Vroome & Hooghe, 2013).

The notion that structural integration may be more consequential for the well-being of immigrants than for natives is reflected in our analyses on national identification. Having a job is associated with higher national identification among immigrants, refugees and natives, but only among the former two groups is higher occupational status associated with higher national identification (De Vroome *et al.*, 2011; De Vroome, Verkuyten, *et al.*, 2014). These results indicate that structural integration – in terms of participating in the labour market and attaining a higher-status position – generally increases the host national identification of immigrants and refugees. Having work and having a job with higher status provides a sense of achievement and of making a contribution, which especially among immigrants can translate into feelings of inclusion and host national belonging (Hagendoorn *et al.*, 2003). For the Dutch natives, 'only' the unemployed were found to form a specific group of concern, which corresponds to research that suggests that the economically marginalized feel 'left out' in society (Heath & Roberts, 2006).

Assimilation theory in sociology argues that immigrants gradually lose their distinctive ethnic identity as a consequence of structural integration in the new society. Migrants would converge into the mainstream leading to a 'decline, and at its endpoint the disappearance, of an ethnic/racial distinction and the cultural and social differences that express it' (Alba & Nee, 1997, p. 863). This would mean that higher structural integration is not only associated with higher host national identification but also with lower ethnic identification. Unfortunately there is very little research on this question. Furthermore, some studies use the Moreno question in which national and ethnic identification are opposites of a scale making it impossible to examine both group identifications separately (e.g. Maliepaard *et al.*, 2010). In one of our studies on Turkish and Moroccan migrants we assessed ethnic identification separately and found that higher structural integration (participation in the labour market and occupational status) is related to lower ethnic identification (De Vroome & Hooghe, 2013). This suggests that structural integration can indeed have a weakening effect on immigrants' sense of ethnic identity.

An additional question is whether structural integration leads to higher (in)compatibility between ethnic and national identification. Further analyses showed a significant interaction effect between occupational level and ethnic identification on host national identification. For immigrants with low-level occupations, the relation between ethnic and national identification was negative, while both group identifications were not significantly associated in higher-level occupations. This shows that, for those having lower occupations, ethnic and national identification were somewhat contradictory and that occupational advancement makes both group identifications more easy to reconcile. In this regard and in terms of acculturation strategies (Berry, 1997), the negative relation between structural integration and ethnic identification might reflect a move from a rather exclusive ethnic identity ('separation') towards a dual identity. Future studies should further investigate to what extent ethnic identification is determined by structural integration in society and the conditions under which structural integration influences the (in)compatibility of ethnic and national identification.

The role of social integration

The idea that social integration in society is a key factor for immigrants' sense of host national belonging has been advanced in the literatures on national identity and social trust (Brown & Hewstone, 2005; Delhey & Newton, 2003; Lubbers *et al.*, 2007). Social integration in itself would be important for psychological integration and would also (partly) explain (mediate) why structural integration leads to psychological integration.

One reason why social ties with majority members can foster host country identification is that these ties contribute to a sense of acceptance and belonging. Social ties can function as a basis for self-identification and shared group membership whereby immigrants consider themselves as belonging to the same community or society. Furthermore, the contact hypothesis holds that close and meaningful contacts with members of different ethnic groups promote positive and tolerant attitudes towards those groups (Allport, 1954; Pettigrew & Tropp, 2006). Contact can lead to a sense of shared belonging and the common ingroup identity model emphasizes that cross-ethnic contacts stimulate a sense of belonging to a larger superordinate category, like an organization or national category (Gaertner *et al.*, 1993). Empirical research on immigrants' psychological integration indeed provides evidence that contact with majority members increases immigrants' feelings of host national belonging (Lubbers *et al.*, 2007; Nesdale, 2002).

Social integration might also play a mediating role in the relation between structural and psychological integration (see Figure 2.1). From the perspective of assimilation theory, it can be argued that structural integration in society is an important condition for social integration to develop. Structural integration facilitates immigrants' contact opportunities and interactions with majority members. In turn, these social ties can lead to a stronger sense of inclusion in the national category. This means that by increasing social ties with majority members, immigrants' structural integration might indirectly increase their sense of host national belonging. There is empirical evidence for this reasoning. Participation in the education system and having a job have been found to increase immigrants' contact opportunities and actual contacts with natives (Kalmijn & Van Tubergen, 2006; Martinovic, 2013). Furthermore, in our research among refugees in the Netherlands we found support for the proposition that increased social contacts with natives is an intermediate step in the association between structural integration and host national belonging (De Vroome *et al.*, 2011). The relation between having work and national identification was partially mediated by having relatively more contact with majority members, as opposed to having a predominantly co-ethnic social network.

Acceptance and discrimination

Labour market discrimination of immigrants is quite common in many countries. For example, in a field experimental study in the Netherlands, professional actors who differed in ethnic background were trained to apply in the same way and with the same qualifications for the same jobs. It turned out that immigrants were almost twice as likely to be rejected by temporary employment agencies (Andriessen *et al.*, 2012). Another study in the Netherlands, in which the résumés of fictitious majority and immigrant applicants with equal qualifications were graded and selected for an interview, showed that both implicit and explicit prejudice can lead to ethnic discrimination in selection and hiring of equally qualified applicants (Blommaert *et al.*, 2012). Similar studies in the United States also demonstrate a clear tendency towards ethnic discrimination in the labour market (Bertrand & Mullainathan, 2004; Pager *et al.*, 2009).

Discrimination in the labour market and in the educational system hampers immigrants' structural integration and thereby, indirectly, the development of a sense of inclusion and host national belonging. Furthermore, discrimination implies unfair treatment, and such treatment tells people that they are not equal members of society and that society itself is less valuable (Tyler, 2001). According to social identity theory (Tajfel & Turner, 1986) and the related rejection–identification model (Branscombe *et al.*, 1999), discrimination is a negative experience that strengthens ethnic identification of minorities. It presents an identity threat that makes people increasingly turn towards the safety and acceptance of their minority group and away from the discriminating majority group. Hence, perceptions of discrimination can result in feeling more Indian and less British, or more Turkish and less Dutch. Studying immigrant youth in Belgium, Sweden and the Netherlands, Fleischmann (2011) found that perceived discrimination was associated with stronger ethnic identification and weaker national identification. In a study among Latino immigrants in the United States it was found that perceived rejection from Americans was associated with lower identification with the United States (Wiley, 2012). Furthermore, in the Netherlands, perceived discrimination has been found to be associated with lower national identification and higher national dis-identification (Verkuyten & Yildiz, 2007). And, in a longitudinal study among Russian immigrants in Finland, it was found that perceived discrimination was causally related to lower national identification (Jasinskaja-Lahti *et al.*, 2009).

Many of these studies have used relatively small, convenient samples and did not take factors such as length of residence, generation, host language proficiency, and social contacts into account. We were able to do so in our large-scale studies and the findings confirm the negative association between perceived discrimination and immigrants' psychological integration in the host society (De Vroome, Martinovic, *et al.*, 2014). In fact, perceived discrimination is one of the most important determinants of national identification among immigrants in the Netherlands. The negative effect of discrimination was also confirmed in our analyses on generalized social trust and trust in political institutions (De Vroome *et al.*, 2013). Stronger feelings of being discriminated against at work and in school were related to lower generalized social and institutional trust. This confirms international research showing that trust is lower among discriminated groups (Alesina & La Ferrara, 2002; Michelson, 2003; Smith, 2010).

Relative deprivation

Structural integration often implies rising expectations, making feelings of not being fully accepted or discriminated against by the majority group even more painful. Immigrants who have a job and are relatively successful in education might therefore perceive higher levels of relative deprivation, which indirectly leads to a lower sense of national belonging. Feelings of relative deprivation contain three aspects (Pettigrew *et al.*, 2008; Smith *et al.*, 2012). First, there must be comparisons made, at the individual or group level. Second, the comparison must lead to the feeling that one is at a relative disadvantage compared to these other individuals or groups. Third, the perceived disadvantage should be considered unfair. For immigrants, perceptions of discrimination and lack of opportunities in the host country combine these three aspects of relative deprivation. When immigrants have the sense of being discriminated against, they feel that they have an unfair disadvantage relative to members of the majority group, either personally or as a group. And, when immigrants have the sense that their group lacks opportunities to succeed economically and to freely enjoy their social and cultural life, they compare their position to the opportunities that are open to other groups in society, most prominently the dominant majority.

There are a number of reasons to expect that feelings of relative deprivation are higher among immigrants who are more integrated structurally, especially in relation to their level of education. First, higher education increases cognitive sophistication which can mean that higher-educated immigrants are more aware of, and have a better understanding of, processes of discrimination and reduced opportunities in society (Kane & Kyyro, 2001; Wodtke, 2012). Education enables immigrants to become more sophisticated social critics who can seek to challenge discrimination and advocate policies that redress group disadvantages. Within the relative deprivation framework, it has been argued that the more advantaged members of disadvantaged groups are most likely to engage in group comparisons (Taylor & Moghaddam, 1994). Higher-educated immigrants may feel more deprived because the relevant comparison to similarly educated majority members turns out unfavourably.

Second, the theory of rising expectations suggests that immigrants who pursue higher education and try to make a contribution to society develop higher expectations. They therefore are more strongly disappointed about unequal treatment whereby their higher expectations are not met with equal rewards (Entzinger & Dourleijn, 2008). The higher educated tend to be more sensitive to acceptance and rejection by the majority population. In contrast to the lower educated, they can more confidently claim that a lack of opportunities and discrimination, rather than a lack of skills and efforts, prevents them and members of their group from gaining economic parity with natives.

Research has found a positive relation between level of education and perceived discrimination among immigrants in countries such as the United States and the Netherlands (Gijsberts & Vervoort, 2007; Sizemore & Milner, 2004; Wodtke, 2012). For example, in a study among various immigrant groups in the Netherlands, Van Doorn *et al.* (2012) found that higher-educated immigrants perceive more discrimination, which could be attributed to their experience of relative deprivation regarding their work and education. The research on the so-called 'integration paradox' further indicates that there can be negative indirect relations between immigrants' structural and psychological integration. This paradox describes the phenomenon of the economically more integrated and higher-educated immigrants turning psychologically away from the host society, instead of becoming more oriented towards it (Buijs *et al.*, 2006; Entzinger & Dourleijn, 2008). Experiences and perceptions of non-acceptance and discrimination, despite their efforts and achievements, would lead them to distance themselves from society. Thus, the more successful ones would be more sensitive to ethnic acceptance and equality, which in turn would drive their reactions to the host society.

We found support for this paradox in one of our studies among groups of Turkish, Moroccan, Surinamese and Antillean immigrants in the Netherlands (De Vroome, Martinovic, *et al.*, 2014). We investigated the relations between immigrants' education and their feelings of relative deprivation, in terms of the perception of discrimination and of belonging to a group that is granted fewer opportunities to succeed and to live freely according to their own cultural values. Levels of perceived deprivation were higher among higher-educated immigrants, and perceived deprivation, in turn, was related to more negative attitudes towards natives and the host society. This was found for the four immigrant groups and for the first and second generation. Importantly, our findings showed that higher education was associated with higher perceived lack of opportunities among immigrants who were educated in the Netherlands and not among those educated in the country of origin. The native majority is an especially relevant and meaningful comparison group for those who are educated in the host society. Their sense of relative deprivation stems from perceiving fewer opportunities despite the fact of having the same level of education as majority members. The education of majority members is probably a less relevant standard of comparison for immigrants who are educated in the country of origin.

These findings on the integration paradox seem contradictory to what was discussed earlier, namely that higher-educated immigrants tend to have more contacts with the majority group (higher social integration) and therefore develop a more positive attitude towards the host society. The integration paradox, however, implies that higher-educated minorities will have a lower sense of national belonging. This might mean that there are two pathways. On the one hand, higher-educated minorities have more frequent contacts with the majority population than lower-educated minorities, and more contact is associated with *higher* national identification. On the other hand, higher-educated minorities will feel less accepted in the country and perceive more discrimination than lower-educated minorities, resulting in *lower* national identification.

We examined these pathways in another study among the same four immigrant groups in the Netherlands (Ten Teije *et al.*, 2012). It turned out that the pattern of associations was quite similar for these four groups. For the first pathway, the findings demonstrated that higher-educated migrants indeed had more contacts with the native Dutch and that contact was associated with stronger national identification. More importantly, there was also empirical evidence for the second pathway. Higher-educated immigrants perceived lower acceptance of ethnic minority groups in Dutch society and more group discrimination than lower-educated migrants. These perceptions were related to weaker national identification. In addition, the unfair treatment of co-ethnics (group discrimination) rather than personal experiences with discrimination, was found to be important for the identification of the higher educated. This supports the idea that the more advantaged members of disadvantaged groups tend to engage in group comparisons and develop more negative attitudes towards the advantaged group (Taylor & Moghaddam, 1994). Higher education might increase one's awareness of and concerns about the vulnerable and relatively marginal position of immigrants in society. In addition, when they perceive and experience ethnic discrimination, higher-status minority members might be more assertive (Baumgartner, 1998). Although we did not explicitly test these interpretations, we did find that the higher educated perceived more group discrimination than the lower educated, whereas there was no difference for personal discrimination. In turn, and independently of personal discrimination, higher perceived non-acceptance of migrant groups and of group discrimination were associated with weaker national identification.

Discussion

Cultural diversity of the workforce has become a common feature of many organizations. This raises challenging questions for the successful management and functioning of these organizations. As discussed in different chapters in this book, cultural diversity can increase productivity, creativity and innovation (Ely & Thomas, 2001), but might also lead to conflicts in work groups and to lower organizational commitment (e.g. Milliken & Martins, 1996; Watson *et al.*, 1998). Positive outcomes at work do not only depend on avoiding unfair treatment but are more likely when the potential added value of diversity is emphasized (see Van der Zee and Otten, Chapter 3) and employees feel that they safely belong and are valued for who they are (see Otten and Jansen, Chapter 5).

In addition to the question of the effects of diversity of the workforce on organizations there is the question of the importance of having an education and a (good) job for feeling included and committed to society. This question on the importance of structural integration is especially relevant for immigrants and ethnic minority members. In plural societies, cultural diversity is a fact of life, and not only assimilationists but also proponents of multiculturalism argue that a feeling of belonging together is necessary for a well-functioning society (Modood, 2007; Parekh, 2000). A society needs unity and cohesion, and a sense of belonging is an important aspect of this.

There are many factors and conditions that stimulate or hamper immigrants' sense of national belonging, and this chapter focused on employment and education (structural integration). The research discussed indicates that structural integration is not only beneficial for the welfare of immigrants and society, but can also contribute to immigrants' sense of national belonging. Structural integration has positive consequences for national identification and trust in societal institutions. Having a job and being successful in education contributes to a sense of host national inclusion because they involve a feeling of achievement and making a contribution to society, and increase social contacts with native majority members.

These findings have implications for the on-going immigration and integration debates in many societies. They suggest that policies aimed at redressing socio-economic inequalities can be expected to increase immigrants' commitment and loyalty to society. The relatively high unemployment and the low occupational status among the employed (De Vroome & Van Tubergen, 2010) implies a rather marginal position and few contact opportunities with majority members. Thus, concerns about immigrants' loyalty to the nation and the fragmentation of society can be addressed by improving their labour market participation and social integration. Labour market and educational policies are probably more important for immigrants to develop a sense of national belonging than lessons in national history and culture or an oath of allegiance, which have been proposed by politicians and policymakers (Kundnani, 2007). Furthermore, anti-discrimination policies are critically important because they improve people's opportunities and tell immigrants that they are equal members of society and that society is fair and has trustworthy institutions. This seems particularly important for the sense of belonging of the more highly educated immigrants who make a strong effort to integrate but have the feeling that key positions in society are not open to them.

Structural integration can contribute to a sense of inclusion and host society belonging among immigrants and minority members. For organizations this means that by hiring immigrants and minorities they can contribute to the social cohesion and unity in society. Many organizations are not exclusively focused on their own targets and goals but also recognize that they have a social responsibility. Providing equal opportunities for immigrants and minorities can yield societal benefits. However, organizations will tend to invest more in equal opportunity initiatives and measures when there are not only benefits for society but also for their own organization. The interest in these kinds of initiatives and measures can be expected to be relatively low when cultural diversity leads to more conflicts in work groups and to lower organizational commitment. It is therefore important to examine and discuss the determinants and conditions of successful inclusive organizations, which is done in the other chapters in this book.

Note

1 The terms used to identify groups of people differ between countries and academic disciplines and all have their specific connotations and problems. Here, we use the terms 'immigrants' and 'migrant groups' to refer to people who themselves *or* their parents have moved to a new country. The terms 'majority' or 'native' are used to refer to the majority population that in European countries comprises natives.

References

Alba, R. & Nee, V. (1997). Rethinking assimilation theory for a new era of immigration. *International Migration Review, 31*, 826–874.

Alesina, A. & La Ferrara, E. (2002). Who trusts others? *Journal of Public Economics*, *85*, 207–234.

Allport, G.W. (1954). *The nature of prejudice*. Cambridge: Addison-Wesley.

Andriessen, I., Nievers, E., & Dagevos, J. (2012). *Op achterstand: Discriminatie van niet-westerse migranten op de arbeidsmarkt*. Den Haag: SCP.

Bartram, D. (2011). Economic migration and happiness: Comparing immigrants' and natives' happiness gains from income. *Social Indicators Research*, *103*, 57–76.

Baumgartner, M.P. (1998). Moral life on the cultural frontier: Evidence from the experience of immigrants in modern America. *Sociological Focus*, *31*, 155–179.

Berry, J.F. (1997). Immigration, acculturation and adaptation. *Applied Psychology: An International Review*, *46*, 5–68.

Bertrand, M. & Mullainathan, S. (2004). Are Emily and Greg more employable than Lakisha and Jamal? A field experiment on labor market discrimination. *The American Economic Review*, *94*, 991–1013.

Blommaert, L., Van Tubergen, F., & Coenders, M. (2012). Implicit and explicit interethnic attitudes and ethnic discrimination in hiring. *Social Science Research*, *41*, 61–73.

Bohnke, P. (2008). Are the poor socially integrated? The link between poverty and social support in different welfare regimes. *Journal of European Social Policy*, *18*, 133–150.

Branscombe, N.R., Schmitt, M.T., & Harvey, R.D. (1999). Perceiving pervasive discrimination among African Americans: Implications for group identification and well-being. *Journal of Personality and Social Psychology*, *77*, 135–149.

Brown, R. & Hewstone, M. (2005). An integrative theory of intergroup contact. *Advances in Experimental Social Psychology*, *37*, 255–343.

Brubaker, R. (2001). The return of assimilation? Changing perspectives on immigration and its sequels in France, Germany, and the United States. *Ethnic and Racial Studies*, *24*, 531–548.

Buijs, F.J., Demant, F., & Hamdy, A. (2006). *Strijders van eigen bodem: Radicale en democratische Moslims in Nederland*. Amsterdam, the Netherlands: Amsterdam University Press.

Constant, A.F. & Massey, D.S. (2003). Self-Selection, earnings, and out-migration: A longitudinal study of immigrants to Germany. *Journal of Population Economics*, *16*, 631–653.

Deaux, K. & Verkuyten, M. (2013). The social psychology of multiculturalism: Identity and intergroup relations. In: V. Benet-Martínez & Y-Y. Hong (Eds.) *The Oxford handbook of multicultural identity: Basic and applied psychological perspectives*. Oxford: Oxford University Press.

Delhey, J. & Newton, K. (2003). Who trusts? The origins of social trust in seven societies. *European Societies*, *5*, 93–137.

De Vroome, T. & Van Tubergen, F. (2010). The employment experience of refugees in the Netherlands. *International Migration Review*, *44*, 376–403.

De Vroome, T. & Hooghe, M. (2013). Life satisfaction among ethnic minorities in the Netherlands: Immigration experience or adverse living conditions? *Journal of Happiness Studies*, doi: 10.1007/s10902-013-9483-2.

De Vroome, T., Hooghe, M., & Marien, S. (2013). Learning how to trust: The dynamics of generalized and political trust among the majority population and ethnic minorities in The Netherlands. *European Sociological Review*, *29*(6), 1336–1350.

De Vroome, T., Martinovic, B., & Verkuyten, M. (2014). The integration paradox: Education and attitudes towards natives among second generation immigrants in the Netherlands. *Cultural Diversity and Ethnic Minority Psychology*, doi: 10.1037/a0034946.

De Vroome, T., Verkuyten, M., & Martinovic, B. (2014). National identification among natives and immigrants in the Netherlands. *International Migration Review*, *48*(1), 76–102.

De Vroome, T., Coenders, M., Van Tubergen, F., & Verkuyten, M. (2011). Economic participation and national self-identification of refugees in the Netherlands. *International Migration Review*, *45*, 615–638.

Dustmann, C. & Weiss, Y. (2007). Return migration: Theory and empirical evidence from the UK. *British Journal of Industrial Relations*, *45*, 236–256.

Elkins, Z. & Sides, J. (2007). Can institutions build unity in multiethnic states? *American Political Science Review*, *101*, 693–708.

Ely, R. & Thomas, D. (2001). Cultural diversity at work: The effects of diversity perspectives on work group processes and outcomes. *Administrative Science Quarterly*, *46*, 229–273.

Entzinger, H. & Dourleijn, E. (2008). *De lat steeds hoger: De leefwereld van jongeren in een multi-etnische stad*. Assen, the Netherlands: Van Gorcum.

Esser, H. (2003). What substance is there in the term 'Leitkultur'? In: R. Cuperus, K.A. Duffek, & J. Kandel (Eds.) *The challenge of diversity*. Innsbruck: Studienverlag.

Fleischmann, F. (2011). *Second-generation Muslims in European societies: Comparative perspectives in education and religion*. Utrecht, the Netherlands: Ercomer.

Gaertner, S.L., Dovidio, J.F., Anastasio, P.A., Bachman, P.A., & Rust, M.C. (1993). The common ingroup identity model: Recategorization and the reduction of inter-group bias. *European Review of Social Psychology*, *4*, 1–26.

Gans, H. (2007). Acculturation, assimilation and mobility. *Ethnic and Racial Studies*, *30*, 152–164.

Gijsberts, M. & Vervoort, M. (2007). Wederzijds beeldvorming. In: J. Dagevos & M. Gijsberts (Eds.) *Jaarrapport Integratie 2007*. The Hague, the Netherlands: Netherlands Institute for Social Research.

Gordon, M.M. (1964). *Assimilation in American life*. London, UK: Oxford University Press.

Hagendoorn, L., Veenman, J., & Vollebergh, W. (2003). Cultural orientation and socio-economic integration of immigrants in the Netherlands. In: L. Hagendoorn, J. Veenman, & W. Vollebergh (Eds.) *Integrating immigrants in the Netherlands: Cultural versus socio-economic integration*. Aldershot, UK: Ashgate.

Headey, B., Muffels, R., & Wooden, M. (2004). Money doesn't buy happiness . . . . Or does it? A reconsideration based on the combined effects of wealth, income and consumption. *IZA Discussion Paper No. 1218*. http://ssrn.com/abstract=571661.

Heath, A. & Roberts, J. (2006). *British identity: Its sources and possible implications for civic attitudes and behaviour*. Oxford, UK: University of Oxford.

Jasinskaja-Lahti, I., Liebkind, K., & Solheim, E. (2009). To identify or not to identify? National disidentification as an alternative reaction to perceived ethnic discrimination. *Applied Psychology – International Review*, *58*, 105–128.

Jensen, P. & Pedersen, P.J. (2007). To stay or not to stay? Out-migration of immigrants from Denmark. *International Migration*, *45*, 87–113.

Kalmijn, M. & Van Tubergen, F. (2006). Ethnic intermarriage in the Netherlands: Confirmations and refutations of accepted insights. *European Journal of Population*, *22*, 371–397.

Kanas, A. & Van Tubergen, F. (2009). The impact of origin and host country schooling on the economic performance of immigrants. *Social Forces, 88*, 893–915.

Kane, E.W. & Kyyro, E.K. (2001). For whom does education enlighten? Race, gender, education, and beliefs about social inequality. *Gender and Society, 15*, 710–733.

Kundnani, A. (2007). Integrationism: The politics of anti-Muslim racism. *Race & Class, 48*, 24–44.

Lubbers, M.J., Molina, J.L., & McCarty, C. (2007). Personal networks and ethnic identifications – the case of migrants in Spain. *International Sociology, 22*, 721–741.

Maliepaard, M., Lubbers, M., & Gijsberts, M. (2010). Generational differences in ethnic and religious attachment and their interrelation. A study among Muslim minorities in the Netherlands. *Ethnic and Racial Studies, 33*, 451–472.

Martinovic, B. (2013). The inter-ethnic contacts of immigrants and natives in the Netherlands: A two-sided perspective. *Journal of Ethnic and Migration Studies, 39*, 69–85.

Michelson, M.R. (2003). The corrosive effect of acculturation: How Mexican Americans lose political trust. *Social Science Quarterly, 84*, 918–933.

Milliken, F.J. & Martins, L.L. (1996). Searching for common threads: Understanding the multiple effects of diversity in organizational groups. *Academy of Management Review, 21*, 402–433.

Modood, T. (2007). *Multiculturalism*. Cambridge, UK: Polity Press.

Moghaddam, M. (2008). Happiness, faith, friends, and fortune: Empirical evidence from the 1998 US survey data. *Journal of Happiness Studies, 9*, 577–587.

Nesdale, D. (2002). Acculturation attitudes and the ethnic and host-country identification of immigrants. *Journal of Applied Psychology, 32*, 1488–1507.

Olgiati, A., Calvo, R., & Berkman, L. (In press). Are migrants going up a blind alley? Economic migration and life satisfaction around the world: Cross-national evidence from Europe, North America, and Australia. *Social Indicators Research*, doi: 10.1007/s11205-012-0151-4.

Pager, D., Bonikowski, B., & Western, B. (2009). Discrimination in a low-wage labor market: A field experiment. *American Sociological Review, 74*, 777–799.

Parekh, B. (2000). *Rethinking multiculturalism: Cultural diversity and political theory*. London, UK: Macmillan.

Park, R.E. (1950). *Race and culture*. New York: Free Press.

Pettigrew, T.F. & Tropp, L.R. (2006). A meta-analytic test of intergroup contact theory. *Journal of Personality and Social Psychology, 90*, 751–783.

Pettigrew, T.F., Christ, O., Wagner, U., Meertens, R.W., Van Dick, R., & Zick, A. (2008). Relative deprivation and intergroup prejudice. *Journal of Social Issues, 64*, 385–401.

Rattan, A. & Ambady, N. (2013). Diversity ideologies and intergroup relations: An examination of colorblindness and multiculturalism. *European Journal of Social Psychology, 43*, 12–21.

Sidanius, J., Feshbach, S., Levin, S., & Pratto, F. (1997). The interface between ethnic and national attachment. *Public Opinion Quarterly, 61*, 102–133.

Sizemore, D.S. & Milner, W.T. (2004). Hispanic media use and perceptions of discrimination: Reconsidering ethnicity, politics, and socioeconomics. *The Sociological Quarterly, 45*, 765–784.

Smith, H.J., Pettigrew, T.F., Pippin, G.M., & Bialosiewicz, S. (2012). Relative deprivation: A theoretical and meta-analytic review. *Personality and Social Psychology Review, 16*, 203–232.

Smith, S.S. (2010). Race and trust. *Annual Review of Sociology*, *36*, 453–475.

Snauwaert, B., Soenens, B., Vanbeselaere, N., & Boen, F. (2003). When integration does not necessarily imply integration: Different conceptualizations of acculturation orientations lead to different classifications. *Journal of Cross-cultural Psychology*, *34*, 231–239.

Staerklé, C., Sidanius, J., Green, E.G.T., & Molina, L.E. (2010). Ethnic minority-majority asymmetry in national attitudes around the world: A multilevel analysis. *Political Psychology*, *31*, 491–519.

Strandh, M. (2000). Different exit routes from unemployment and their impact on mental well-being: The role of the economic situation and the predictability of the life course. *Work Employment and Society*, *14*, 459–479.

Tajfel, H. & Turner, J.C. (1986). The social identity theory of intergroup behavior. In: S. Wörchel & W. Austin (Eds.) *The social psychology of intergroup relations*. Pacific Grove: Brooks/Cole.

Taylor, C. (1992). The Politics of Recognition. In: A. Gutmann (Ed.) *Multiculturalism: Examining the politics of recognition*. Princeton: Princeton University Press.

Taylor, D.M. & Moghaddam, F.M. (1994). *Theories of intergroup relations*. New York: Praeger.

Ten Teije, I., Coenders, M., & Verkuyten, M. (2012). The paradox of integration: Educational attainment and immigrants' attitudes towards the native population. *Social Psychology*, doi:10.1027/1864-9335/a000113.

Tyler, T.R. (2001). Public trust and confidence in legal authorities: What do majority and minority group members want from the law and legal authorities? *Behavioral Sciences and the Law*, *19*, 215–235.

Uberoi, V. (2008). Do policies of multiculturalism change national identities? *The Political Quarterly*, *79*, 404–417.

Van Doorn, M., Scheepers, P., & Dagevos, J. (2012). Explaining the integration paradox among small immigrant groups in the Netherlands. *International Migration and Integration*, doi:10.1007/s12134-012-0244-6.

Vasta, E. (2007). From ethnic minorities to ethnic majority policy: Multiculturalism and the shift to assimilationism in the Netherlands. *Ethnic and Racial Studies*, *30*, 713–740.

Verkuyten, M. & Yildiz, A.A. (2007). National (dis)identification and ethnic and religious identity: A study among Turkish-Dutch Muslims. *Personality and Social Psychology Bulletin*, *33*, 1448–1462.

Walters, D., Phythian, K., & Anisef, P. (2007). The acculturation of Canadian immigrants: Determinants of ethnic identification with the host society. *Canadian Review of Sociology and Anthropology*, *44*, 37–65.

Watson, W.E., Johnson, L., Kumar, K., & Critelli, J. (1998). Process gain and process loss: Comparing interpersonal processes and performance of cultural diverse and non-diverse teams across time. *International Journal of Intercultural Relations*, *30*, 671–682.

Wiley, S. (2012). Rejection-identification among Latino immigrants in the United States. *International Journal of Intercultural Relations*, doi:10.1016/j.ijintrel.2012.08.018.

Wodtke, G.T. (2012). The impact of education on intergroup attitudes. A multiracial analysis. *Social Psychology Quarterly*, *75*, 80–106.

Zimmermann, L., Zimmermann, K., & Constant, A. (2007). Ethnic self-identification of first-generation immigrants. *International Migration Review*, *41*, 769–781.

3 Organizational perspectives on diversity

Karen van der Zee and Sabine Otten

Influenced by the increasing ethnic variation in Western societies, cultural diversity in organizations is also on the rise. As a consequence, and as the following example of IBM illustrates, prominent organizations incorporate diversity-related ideologies in their mission statements:

> IBM's enduring commitment to diversity is one of the reasons we can credibly say that IBM is one of the world's leading globally integrated enterprises. We also understand that diversity goes beyond fair hiring practices and protection for all employees. It also includes a focus on how those disparate pieces fit together to create an innovative, integrated whole. We call this approach "inclusion."
>
> While our differences shape who we are as individual IBMers, our shared corporate culture and values remain central to our mutual success. IBMers around the world work in an environment where diversity— including diversity of thought—is the norm, which yields a commitment to creating client innovation in every part of our business.
>
> ("Diversity & Inclusion," p. 10, www-03.ibm.com/employment/us/ diverse/downloads/ibm_diversity_brochure.pdf)

In theory, diversity seems to offer organizations opportunities for flexibility and innovation. The literature has repeatedly stressed the potential for diverse groups to be more creative and to generate better decisions (e.g. Mannix & Neale, 2005). This is because, with more available perspectives on a situation, there should be a greater potential for having the "right solution" or for generating unconventional approaches. The mission statement of IBM (which is representative of that of a great many other companies) clearly reflects such a belief that diversity among its staff may help stimulate such desirable outcomes for their company.

Unfortunately, reality is less cheerful than beliefs expressed in mission statements. The daily practice of organizations reveals a strong preference for similarity and homogeneity (e.g. Schneider et al., 1995). Organizations have a special attraction for people who resemble current members of the organization, and therefore recruiters have a tendency to choose applicants who are alike. For this reason, people who are different have a lower probability of getting a job. In a recent study in the Netherlands, it was found that an indigenous Dutch job-seeker had a 1.6 times greater chance of getting a job than an equally qualified job-seeker from a Non-Western ethnic minority (Andriessen et al., 2012). And, even if accepted, minority employees have a higher likelihood of experiencing tensions in the workplace and, as a consequence, leaving the organization (Hofhuis et al., 2008; see also Hofhuis, 2012). A quote from an employee participating in the study by Hofhuis et al. (2008) illustrates this:

> When I entered the department it consisted of a staunch clique of people who had been colleagues for years. I tried to establish contacts with them but we actually had little in common. I am from quite a different world; I just didn't manage to become included.

There are not only problems with the actual implementation of diversity at the workplace; its outcomes are also mixed (e.g. Mannix & Neale, 2005; Van Knippenberg et al., 2004; Van Knippenberg & Schippers, 2007; Williams & O'Reilly, 1998). On the one hand, studies suggest detrimental outcomes of diversity such as negative affect, communication difficulties, and enhanced turnover (McLeod et al., 1996). Observable differences between employees, such as race and gender, are often associated with stereotypes and prejudice, which hamper interactions on the work floor (Milliken & Martins, 1996). A prominent explanation for these negative consequences stems from social identity theory (see Abrams & Hogg, 1990; Tajfel, 1982; Tajfel & Turner, 1979), which assumes that us–them distinctions, and people's associated favoritism for their own groups, will enhance group members' positive identity. Moreover, the similarity-attraction principle (e.g. Byrne, 1999; cf. Newcomb, 1956) implies a preference for similar rather than different others, and, therefore, more satisfaction with homogeneous rather than heterogeneous groups.

On the other hand, informational approaches to diversity have emphasized that the variety of input associated with diversity may also encourage innovation, creativity and higher-quality solutions to complex problems (Ling, 1990; McLeod & Lobel, 1992; Nakui et al., 2011; Watson et al., 1993). With more available ways of viewing a situation, there is a greater potential for generating the "right solution" or for generating unconventional approaches (see also Paulus and Van der Zee, this volume). Research has shown that multicultural groups develop more and better alternatives to a problem and criteria for evaluating those alternatives than do culturally homogeneous groups (McLeod & Lobel, 1992) and that they are more creative than homogenous groups (Ling, 1990; Nakui et al., 2011). Indeed, a study by Watson et al. (1993) suggests that in the long run diverse groups outperform homogeneous groups.

In sum, the best answer to the question of whether diversity is beneficial for organizations is probably: "It depends." The focus of the present chapter is on a boundary condition that we consider especially relevant for the success of cultural diversity at the workplace, namely, the diversity management perspective endorsed by leaders in the organization. We will first define and differentiate diversity management perspectives and then discuss the empirical evidence that links these perspectives to relevant outcome variables.

Managing diversity

Whether positive or negative consequences of diversity will occur may largely depend on the way in which diversity is valued and subsequently managed (e.g. Cox, 1993; Cox & Blake, 1991; Ely & Thomas, 2001; Harquail & Cox, 1993; Kochan et al., 2003; Mannix & Neale, 2005; Pless & Maak, 2004; Van Knippenberg & Haslam, 2003). To this end, organizations have developed a range of different approaches (Thomas & Ely, 1996).

As a first step, these management perspectives on diversity can generally be distinguished in terms of approaches that aim primarily to safeguard the psychological well-being of the organizational members by reducing possible detrimental consequences of diversity, versus approaches that aim to increase the organization's productive work outcomes. We will refer to these perspectives as 'colorblind' versus 'colorful,' respectively (e.g. Luijters, 2008; cf. the distinction between colorblindness versus multiculturalism; see, for an overview, Rattan & Ambady, 2013).

Colorblind perspectives are characterized by approaches that do not wish to differentiate employees on the basis of category membership. Organizations adopting a colorblind approach typically stress qualifications over any other factor (Stevens et al., 2008). Category membership is defined as irrelevant. Hence, colorblind organizations emphasize the affiliation with the broader organization, which enhances shared organizational identity and reduces the salience of employees' identities on the subgroup level, such as their cultural background or religion. Colorblindness can be recognized in American and Western European ideals of individualism, meritocracy and equality (Markus et al., 2000; Thomas et al., 2004).

In contrast, *colorful perspectives* focus on the benefits of incorporating cultural diversity and suggest that exploration of differences is an important strategic strategy for the organization that offers competitive advantage. Organizations that adopt colorful approaches assert that differences between cultural groups should be recognized and acknowledged, in light of the proposed beneficial influence of these group differences on work processes (Cox, 1991; Stevens et al., 2008). In the literature, the colorful perspective is also termed 'multiculturalism' (Stevens et al., 2008). For our focus, we prefer the term colorful over multiculturalism. Whereas the concept of multiculturalism explicitly refers to cultural differences, the term colorful reflects an appreciation of differences in general.

Diversity perspectives

Ely and Thomas's three diversity perspectives

How do the general principles of colorblindness and colorfulness translate into more specific diversity approaches? By studying a consulting firm, a financial services firm, and a law firm in the United States, Ely and Thomas (2001) identified three perspectives towards workforce diversity, namely the *Discrimination-and-Fairness* perspective, the *Access-and-Legitimacy* perspective and the *Integration-and-Learning* perspective. These perspectives reflect different normative beliefs and expectations about the reason to diversify, the value of cultural diversity, and its connection to work processes (Stevens et al., 2008).

The first perspective on diversity defined by Ely and Thomas (2001) is the *Discrimination-and-Fairness* perspective, which is characterized by a belief in a diverse workforce as a moral imperative to ensure justice and the fair treatment of all members of society. Central to this perspective is the assumption that employees, regardless of their background, deserve equal (or rather equitable) treatment. On the basis of the idea of equal treatment, the Discrimination-and-Fairness perspective has in the literature sometimes been classified as colorblind (e.g. Luijters, 2008), although this idea can be challenged, as we will discuss later.

A well-known policy tool linked to this perspective concerns formulating target numbers of cultural minorities for each department in the organization and holding departments responsible for achieving those numbers. Another example concerns anti-discriminatory measures, such as anti-discrimination laws, bias-free selection devices, and training of recruiters and assessors. Training methods that focus on helping cultural minorities to reduce "handicaps" in their skill-levels (e.g. by language training) also fit in this perspective. Ely and Thomas (2001) clearly point at disadvantages of the Discrimination-and-Fairness perspective. In particular, one of the by-products is that in many cases assimilation to the dominant standard becomes the norm. In this sense, the perspective reflects the assimilationist approach towards integration of cultural minorities in society, putting pressure on giving up one's original culture (e.g. Bourhis et al., 1997).

The second perspective on the value of diversity is the *Access-and-Legitimacy* perspective, characterized by the belief that diversity in the organization helps in gaining *access* to the diverse market (Ely & Thomas, 2001, p. 244). An example might be the supermarket in a multicultural neighborhood that has a large number of cultures represented among its customers. In such an environment, it is an advantage for the supermarket chain if it employs staff members who are sensitive to the special needs of the various customer groups. The Access-and-Legitimacy perspective is a colorful perspective, as it assumes that diversity can bring extra value to the organization.

An important risk of the Access-and-Legitimacy perspective is that managers "tend to emphasize the role of cultural differences in a company without really analyzing those differences to see how they actually affect the work that is done" (Thomas & Ely, 1996, p. 7). In addition, the division of tasks according to cultural background may induce separation. In the Access-and-Legitimacy perspective, differences are acknowledged and used instrumentally in business. However, management does not see the necessity to learn from diversity. Probably as a result, various cultural backgrounds may be represented at the lower levels of the organization, but not at the higher management levels. In that sense, this perspective can be seen as being not fully 'colorful'. An example can be found in a Dutch police department that specifically seeks to employ Moroccans in the police force in order to have them patrolling in neighborhoods where many Moroccans get in trouble with the police, or to let them, for example, be present at a soccer match when the Dutch national team plays against the Moroccan team. Though such distribution of duties along ethnic backgrounds is certainly useful for the organization, this approach has its drawbacks. As long as the specific expertise contributed by Moroccan police officers is not shared by the organization as a whole, the company cannot be considered a truly intercultural organization. Conversely, the Moroccan police officers are likely to feel only partly appreciated by the organization. This is because they are only allowed to think "in color" at an operational level, whereas at a strategic level they have to conform.

Finally, in the *Integration-and-Learning* perspective, diversity is seen as a resource for learning, change, and renewal. In addition, diversity is included in the organization's mission. Managers stimulate diversity in all the segments of their organization, and truly value and stimulate different approaches to work, and encourage the exchange of different opinions and insights (Thomas & Ely, 1996). The mission statement at the beginning of this chapter clearly reflects such a perspective. Importantly, according to Ely and Thomas, all three perspectives can be successful in motivating managers to diversify their workforce, but only the Integration-and-Learning perspective produces sustained benefits from diversity. The Integration-and-Learning perspective can be regarded as a colorful perspective, as it clearly links diversity among employees to organizational outcomes.

Diversity perspectives and person–environment fit

The three diversity perspectives by Ely and Thomas (2001) also reflect different views on the fit between employees and their work environment (P–E fit, cf. Kristof-Brown et al., 2005). P–E fit perceptions refer to the perceived compatibility between an individual and his/her environment (Kristof-Brown et al., 2005). According to Kristof-Brown et al. (2005), in the typical work environment, P–E fit perceptions may include perceptions of person–organization (P–O) fit, person–group (P–G) fit, and person–job (P–J) fit. Specifically, P–O fit perceptions refer to judgments of the congruence between an employee and an organization's values and goals. P–G fit perceptions refer to judgments of the interpersonal compatibility between an employee and his/her work group (Cable & DeRue, 2002). Finally, P–J fit occurs when employees' knowledge, skills, and abilities are perceived to be commensurate with what the job requires.

When we consider these definitions, it becomes clear that the three perspectives ask for new and different conceptualizations of how the fit between employees and their work environment is determined. As we argued above, the Discrimination-and-Fairness perspective reflects an assimilationist approach. Employees are assumed to fit in the work environment when their characteristics fit with the dominant values of the organization or their work group (cf. P–O and P–G fit, e.g. Kristoff-Brown et al., 2005). The Access-and-Legitimacy and Integration-and-Learning perspective cannot so easily be described in terms of existing approaches to P–E fit. In the Access-and-Legitimacy perspective, fit between employees and the work environment is defined at the work group or organizational level. Organizations with this perspective strive for a composition of their staff that fits the cultural diversity of the external environment, that is, their clients and customers. Finally, in the Integration-and-Learning perspective, the idea of person–environment fit is approached from a reversed angle: the basic idea is that the organization or work group is adjusted to accommodate the potentials of its employees rather than the other way around. Therefore, it is rather an environment–person (E–P)-fit. The change in conceptualization of fit in these perspectives is important, because it has clear implications for personnel selection. For example, organizations with an Integration-and-Learning perspective need other, more curiosity driven, methods of selecting staff than traditional methods that depart from assessing candidates against static job requirements (P–J fit).

Empirical evidence

Ely and Thomas (2001) developed their distinction of the three approaches that organizations can take towards diversity management on the basis of one study performed in a consulting firm within a US context. To replicate their findings in different organizations in a different national context, Luijters (2008) undertook a study in which 15 managers from different organizations in the Netherlands were interviewed on the diversity policies they adopted in their teams. The data provided support for the three perspectives as distinguished by Ely and Thomas (2001), as can be derived from examples of statements that the managers made during the interviews (Box 3.1) that are indicative of each perspective. Additionally, the results indicated that practices in the majority of participating organizations reflected the Discrimination-and-Fairness and the Access-and-Legitimacy perspective

Box 3.1 Statements representative of the Ely & Thomas (2001) diversity perspectives

Discrimination and fairness

"We act in ways that support the Employment of Minorities Act." "The community here is very culturally diverse. The company automatically became diverse as a result."

"I don't think it matters if someone is Dutch or non-Dutch, After all it's just a person."

"We don't really talk about culture, it is a nice team, but I don't think it is different because of its diversity."

"Cultural background has no value for their work, they are just good care takers."

Access and legitimacy

"In order to get in the mindset of foreign customers, you need to have foreign employees."

"The (ethnic) marketing group offers different products and services."

"Moroccan advisors simply sell more insurances."

"When a Suriname customer needs help, then we send the Suriname employee. Even if she explains the situation to me, I don't know what to do with that: I am Dutch. She knows how things work in her culture."

Integration and learning

"I once deliberately chose a Turkish employee for a job, because he brings to his team what he knows about his culture. As a result cultural differences become part of the usual for more colleagues."

"Our group is a rich collection of cultures, which enriches peoples' experience and contributes to the joy perceived in the work."

"The cultural background of our company is the oil that runs the machine."

"We have built some sort of pride in the mix of different cultures. This sort of 'feel good' out of 'multiculturality' is recognized by the market."

(adopted from Luijters, 2008)

rather than the Integration-and-Learning perspective. Although it is difficult to draw generalizations from a single and relatively small study, this may be a reflection of the integration policy at that time in the Netherlands. In the period 2000–2004, the Netherlands used to strive for 'equal representation of minority groups in organizations and communities' (Employment of Minorities Act), taking policy measures to ensure fair treatment and stimulate equal representation of cultural minorities in companies and governmental institutions across the nation.

From three to five diversity perspectives: refining the model by Ely and Thomas

Although the results presented by Luijters (2008) nicely reflect the perspectives as distinguished by Ely and Thomas (2001), the outcomes also suggest some refinements to their distinction (see also Podsiadlowski et al., 2013). For example, the Discrimination-and-Fairness perspective seems to include both strategies in which organizations are not concerned about cultural differences and strategies in which organizations are actively involved in promoting fairness and preventing discrimination. The former case concerns organizations who are not consciously seeking to become more diverse, but who are simply aiming to hire the best candidate for each position. If such organizations happen to attract more people from diverse cultural backgrounds, this is because they are the candidates who best fit the requirements for available positions. Because this perspective most strongly reflects the characteristics of what is referred to in the literature as colorblind (e.g. Stevens et al., 2008) we also term this perspective *colorblind.*

The second type of organizations subsumed under the Discrimination-and-Fairness perspective is not properly described as being "colorblind," but does explicitly have diversity as its mission. These organizations depart from the basic premise that all humans are equal and deserve an equal chance. They actively strive for providing such equal chances by hiring people of various cultural backgrounds. In order to promote their minority members' advancement in the organization, extra measures are taken to support them. We will refer to this perspective as *fairness*[1].

The difference between the colorblind and the fairness perspectives becomes clear when one compares the statements "We don't really talk about culture, it is a nice team, but I don't think it is different because of its diversity" and "We act in ways that support the Employment of Minorities Act" (see Box 3.2). While, in colorblind organizations, individuals fit in the organization when they possess the characteristics that are required for the job (P–J fit), in organizations that emphasize fairness, fit is most likely to be defined in terms of a representation of cultural groups that equals their representation in the environment of the organization or among graduates with the required educational profile. Note that, just as we discussed for the Access-and-Legitimacy perspective, fit in this sense is defined at the work group or organizational level rather than at the level of individual employees.

In addition, the study by Luijters (2008, chapter 4) suggests that the legitimacy component of the Access-and-Legitimacy perspective is difficult to disentangle from the fairness perspective, although its original definition by Ely and Thomas (2001) more explicitly focused on the external environment (society, customers, and clients) rather than the internal environment as is the case in the Discrimination-and-Fairness perspective. That is, legitimacy in terms of being a reflection of specific customer groups or of society in general refers to *not excluding* specific groups, which is also central to the *fairness* perspective. New in the Access-and-Legitimacy perspective is the

Box 3.2 Extended model of diversity perspectives

Perspective	Basic ideology	Value of diversity	Definition of fit
reinforcing homogeneity	unity from assimilation	negative; source of conflicts and coordination losses	being similar • P–O fit • P–G fit
colorblind	qualifications count, not background	unspecified	being qualified • P–J fit
fairness	equal chances	unspecified	equal representation • P–E fit at the group level
access	profit	positive; source of profit	representing backgrounds of customers and clients • P–E fit at the group level
integration	learning	positive; source of learning	fitting organization to employee characteristics • E–P fit

idea that diversity helps in *gaining* the knowledge that is necessary to be able to respond to the needs of different groups (i.e. getting access). We will therefore exclude the legitimacy component from the Access-and-Legitimacy perspective and distinguish a third perspective that focuses on gaining access to the needs of different cultural groups as *access*.

A final limitation of the classification by Ely and Thomas (2001) is that they focused solely on perspectives that depart from a positive or at least neutral attitude towards diversity. However, considering the limited evidence favoring positive outcomes of diversity over negative outcomes (Mannix & Neale, 2005; Van Knippenberg et al., 2004; Williams & O'Reilly, 1998), combined with the previously mentioned fact that in practice most organizations have tendencies towards homogeneity rather than towards diversity, it is not realistic to assume that all organizations actually strive for diversification of their workforce. We therefore added a fifth perspective called '*reinforcing homogeneity*'. This perspective is characteristic of organizations that explicitly value, and strive for, similarity. These organizations hold a strong belief that organizational targets are best reached under conditions of shared values and common goals within the workforce. In order to create or foster such unity, they attract and retain staff members who embrace the dominant culture and values of the organization. The original definition of person–environment fit by Kristoff-Brown et al. (2005), in terms of a fit between the employee and the work group or organization (respectively P–G and P–O fit), applies to this perspective.

By way of summary, Box 3.2 presents an overview of the above five perspectives in terms of their basic ideology, the perceived value of diversity and the sense of what makes people fit into the organization. In the following, we will summarize empirical evidence regarding the outcomes associated with these different diversity perspectives. Because evidence regarding the outcomes of more specific approaches as summarized above is scarce, in doing so we have to rely partly on more global distinctions related to color-blind and colorful perspectives on diversity. Future studies need to study in more depth how our five specific perspectives are perceived by employees and in what way they are related to relevant work outcomes.

Effectiveness of different diversity management perspectives

So far, there is only very little research dealing explicitly with the effectiveness of different practices of diversity management. It has been suggested that diversity management policies have an impact on important outcome variables, such as organizational climate (Wentling & Palma-Rivas, 2000), inclusiveness (Roberson, 2006) and performance (Kochan et al., 2003), but empirical data supporting this assumption are almost non-existent. An exception is a study performed by Ely and Thomas (2001) in a financial services company in the United States. Members of the organization, from different branches, filled out a four-item questionnaire to indicate the extent to which they adopted an Integration-and-Learning perspective. Their data revealed that ethnic diversity was associated with higher overall performance in branches that endorsed an Integration-and-Learning perspective on diversity, relative both to ethnically diverse branches that did not embrace this perspective and to ethnically homogeneous branches (see Kochan et al., 2003).

In our own research group, we tried to extend these findings to cultural diversity in Dutch organizational contexts, focusing on indicators of organizational climate and inclusion, as well as work processes and work outcomes. In what follows, we will summarize the main findings from our research group.

The idea that perspectives towards diversity that explicitly stress the link between diversity and positive organizational outcomes may successfully promote openness towards and appreciation of diversity was empirically tested in an experimental study by Hofhuis (2012). Subjects were instructed to focus either on potential positive outcomes of cultural diversity in the workplace or on potential negative outcomes of cultural diversity by first writing these down individually and then discussing them in a group context and identifying the best examples. The data suggested that recruiters who focused on positive diversity outcomes in the workplace showed more appreciation of minority candidates who displayed strong cultural maintenance in the workplace.

The previously mentioned study by Luijters (2008, chapter 4) provided a more direct test of the impact of diversity perspectives on organizational outcomes. Here, team leaders' diversity perspectives were classified according to the distinction suggested by Ely and Thomas (2001), and it was also investigated how the three diversity perspectives related to team members' ratings of *organizational climate* and work outcomes. An important characteristic of colorful diversity perspectives is that diversity is perceived as being of value to the organization (Cox, 1991; Cox & Blake, 1991; Harquail & Cox, 1993). When the management of an organization endorses such a perspective, this should be reflected in perceptions by employees of an organizational climate that is *open* and *appreciative* of diversity (Harquail & Cox, 1993; Luijters et al., 2007). An *open* climate is reflected in the possibility for employees to choose their own work style and maintain important cultural habits, even though these habits may differ from what is perceived as normal (e.g. allowing female Muslim employees in a Dutch organization to wear headscarves). Differences are not only allowed, but also discussed openly. Moreover, a climate that is *appreciative* of diversity is characterized not only by a general attitude that positively values diversity but also by a willingness to use this diversity rather than perceiving it as a problem.

The results by Luijters (2008) not only supported the idea that a colorful perspective goes along with a more positive diversity climate, but also that it is associated with more positive team processes and outcomes than the colorblind perspective. More specifically, teams whose leader endorsed a Discrimination-and-Fairness perspective scored lower on the climate factor 'openness' and team processes and output were less favorable compared to teams with an Access-and-Legitimacy or an Integration-and-Learning perspective. In addition, both 'openness' and 'appreciation' turned out to be important climate aspects that were associated with positive outcomes of diversity, not only through their association with diversity perspectives, but also independently (see also Luijters et al., 2007; Hofhuis et al., 2012). Interestingly, with regard to the appreciation component of the diversity climate, all three diversity perspectives from the taxonomy by Ely and Thomas (2001) scored equally high, thereby confirming our earlier argument that they all depart from the general assumption that diversity in the organization is positively valued.

Group differences in the effectiveness of diversity management perspectives

The majority of studies on diversity perspectives have focused on enhancing the inclusion of *minority members* in the organization. However, the same policies that may be perceived positively by minority members may not evoke positive responses among majority members. This is of great importance, because being the dominant force in organizations, the positive attitudes of majority members would seem to be crucial to successful diversity management. In this regard, most studies that investigate minority and majority members' responses to colorblindness versus colorful approaches have focused on national integration policies rather than on diversity policies in organizations (e.g. Karafantis et al., 2010; Levin et al., 2012; Plaut et al., 2011; Ryan et al., 2007; Wolsko et al., 2000). In general, it has been suggested that majority group members show higher levels of endorsement of color-blindness, whereas minority members tend to support multiculturalism to a greater extent (Plaut et al., 2011; Ryan et al., 2007; Verkuyten, 2005; Wolsko et al., 2006).

How do these findings translate into an organizational context? In a recent study among a sample of employees from different organizations, we were able to replicate the finding that, for majority members, the extent to which organizations adopted a fairness perspective was positively related to work outcomes in terms of work satisfaction and innovation. In contrast, for minority members, the extent to which an organization supported an approach in which differences between cultural groups are recognized and acknowledged (*integration*), positively predicted work outcomes (Vos et al., 2013). Moreover, for both majority and minority members, the relationship between the organizational strategy towards diversity and work outcomes was mediated by the extent to which employees perceived themselves to be included in the organization. Whereas majority members perceived themselves to be included in organizations that stress equality regardless of cultural background, feelings of inclusion for minority members were particularly secured in organizations that adopted a multicultural approach (see also Otten and Jansen, this volume).

In another study, Meeussen et al. (2014) examined how leaders' colorblind-ness versus multiculturalism affected the work experiences of cultural minor-ity and majority members, who collaborated in teams over a period of six months. Their findings indicate that leaders' colorblindness is associated with more task conflict for all group members, and with more relationship conflict and more distancing from the work group for minority members only. In contrast, leaders' multiculturalism was associated with higher feelings of inclusion among both minority and majority members. Interestingly, these findings suggest that not only the minority group members, but also the majority, may profit from a colorful approach towards diversity, and that a diversity perspective stressing the value in diversity need not be detrimental for majority members.

Towards effective diversity perspectives

As the previous section suggests, it seems important for organizations to develop an approach that makes both minority and majority members feel included. In this vein, Stevens et al. (2008) have proposed a new per-spective that they refer to as *all-inclusive multiculturalism*. Crucial to the idea of all-inclusive multiculturalism is that there are positive relationships between employees who are dissimilar, and that it is these relationships that encourage positive affect and mutual learning in diverse groups. With the focus on contact between members of different subgroups, minority and majority members become equally important and equally irreplaceable, thereby guaranteeing inclusion for both sides. The term multiculturalism is akin to what Haslam (2001) referred to as "organic pluralism," referring to a superordinate organizational identity that recognizes, accommodates, and encourages subgroup identities that reflect the shared self-determined interests and aspirations of employees.

The idea that positive interpersonal bonds may promote positive outcomes of diversity has also been stressed by other researchers (e.g. Brickson & Brewer, 2001; Cross et al., 2000). In this regard, in social psychology, Brickson and Brewer (2001) introduced the concept of *relational identity orientation* referring to an individual's conception of his or her relatedness to other individuals. This orientation refers to the degree to which the representations of (close) relationships with others are included into the mental representation of the self (cf. Aron et al., 1992). For example, as a team member I can perceive myself in terms of my membership of a collective or in terms of the relationship that I have developed with two of my team mates, by being their mentor or by providing materials or technical knowledge they need in order to perform their tasks. Positive feelings about the self will derive from developing and maintaining such close relationships with other individuals (see also Ashforth et al., 2008). In that sense, trust and empathy form an important basis for dealing with the social world. Accordingly, Brickson (2000) argues that mutual cognitive understanding and concern among members of different subgroups are most likely to occur from a relational identity orientation. A relational identity orientation is likely to emerge from dyadic relationships, for example organized in small face-to-face groups or dense and integrated networks. The situation is framed in terms of mutual relations rather than in terms of group membership and the norms that go along with it. Regarding diversity in organizations, this suggests that providing opportunities for contact across cultural subgroups is a crucial first step. Future studies may try to integrate these theoretical perspectives by linking diversity perspectives in organizations to such relational processes and subsequent outcomes.

An alternative approach to diversity management that has been put forward by Markus and colleagues (2000) focuses on *identity safety*. The idea of identity safety is again rooted in assumptions put forward in social psychology. Probably most relevant here is intergroup threat theory by Stephan and Stephan (2000), who state that positive relations among cultural groups are endangered by different sources of "intergroup threat," such as interaction anxiety (difficulties in interaction with members of different cultural groups), symbolic anxiety (threat associated with different value systems), negative stereotypes (cf. Steele and Aronson's (1995) construct of stereotype threat), and realistic anxiety (threat associated with depletion of resources resulting from the presence of an outgroup). Diversity management should explicitly focus on reducing these threats (see, for a discussion, Purdie-Vaughns & Ditlmann, 2010).

Like multiculturalism, identity safety explicitly acknowledges that diversity can be a source of value. Unlike multiculturalism, however, it also emphasizes that while people from different social groups and backgrounds can experience the same social contexts in similar ways, various barriers in mainstream institutions (i.e. identity threats) can also prevent them from doing so. Think, for example, of the police deciding to promote employees of Moroccan descent to leadership positions because their leadership helps the organization to be more effective in handling problems of the Moroccan-Dutch community. In this case, white male policemen may very well agree with this perspective, but nevertheless show resistance, because this policy may threaten their own chances for promotion in the organization (cf. Stephan & Stephan, 2000; intergroup threat theory).

Interestingly, both the perspective of all-inclusive multiculturalism (Stevens et al., 2008) as well as the identity safety perspective (Markus et al., 2000) provide solutions for diversity management that are based on preventing potentially negative relational aspects of diversity rather than on actualizing the actual value that diversity may have for the organization. Similarly, the ASPIRe-model by Haslam et al. (2003; see also Peters et al., this volume) argues that giving voice to all groups in organizations will have relational benefits by satisfying needs for procedural and distributive justice (see Chapter 6 for a detailed description of this model on how organizations may *a*ctualize *s*ocial and *p*ersonal *i*dentity *r*esources in their employees). Therefore, we propose a third strategy that is closely linked to the Integration-and-Learning perspective as identified by Ely and Thomas (2001), and which focuses on how to generate positive outcomes for both majority and minority members. More specifically, we pose that members of the cultural majority will feel more included when organizations adopt a definition of 'colorful' that is not limited to cultural background, but also includes other dimensions, such as age, competencies, or functional background. For example, based on the ethnic composition of their work force, a law firm can attune their services to specific cultural groups of clients, while at the same time aiming at products that fit specific areas of legal knowledge among their employees. This idea implies that, by creating structures that necessitate cooperation across various categorical distinctions, organizations may help build complex social identities, which may promote openness to change and tolerance towards diversity (Roccas & Brewer, 2002).

Conclusions

We started this chapter with quoting from IBM's diversity perspective, stating that "diversity goes beyond fair hiring practices and protection for all employees. It also includes a focus on how those disparate pieces fit together to create an innovative, integrated whole." This passage clearly reflects an integration perspective towards diversity, and an intention to move beyond merely offering fairness to employees from various cultural groups in society. In this chapter, we provided an overview of the different perspectives that organizations can take towards diversity in terms of their basic ideology, and their assumption about the value that diversity may have for the organization. We also gave examples of the scarce empirical evidence suggesting that management perspectives that do acknowledge the value of diversity are more effective in terms of stimulating an open climate as well as favorable work processes and outcomes. Hence, trying to avoid unfair treatment of minority groups might not provide the same benefits to the organization as does promoting the potential added value of diversity. Interestingly, the ASPIRe model by Haslam and collaborators (Haslam et al., 2003; see Peters et al., this volume) describes a 4-stage model of how to achieve such a goal. Though the evidence for the effectiveness of this approach is still in its initial stage, first results are promising.

In terms of how different approaches to diversity are perceived, findings may differ for minority and majority members. Particularly minority members seem to appreciate "multicultural" perspectives, whereas majority member might feel more comfortable with approaches that focus on color-blindness and fairness without attaching specific value to differences. We presented the all-inclusive multiculturalism perspective (Stevens et al., 2008) as well as the identity safety perspective (Markus et al., 2000) as approaches that may help avoid negative responses among both majority and minority members. Alternatively, we proposed an approach that can be regarded as an extension of the Integration-and-Learning perspective by Ely and Thomas (2001) in that it departs from a definition of 'colorful' that is not limited to cultural background, but also includes other dimensions, such as competencies, age or gender.

The first step for organizations striving to develop such a diversity perspective is to form an integral vision of diversity. The question then becomes: "What does diversity mean to us? How do we use diversity to learn and excel as an organization?" In turn, an integral vision requires continuous communication about the vision and its translation to all levels of the organization. To translate this vision to the daily reality at work, leadership and team development methods seem crucial (Haslam et al., 2011). In recent work we found evidence that an open climate appreciative of learning is facilitated by participative leadership stimulating the unique input of individual employees in the work process and decision making (De Poel et al., 2012).

A learning climate is crucial for positive diversity outcomes (Ely et al., 2012). Training of leaders can capitalize on this. In addition, research suggests that it is possible to have teams actively develop new and more inclusive identities in group sessions themselves, through negotiation or observation of one another's behaviour that allow for unique input of individuals but that also lead to a sense of sharedness (e.g. Postmes et al., 2005; Jans et al., 2011; see also Chapter 6 by Peters et al., who discuss the beneficial effects of combining subgroup and organizational identity). By focusing on unique input of individuals rather than on their group membership, such methods may lead to positive outcomes among both minority and majority members. The present review of various approaches to diversity may help to further develop and refine human resource tools.

We realize that the present overview may evoke a strong good–bad association linked to the colorblind–colorful distinction. It is important to note that the current state of the literature on colorblindness and colorful diversity approaches suggests that neither of them will be a panacea for improving intergroup relations (Rattan & Ambady, 2013). Moreover, it is important to realize that diversity approaches are not static, but subject to transitions. For a previously homogeneous organization it may be a very good first step to implement, for example, unbiased selection procedures in order to provide fair chances also to minority group members. Moreover, organizations that do adopt an Integration-and-Learning perspective may nonetheless keep using methods that fit with a different perspective. For example, when moving towards an Integration-and-Learning perspective an organization will probably not abandon unbiased selection procedures, which are based on ideas of fairness. However, to really get added value and mutual learning from diversifying, managers' perspectives on diversity need to go beyond a concern about fairness and need to develop further towards openly acknowledging and encouraging differences on the work floor (as is also an important aspect in the ASPIRe model as described by Peters et al., this volume). When this appreciation of differences is not realized at the expense of those who belong to the mainstream, and when the work is structured such that interpersonal relations can be built across cultural boundaries, there will be a great deal to gain from diversity.

Note

1 Note that labelling this perspective "fairness" refers to the explicitly stated goal of such a perspective to provide fair treatment to minority groups in society. Whether such an ideology actually serves this goal, or, as some critics argue, actually reinforces status inequalities, is not covered by this label.

References

Abrams, D. & Hogg, M. A. (Eds.) (1990). Social identification, self-categorization, and social influence. *European Review of Social Psychology*, *1*, 195–228.

Andriessen, I., Nievers, E., & Dagevos, J. (2012). *Op achterstand. Discriminatie van niet-westerse migranten op de arbeidsmarkt. [Falling behind: Discrimination of non-Western migrants on the labor market.]* Den Haag: Sociaal en Cultureel Planbureau, November.

Aron, A., Aron, E. N., & Smollan, D. (1992). Inclusion of Other in the Self Scale and the structure of interpersonal closeness. *Journal of Personality and Social Psychology*, *63*, 596–612.

Ashforth, B., Harrison, S., & Corley, K. (2008). Identification in organizations: An examination of four fundamental questions. *Journal of Management, 34*(3), 325–374.

Bourhis, R. Y., Moïse, L., Perreault, S., & Senécal, S. (1997). Towards an interactive acculturation model: A social psychological approach. *International Journal of Psychology, 32*(6), 369–386. doi:10.1080/002075997400629.

Byrne, D. S. (1999). *Social exclusion.* Buckingham: Open University Press.

Brickson, S. (2000). The impact of identity orientation on individual and organizational outcomes in demographically diverse settings. *Academy of Management Review, 25*(1), 82–101.

Brickson, S. & Brewer, M. B. (2001). Identity orientation and intergroup relations in organizations. In M. Hogg & D. Terry (Eds.), *Social identity processes in organizational contexts* (pp. 49–65). Philadelphia: Psychology Press.

Cable, D. M. & DeRue, D. S. (2002). The convergent and discriminant validity of subjective fit perceptions. *Journal of Applied Psychology, 87*, 875–884.

Cox, T. (1991). The multicultural organization. *Academy of Management Executive, 5*(2), 34–47.

Cox, T. (1993). *Cultural diversity in organizations: Theory, research and practice.* San Francisco, CA: Berrett-Koehler.

Cox, T. H. & Blake, S. (1991). Managing cultural diversity: Implications for organizational competitiveness. *The Executive, 5*, 45–56.

Cross, S. E., Bacon, P. L., & Morris, M. L. (2000). The relational-interdependent self-construal and relationships. *Journal of Personality and Social Psychology, 78*, 791–808.

De Poel, F., Stoker, J. I., & Van der Zee, K. I. (2012). Climate control? The relationship between leadership, climate for change, and work outcomes. *The International Journal of Human Resource Management, 23*, 694–713.

Ely, R. J. & Thomas, D. A. (2001). Cultural diversity at work: The effects of diversity perspectives on work group processes and outcomes. *Administrative Science Quarterly, 46*, 229–273.

Ely, R. J., Padavic, I., & Thomas, D. A. (2012). Racial diversity, racial asymmetries, and team learning environment: Effects on performance. *Organization Studies, 33*, 341–362.

Harquail, C. V. & Cox, T. C. (1993). Organizational culture and acculturation. In T. Cox, Jr., *Cultural diversity in organizations. Theory, research & practice* (pp. 161–176). San Francisco: Berrett-Koehler Publishers.

Haslam, S. A. (2001). *Psychology in organizations: The social identity approach.* London: Sage.

Haslam, S. A., Eggins, R. A., & Reynolds, K. J. (2003). The ASPIRe model: Actualizing social and personal identity resources to enhance organizational outcomes. *Journal of Occupational and Organizational Psychology, 76*, 83–113.

Haslam, S. A., Reicher, S. D., & Platow, M. J. (2011). *The new psychology of leadership: Identity, influence and power.* London: Psychology Press.

Hofhuis, J. (2012). *Dealing with differences: Managing the benefits and threats of cultural diversity at the workplace.* Kurt Lewin Institute Dissertation Series; University of Groningen, The Netherlands.

Hofhuis, J., Van der Zee, K. I., & Otten, S. (2008). *Uitstroom van allochtonen bij de Rijksoverheid [Turnover among cultural minorities employed at the Dutch Public Service].* Den Haag: A&O-fonds Rijk.

Hofhuis, J., Van der Zee, K. I., & Otten, S. (2012). Social identity patterns in culturally diverse organizations: The role of diversity climate. *Journal of Applied Social Psychology, 42*, 964–989.

Jans, L., Postmes, T., & Van der Zee, K. I. (2011). The induction of shared identity: The positive role of individual distinctiveness for groups. *Personality and Social Psychology Bulletin, 37*, 1130–1141.

Karafantis, D. M., Pierre-Louis, J., & Lewandowski, G. W. J. (2010). A comparison of the multicultural and colorblind perspectives on the intergroup attitudes of college students. *Journal of Human Behavior in the Social Environment, 20*(5), 688–710.

Kochan, T., Bezrukova, K., Ely, R., Jackson, S., Joshi, A., Jehn, K., Leonard, J., Levine, D., & Thomas, D. (2003). The effects of diversity on business performance: Report of the diversity research network. *Human Resource Management, 42*, 3–22.

Kristof-Brown, A. L., Zimmerman, R. D., & Johnson, E. C. (2005). Consequences of individuals' fit at work: A meta-analysis of person–job, person–organization, person–group, and person–supervisor fit. *Personnel Psychology, 58*, 281–342.

Levin, S., Matthews, M., Guimond, S., Sidanius, J., Pratto, F., Kteily, N., Pitpitan, E. V., & Dover, T. (2012). Assimilation, multiculturalism, and colorblindness: Mediated and moderated relationships between social dominance orientation and prejudice. *Journal of Experimental Social Psychology, 48*, 207–212.

Ling, S. C. (1990). The effects of group cultural composition and cultural attitudes on performance of blacks and whites, using a black and white TAT. With black and white administrators. *Journal of Applied Psychology, 65*, 685–696.

Luijters, K. (2008). *Making diversity bloom: Coping effectively with cultural differences at work*. Kurt LewinInstitute Dissertation Series, Enschede, the Netherlands: Print Partners Ipskamp.

Luijters, K., Van der Zee, K. I., & Otten, S. (2007). Cultural diversity in organizations: Enhancing identification by valuing differences. *International Journal of Cross-cultural Relationships, 32*, 154–163.

McLeod, P. L. & Lobel, S. A. (1992). The effect of ethnic diversity on idea generation in small groups. *Academy of Management Annual Meeting Best Papers Proceedings*, 227–231.

McLeod, P. L., Lobel, S. A., & Cox, T. H. (1996). Ethnic diversity and creativity in small groups. *Small Group Research, 27*, 248–264.

Mannix, E. & Neale, M. A. (2005). What difference makes a difference: The promise and reality of diverse groups in organizations. *Psychological Science in the Public Interest, 6*, 31–55.

Markus, H. R., Steele, C. M., & Steele, D. M. (2000). Colorblindness as a barrier to inclusion: Assimilation and nonimmigrant minorities. *Daedalus, 129*(4), 233–259.

Meeussen, L., Otten, S., & Phalet, K. (2014). Managing diversity: How leaders' multiculturalism and colorblindness affect work group functioning. *Group Processes & Intergroup Relations*. doi: 10.1177/1368430214525809.

Milliken, F. J. & Martins, L. L. (1996). Searching for common threads: Understanding the multiple effects of diversity in organizational groups. *Academy of Management Review, 21*, 403–433.

Nakui, T., Paulus, P. B. & Van der Zee, K. I. (2011). The role of attitudes in reactions to diversity in work groups. *Journal of Applied Social Psychology, 41*, 2327–2351.

Newcomb, T. M. (1956). The prediction of interpersonal attraction. *Psychological Review, 60*, 393–404.

Plaut, V. C., Garnett, F. G., Buffardi, L. E., & Sanchez-Burks, J. (2011). "What about me?" Perceptions of exclusion and whites' reactions to multiculturalism. *Journal of Personality and Social Psychology, 101*(2), 337–353.

Pless, N. M. & Maak, T. (2004). Building an inclusive diversity culture: Principles, processes and practice. *Journal of Business Ethics, 54*(2), 129–148.

Podsiadlowski, A., Gröske, D., Kogler, M., Springer, C., & Van der Zee, K. I. (2013). Managing a culturally diverse workforce: Diversity perspectives in organizations. *International Journal of Intercultural Relations, 37*, 159–175.

Postmes, T., Haslam, S. A., & Swaab, R. (2005). Social influence in small groups: An interactive model of social identity formation. *European Review of Social Psychology, 16*, 1–42.

Purdie-Vaughns, V. & Ditlmann, R. (2010). Reflection on diversity science in social psychology. *Psychological Inquiry, 21*(2), 153–159.

Rattan, A. & Ambady, N. (2013). Diversity ideologies and intergroup relations: An examination of colorblindness and multiculturalism. *European Journal of Social Psychology, 43*, 12–21.

Roberson, Q. M. (2006). Disentangling the meanings of diversity and inclusion in organizations. *Group and Organization Managament, 31*, 212–236.

Roccas, S. & Brewer, M. B. (2002). Social identity complexity. *Personality and Social Psychology Review, 6*, 88–106.

Ryan, C. S., Hunt, J. S., Weible, J. A., Peterson, C. R., & Casas, J. F. (2007). Multicultural and colorblind ideology, stereotypes, and ethnocentrism among black and white Americans. *Group Processes & Intergroup Relations, 10*(4), 617–637.

Schneider, B., Goldstein, H. W., & Smith, D. B. (1995). The ASA-framework; An update. *Personnel Psychology, 48*, 748–769.

Steele, C. & Aronson, J. (1995). Stereotype threat and the intellectual test performance of African Americans. *Journal of Personality and Social Psychology, 69*, 797–811.

Stephan, W. G. & Stephan, C. (2000). An integrated threat theory of prejudice. In S. Oskamp (Ed.), *Reducing prejudice and discrimination* (pp. 23–45). Mahwah, NJ: Lawrence Erlbaum Associates.

Stevens, F. G., Plaut, V. C., & Sanchez-Burks, J. (2008). Unlocking the benefits of diversity: All-inclusive multiculturalism and positive organizational change. *Journal of Applied Behavioral Science, 44*(1), 116–133.

Tajfel, H. (1982). Instrumentality, identity and social comparisons. In H. Tajfel (Ed.), *Social identity and intergroup relations* (pp. 483–507). Cambridge, UK: Cambridge University Press.

Tajfel, H. & Turner, J. C. (1979). An integrative theory of intergroup conflict. In W. G. Austin & S. Worchel (Eds.), *The social psychology of intergroup relations* (pp. 33–48). Monterey, CA: Brooks/Cole.

Thomas, D. A. & Ely, R. J. (1996). Making differences matter: a new paradigm for managing diversity. *Harvard Business Review*, Sept.–Oct. 1996, 1–12.

Thomas, K. M., Mack, D. A., & Montagliani, A. (2004). The arguments against diversity: Are they valid? In M. S. Stockdale & F. J. Crosby (Eds.), *The psychology and management of workplace diversity* (pp. 31–51). Malden: Blackwell Publishing.

Van Knippenberg, D. & Haslam, S. A. (2003). Realizing the diversity dividend: Exploring the subtle interplay between identity, ideology and reality. In S. A. Haslam, D. V. Knippenberg, M. Platow, & N. Ellemers (Eds.), *Social identity at work: Developing theory for organizational practice* (pp. 61–77). New York: Taylor & Francis.

Van Knippenberg, D. & Schippers, M. C. (2007). Work group diversity. *Annual Review of Psychology, 58*, 515–541.

Van Knippenberg, D., De Dreu, C. K., & Homan, A. C. (2004). Work group diversity and group performance: An integrative model and research agenda. *Journal of Applied Psychology, 89*, 1008–1022.

Verkuyten, M. (2005). Ethnic group identification and group evaluation among minority and majority groups: Testing the multiculturalism hypothesis. *Journal of Personality and Social Psychology, 88*(1), 121–138.

Vos, M. W., Jansen, W. S., Otten, S., Podsialowski, A., & Van der Zee, K. I. (2013). Colorblind or colorful? The impact of diversity approaches on inclusion and work outcomes among majority and minority employees. Manuscript under review.

Watson, W. E., Kumar, K., & Michaelsen, L. K. (1993). Cultural diversity's impact on interaction process and performance: Comparing homogeneous and diverse task groups. *Academy of Management Journal, 36*, 590–602.

Wentling, R. M. & Palma-Rivas, N. (2000). Current status of diversity initiatives in selected multinational corporations. *Human Resource Development Quarterly, 11*, 35–60.

Williams, K. & O'Reilly, C. (1998). The complexity of diversity: A review of forty years of research. In D. Gruenfeld & M. Neale (Eds.), *Research on managing in groups and teams*. Greenwich CT: JAI Press.

Wolsko, C., Park, B., & Judd, C. M. (2006). Considering the Tower of Babel: Correlates of assimilation and multiculturalism among ethnic minority and majority groups in the united states. *Social Justice Research, 19*(3), 277–306.

Wolsko, C., Park, B., Judd, C. M., & Wittenbrink, B. (2000). Framing interethnic ideology: Effects of multicultural and color-blind perspectives on judgments of groups and individuals. *Journal of Personality and Social Psychology, 78*(4), 635–654.

4 Respect and the viability of ethnically diverse institutions

Yuen J. Huo,[1] Kevin R. Binning, and Christopher T. Begeny

Projections from the 2010 national census indicate that within the next 20 years the United States will become a plurality nation in which no one cultural, ethnic, or racial group will constitute the numerical majority (U.S. Census Bureau, 2012). This unprecedented shift is due in large part to recent waves of immigration from Asian and Latin American nations. Similarly, the U.S. labor force will become substantially more diverse in the next few decades. Between 2000 and 2050, the share of Whites in the labor force is expected to drop by 20 percent (from 73 percent to 53 percent), while all major ethnic minority groups are expected to grow. Notably, the share of Hispanics will more than double (from 11 percent to 24 percent), and Asians will increase by 6 percent (from 5 percent to 11 percent; Toossi, 2002). As a consequence, institutions and communities across the U.S. must face the challenges posed by this demographic shift. The more immediate challenge is the incorporation of large numbers of new immigrants in addition to historical minority groups. A second challenge is how Whites, the traditional majority ethnic group and the dominant political force in the U.S., will respond to these demographic changes.

Within this context, how can institutions continue to build human capital while maintaining cohesion and productivity within the workplace and other institutions? To address this question, we review past research and introduce recent findings on the psychological experience of respect in groups. We argue that the desire to feel valued by other group members is key to maintaining strong and viable, diverse institutions. That is, individuals are attuned to information that indicates how much they are valued (respected) by ingroup members. In turn, these perceptions of respect promote not only a sense of institutional belonging and commitment but also psychological well-being. Together, this set of attitudes and behaviors can strengthen the institution as a whole.

A key insight of the research we will review is that the specific identity concerns experienced by individuals depend, in part, on where their ethnic group falls in the societal hierarchy. In the U.S., there is wide consensus that Whites represent the dominant ethnic group, whereas the other ethnic groups (e.g. African Americans, Asians, and Latinos) hold subordinate

Source of evaluation	Target of evaluation	Type of respect
Institution	Individual members of the institution	Personal respect
Institution	Ethnic groups within the institution	Ethnic subgroup respect
Ethnic group	Individual members of the ethnic group	Ethnic intragroup respect

Figure 4.1 Typology of respect.

status (Sidanius et al., 1997). As a consequence, individuals may be aware of and respond to several distinct manifestations of the experience of respect. These experiences vary in terms of the source of respect (the institution or the individual's ethnic group) as well as the target (the individual or his or her ethnic group). We focus on three manifestations of the experience of respect: 1) personal respect (institution members' views about the individual); 2) ethnic subgroup respect (institutional members' views about the ethnic group); and 3) ethnic intragroup respect (ethnic group members' views about the individual) (see Figure 4.1). In this chapter, we provide empirical evidence for the distinctiveness of each form of respect and their consequences for the institution and its individual members. We also discuss actions that institutions can take to promote feelings of respect among its members.

The psychology of respect: theory and background

The theoretical framework for the present analysis draws from research on the individual's relationship to others within organized groups (workplace, school, community). The psychological construct we refer to as personal respect captures people's views of their value to and standing within important reference groups (Huo et al., 2010a; Smith et al., 2003; Spears et al., 2006). Personal respect from the group represents the group's opinion of individuals rather than a reflection of views derived from idiosyncratic interpersonal relationships (Emler & Reicher, 1995). Thus, the respect that individuals are shown by the group is a central part of their social identity (Smith et al., 2003). This conceptualization is distinct from the majority of work on social identity and self-categorization which highlights individuals' knowledge of, attachment to, and evaluations of groups they belong to (Leach et al., 2008). Whether people view the group as valuable is clearly important. However, people's beliefs about whether the group values them can be equally, if not more, important.

Because a defining feature of the experience of respect is that it reflects the group's collective opinion, the actions of important group representatives (i.e. group leaders, authorities) carry particular weight. Related research indicates that group authorities, by enacting decisions in a fair way, communicate the group's respect for individual members. This, in turn, elicits loyalty and attachment to the group (Smith et al., 2003; Tyler et al., 1996). Similar responses are produced when group members directly communicate their collectively shared opinion of individual members (Ellemers et al., 2004; Huo et al., 2010b; Simon & Stürmer, 2003).

Individuals' feelings of the extent to which they are respected by the group predict a wide range of attitudes and behaviors including organizational citizenship behavior, trust in and deference to group leaders, and engaging in workloads above and beyond what is required (for a review, see Smith et al., 2003). Other research has demonstrated another important outcome: individuals who perceive respect from their reference groups report higher levels of self-esteem (Koper et al., 1993; Smith et al., 2003; Smith et al., 1998). The close tie between perceived respect and the self-concept suggests that the communication of respect from the reference group facilitates the bond between the self and the group. When individuals feel valued by the group, they are motivated to think of themselves and to act as a group member (Huo et al., 2010a). In sum, the communication of respect (or lack thereof) from the group is an important mechanism that has potential to shape the health of the group and its individual members.

Our analysis thus far provides a basic framework for understanding the experience of respect as communication from one group to one individual. In many institutions, social relations are more complex (Dovidio et al., 2009). For example, at the workplace, employees are organized into departments and work groups. In ethnically and culturally diverse institutions, ethnicity and race also become salient forms of social categorization (Huo & Tyler, 2001). Within these more complexly organized institutions, evaluative feedback about one's subgroup (e.g. one's ethnic group) takes on special meaning and may independently influence the dynamics of intragroup relations.

Below, we first explore the basic relationship between personal respect and indicators of the vitality of the institution and its individual members. We then focus on the relationship between subgroup respect and these outcomes. Lastly, we introduce the concept of ethnic intragroup respect and focus on how the ethnic ingroup, itself, is a potential source of important social evaluative feedback, particularly for members of ethnic minority groups. Throughout, we pay particular attention to how these three manifestations of the experience of respect may have differential consequences for institutions and their members, and also whether these processes are similar or different for the dominant ethnic group (e.g. White Americans) and for ethnic minority groups (e.g. African Americans, Asians, and Latinos).

Personal respect

In this section, we examine the relationship between personal respect and each of two categories of outcomes. The first, *group-oriented outcomes*, reflects individual attitudes and behavioral intentions that directly affect the group, such as group commitment and the desire to engage in actions to improve the group. The second, *individual-oriented outcomes*, reflects indicators of personal well-being including self-esteem and low levels of perceived stress.

Personal respect and group-oriented outcomes

As noted earlier, individuals' perceptions that they are respected by other ingroup members have been linked to attitudes and behaviors that affect the welfare of the group, including group loyalty, commitment, and trust in the decisions of group authorities (for reviews see Huo et al., 2010a; Smith et al., 2003; Spears et al., 2006). These relationships are robust and have been demonstrated across different institutional contexts. In the workplace, feelings of respect promote organizational citizenship and greater compliance with workplace rules and with supervisor decisions, even after controlling for economic incentives (Tyler & Blader, 2000). In the educational context, our research shows that when high school students feel valued by their school community, they identify more with the school, volunteer to help at school, and report lower levels of social alienation (Huo et al., 2010a). Finally, in a study of at-risk youths in urban areas, young men who perceived high levels of respect within their local community were less likely to engage in future violent behavior that harms the community (Leary et al., 2005). Together, these field studies show a clear relationship between individuals' perceptions of being valued by the group and their motivation to act on behalf of the group. Studies that experimentally manipulate the experience of respect, similarly, show that when the group conveys their approval of and regard for individual members, they respond with more positive views about the group and greater willingness to engage in behavior that promotes group goals (Simon & Stürmer, 2003; Smith et al., 1998).

These research findings show that perceptions of respect from other members of the institution are associated with a range of attitudes and behaviors that facilitate collectively shared goals. However, a stronger test would be one in which we evaluate whether these relationships hold up during a time of institutional distress. To test this possibility, we reanalyzed data from a study of faculty employed by universities in California during the height of the U.S. economic recession in 2009. In response to severe cutbacks in public funding for California's public university systems, administrators implemented a controversial year-long work furlough for faculty. The furlough was not accompanied by reductions in teaching load and/or other adjustments for amount of service provided. Thus, the furlough was equivalent to a 10 percent salary reduction. Given the high level of uncertainty and discontent surrounding the furlough, the situation provided a unique opportunity to evaluate the robustness of the influence of perceived respect on individuals' attitudes and behavioral intentions.

Faculty members from three campuses were recruited via e-mail to complete a web-based survey ($N = 953$) (for study details, see Osborne et al., 2012). We measured the extent to which individuals felt that they were respected by the university community with three items. Each began with the stem: *Most of the time, I feel that people at my university . . .* followed by: 1) *value my opinions and ideas*; 2) *think highly of my abilities and talents*, and 3) *admire my achievements*. These items were adapted from previous research that assessed feelings of respect from group members (see for example, Huo et al., 2010b).

To evaluate whether perceived respect would predict views about a workplace during a time of organizational crisis, we examined the predicted relationship using four different outcome variables: organizational belongingness, strength of organizational identification, support for the work furlough, and intention to protest the furlough. In addition to individuals' perceptions of respect within the workplace, we included in our model indicators that reflect a number of more objective indicators of status (e.g. years of service, gender).

Table 4.1 shows that perception of personal respect was a significant predictor of each of the four outcomes. It is notable that in a model that includes objective indicators of status, perceived respect was a significant predictor of organizational belongingness, organizational identification, support for the work furlough, and intention to protest the work furlough. The findings show that the relationship between perceived respect and group-oriented outcomes is robust and persists even during a highly stressful time for the organization and its employees. With what amounts to a sizable pay cut, faculty members who perceived that they were valued within the university community continued to support their workplace. Moreover, feelings of respect predicted whether or not these individuals went along with or actively

Table 4.1 Perceived respect for the individual and organizational outcomes

	Outcome variables			
	Organizational belongingness	*Organizational identification*	*Support work furlough*	*Protest work furlough*
Predictors				
Personal Respect	0.69**	0.42**	0.13**	−0.14**
Research Grant (No/Yes)	0.01	0.03	0.10*	−0.08[+]
Admin. Position (No/Yes)	−0.03	−0.08*	0.05	−0.03
Tenure (No/Yes)	−0.01	−0.05	−0.22**	0.15**
Years of Employment	−0.05	0.17**	0.12[+]	−0.06
White (No/Yes)	0.00	0.06	0.02	−0.08[+]
Gender (Male/Female)	0.07*	0.02	0.00	−0.11[+]
Age	0.00	0.00	0.02	−0.10[+]
R-squared	0.69**	0.21**	0.06**	0.07**

Notes: [+] $p < 0.10$, * $p < 0.05$, ** $p < 0.01$.

protested the furlough. Together with existing studies, these findings suggest that perceived respect is an important contributor to institutional cohesion, not only under normal conditions but also during highly difficult times.

Personal respect and psychological well-being

We have introduced evidence to show that experiences of personal respect can promote attitudes and behaviors that help to maintain institutional vitality. An arguably equally important indicator of how well an institution is doing is whether its individual members are physically and psychologically healthy and well adjusted. If we think of individual well-being as a partial reflection of institutional climate, then institutions comprised of healthy individuals should have a distinct advantage over those that do not.

Findings across a number of disciplines suggest that an individual's social position (an objective form of status distinct from but related to respect; see discussion in Binning & Huo, 2012) is associated with measurable psychological and physical health outcomes. Analyses of large-scale epidemiological datasets, for example, show that even after controlling for obvious predictors of health and longevity (e.g. income, lifestyle), status (defined as social position within a community) independently predicted health outcomes (Marmot, 2004). Individuals in positions consensually recognized as having higher social status are physically healthier and live longer. Furthermore, attesting to the link between subjective experiences of respect and health outcomes, large-scale surveys of workers found that perceptions of respectful treatment by supervisors predicted fewer sick days and reports of work-related illnesses (Elovainio et al., 2005; Schmitt & Dörfel, 1999). While these findings draw from correlational data, experimental data produce converging findings. A field experiment of nurses who received an involuntary salary reduction found that those with supervisors trained to behave in a respectful and fair manner reported fewer occurrences of psychosomatic stress symptoms (e.g. sleep problems; Greenberg, 2006). Recent work in health psychology has begun to uncover the biological pathways through which the experience of respect affects health. Experimentally inducing acute threat to individuals' social standing has produced short-term but measurable physiological changes (Gruenewald et al., 2006; Murphy et al., 2013).

Research linking respect from the group to the self-concept provides insight into why social evaluations from the group would affect health-related outcomes. Consistent with the findings described above, an early experiment documented that the communication of respect from a referent group leads to higher levels of self-esteem (Koper et al., 1993). Moreover, the effect of respect on self-esteem is moderated by social categorization. Individuals report higher levels of self-esteem when the communication of respect comes from an ingroup authority than when it comes from an outgroup authority (Smith et al., 1998). This finding suggests that the influence of respect on the individuals' sense of subjective well-being is tied specifically to the group that individuals identify with. One implication of this finding is that it can be thought of as a double-edged sword. On the one hand, the communication of respect would have positive benefits for the well-being of individuals who identify strongly with the organization. On the other hand, when the communication of respect is absent, these same individuals also bear the negative consequences.

In our own recent research, we sought to expand upon this work by examining the possibility that experiences with personal respect can be detected not just in self-evaluations but also in measurable outcomes that more directly reflect psychological health. To do so, we draw upon work on the group-value model which suggests that individuals are highly motivated to seek information about their value to self-relevant groups (Lind & Tyler, 1988). Research motivated by the group-value model demonstrates that the actions of group leaders convey important information about how the group as a whole feels about individual members. Specifically, when leaders or other key group representatives treat individuals in a way that is consistent with standards of fairness (neutrality, politeness, consideration of different views), they communicate the individual's value or worth to the group. In contrast, when leaders act in a way that deviates from fairness standards, they communicate that the individual has a marginal status. Other research suggests that members of small work groups who collectively treat individual group members in a fair or unfair way can elicit similar responses (Simon & Stürmer, 2003).

Building on this research, we examined whether how individuals are treated by group members would shape their well-being, mediated by perceptions of personal respect. That is, individuals who are treated in a fair way by the group are likely to recognize that they are respected members of the group. The perception that they are valued by the group, in turn, predicts higher levels of subjective well-being. We tested these hypothesized relationships using data from a field study (for details, see, Huo et al., 2010b). In the study, students at an ethnically diverse, urban high school were interviewed about their everyday experiences at school. Students were asked to report how they are treated by most peers, teachers, and staff at the school. They also reported perceptions of how they are viewed by most people in their school community (i.e. personal respect). Several measures of psychological well-being were assessed including self-esteem, anxiety, and depressive symptoms. The findings show that experiences with both teachers/staff and peers shape perceptions of respect from the group and indicators of psychological well-being. Individuals who feel that they are generally treated fairly by peers, teachers, and staff report more positive psychological adjustment, and this relationship was mediated by perceptions of respect.

Concerns about personal respect across ethnic groups

The research we have reviewed suggests that the communication of respect can contribute to organizational vitality in multiple ways—by motivating group-oriented attitudes and behaviors and promoting the well-being of individuals. However, in diverse institutions, an important question that begs to be answered is whether these relationships hold up across different ethnic groups. The high school field study drew from a highly diverse sample and thus provided an opportunity to test the robustness of the communication of respect as a mechanism for creating inclusion. Interestingly, we found that the link between perceptions of being valued by the school community and psychological well-being is stronger among African American and Latino students than it is among White and Asian students. While Asians are a numerical minority in American society, in studies that asked individuals to rank the relative standing of different ethnic groups, Asians are generally ranked higher than African Americans and Latinos and closer to Whites (Begeny & Huo, 2013; Sidanius et al., 1997). Thus, one possible explanation for the differences across ethnic groups is that membership in lower-status subgroups within an institution may increase the motivation to search for status-affirming information (Jetten et al., 2002).

Together, the findings suggest that perceived respect, derived from interactions with group members, is a potentially effective tool for promoting feelings of inclusion in diverse institutions. However, the observed interaction between ethnic group membership and perceptions of respect suggests that structural elements within the institution such as the relative standing of ethnic group must be considered.

Subgroup respect

In diverse institutions, individuals are not only members of the institution but also members of salient subgroups within the institution (e.g. members of their ethnic groups). Thus, ethnic, cultural, and other subgroup-based divisions may shape individuals' perceptions and experiences of respect. Self-categorization theory suggests that personal and social identities are distinct (Turner, 1987). Here, we consider how the experience of subgroup respect may be similar to or different from the experience of personal respect.

Past research demonstrates that recognition and acknowledgement of ethnic identities are more important to ethnic minorities than to majority group members (Hehman et al., 2012; Plaut et al., 2011). One reason may be that ethnic identity is more salient among ethnic minority group members (Phinney, 1996; Waters, 1990). Alternatively, ethnic minorities may be more concerned about the standing of their ethnic subgroup when their subgroup is seen as marginalized or peripheral to a broader group (Van Kleef et al., 2012). Evaluations of the ethnic subgroup by others can serve as a gauge of the extent to which the institution values an important component of individuals' social identity (Huo & Molina, 2006). Thus, in contrast to Whites, ethnic minorities may pay particular attention to information about the extent to which their ethnic subgroup is respected.

Subgroup respect and group-oriented outcomes

Datasets we have collected allowed us to test the prediction that subgroup respect would matter more to ethnic minority group members than to dominant group members. In each study, we measured subgroup respect with multiple items that are adapted from parallel items previously used to measure personal respect. Each subgroup respect item was framed to assess individuals' perceptions of the extent to which the ethnic subgroup they belong is valued by the members of the institution (e.g. *Most Americans value the opinions and ideas of most [participant's ethnic group]*). We first focused on the relationship between subgroup respect and the individual's views of and commitment to the institution and then on the relationship between subgroup respect and psychological well-being.

In a large-scale random-digit telephone survey of African Americans, Latinos, and Whites, we evaluated whether our prediction about the moderating effect of ethnic subgroup membership would hold up in the context of U.S. ethnic relations. We assessed the extent to which individuals feel that other Americans respect them (personal respect) and also the extent to which they feel that Americans respect their ethnic group (subgroup respect). Controlling for strength of identification with the nation and with their ethnic group, subgroup respect predicted attitudes toward America and toward ethnic outgroups—but only among ethnic minority respondents and not among Whites (Huo & Molina, 2006). Specifically, African Americans and Latinos who perceive that most Americans value and respect their ethnic group (i.e. high levels of subgroup respect) report more positive feelings toward the nation, higher levels of trust in its institutions, and lower levels of ethnic ingroup bias. These relationships were not present among White respondents. In contrast, among Whites, perceptions that Americans respect them as individuals (i.e. high levels of personal respect) predicted each indicator.

In a second dataset, we sought to replicate the observed group-based asymmetry in a school context (Huo et al., 2010). The school from which we drew our sample is highly diverse and characterized by a history of ethnic tension. The findings again showed that ethnic subgroup respect predicted individuals' views about the institution but only among ethnic minority students and not among White students. In particular, subgroup respect predicted more positive feelings toward the school, lower levels of school disengagement, and lower levels of ethnic ingroup bias. These relationships held among each of the ethnic minority groups included in the study: African Americans, Asians, and Latinos. In contrast, none of these relationships held among Whites.

Subgroup respect and psychological well-being

In contrast to the robust and consistent relationship between personal respect and self-esteem (Smith et al., 2003), the relationship between subgroup respect and psychological well-being is more tentative. In two studies, one of adolescents that we described earlier and another of young adults, both at ethnically diverse environments (urban high school and large public university), we did not find clear evidence of a link between perceived subgroup respect and psychological well-being (Huo et al., 2012). We did, however, replicate the relationship between personal respect and indicators of psychological well-being including self-esteem, general mental health, and self-reported physical health. These relationships held for both Whites and ethnic minorities. Subgroup respect, when controlling for personal respect, did not predict psychological well-being for any of the ethnic groups we investigated, including Whites, African Americans, Asians, and Latinos.

For Whites who historically have been the dominant ethnic group in the United States, it is reasonable to conclude that ethnic identity may be less salient and central to the self-concept. Moreover, any attention to their status as members of the dominant group may further serve as unwelcome reminders of unearned privilege (Knowles & Marshburn, 2010). The absence of a relationship between subgroup respect and psychological well-being among ethnic minorities, while counter-intuitive at first glance, is not inconsistent with related research. For example, Crocker et al. (1994) found that general public evaluations of the ethnic group predicted well-being (self-esteem, life satisfaction, depression, and hopelessness) for Whites, to a lesser extent for Asians, and no relationship among African Americans. Analyses of data from Black immigrants to the United States found that the strength of relationship between how Americans view them and their self-evaluations decreased with the duration of time that this group of socially devalued immigrants had been in the U.S. (Wiley et al., 2008). The pattern of finding suggests the evolution of an adaptive strategy, with immersion in the host country predicting greater separation of group-based feedback from self-evaluations. It is also consistent with the argument that targets of prejudice and discrimination can adapt and develop alternative strategies for seeking valid evaluative feedback. Such strategies may include separating group-based feedback from the self-concept (Crocker & Major, 1989) as well as seeking out alternative sources of feedback (Jones, 2003; Postmes & Branscombe, 2002).

Subgroup respect: some caveats

Together, the findings suggest that there are identifiable constraints on the influence of group-level respect. Respect targeted toward subgroups within an institution shapes attitudes and behaviors that benefit the organization but only among minority group members. Moreover, subgroup respect does not predict subjective well-being among individuals regardless of whether they are White or members of an ethnic minority group. Thus, in contrast to the broad influence of personal respect which predicts both group-oriented outcomes and psychological well-being among both dominant and subordinate group members, the influence of subgroup respect is more limited.

One implication of the findings reviewed is that attention must be paid not only to the individual's relationship with the institution but also to the bond between each subgroup and the institution. In the context of increasing levels of population diversity, ethnic, racial, and cultural divisions are likely to emerge within both public and private institutions such as schools and the workplace. Moreover, these divisions come with the knowledge and history of differences in access to power and resources among higher-status and lower-status ethnic groups in the broader society. While individuals' perceptions that a referent subgroup (e.g. one's ethnic group) is valued by the organization is not related to their psychological well-being, these beliefs do predict attitudes toward and willingness to engage in behavior on behalf of the institution at least among ethnic minority group members. With Latinos and Asians as the two fastest growing subpopulations in the U.S., to fully exercise all available tools for creating a sense of belonging, inclusion, and commitment among its diverse membership, institutions must take into account the distinct identity needs of these and other traditionally recognized ethnic minority groups.

Ethnic intragroup respect

Thus far, we have explored the institution as a source of identity-relevant feedback both directed toward individuals and directed toward ethnic subgroups. While this focus has generated important insights about the role of respect in ethnically diverse institutions, there is another, often overlooked source of feedback. In institutions within societies that acknowledge a consensually shared hierarchy of ethnic groups, the ethnic minority group is potentially a yet uninvestigated source of social evaluative feedback and support, independent of personal and subgroup respect. In this section, we examine the third form of respect, ethnic intragroup respect, which we conceive of as the respect for individuals that comes from other members of their ethnic ingroup.

Related research suggests that perceptions of being valued and respected by fellow ethnic group members can positively shape individuals' psychological health and well-being. In a study that examined African Americans' perceptions of being accepted by other African Americans, findings indicate that perceived acceptance predicted individuals' self-esteem, life satisfaction and general well-being (Postmes & Bramscombe, 2002). Moreover, African Americans who felt more rejected by ethnic ingroup members reported lower levels of self-esteem and well-being. Other research has found a similar pattern with multiracial individuals drawing their sense of well-being from within the community of other multiracials (Giamo et al., 2012).

In one study we conducted, we examined the relationship between ethnic intragroup respect and psychological well-being (Begeny & Huo, 2013). We examined this link not only among African Americans ($N = 173$), but also among Asians ($N = 145$), Latinos ($N = 156$), and Whites ($N = 129$).

Individuals recruited through the internet were asked to respond to a set of items that assess ethnic intragroup respect, adapted to reflect their perceptions of being valued and accepted by members of their own ethnic group. They also completed measures of self-esteem, psychological stress, anxiety, and self-reported physical health. Additionally, because prior research has focused on perceived discrimination as a predictor of individuals' well-being (e.g. Postmes & Branscombe, 2002), we also assessed experiences with ethnic discrimination and controlled for this factor in our analysis. Thus, we can evaluate how ethnic intragroup respect shapes individuals' well-being over and above what is explained by perceived discrimination.

Table 4.2 shows the results of regression analyses in which ethnic discrimination and ethnic intragroup respect were used to predict self-esteem, psychological stress, anxiety, and self-reported physical health. Even after controlling for perceived ethnic discrimination (as well as age, sex, and education), ethnic intragroup respect was a significant predictor of each indicator of psychological well-being among all four ethnic groups. The more individuals perceive respect from other ethnic ingroup members, the higher their self-esteem and physical health and the lower their levels of psychological stress and anxiety. Although the relationship between ethnic intragroup respect and physical health was not statistically reliable among Asians and Whites, the direction of the relationship was similar.

These findings indicate that respect from ethnic ingroup members shapes psychological well-being. In particular, when individuals perceive discrimination directed toward their ethnic group, perceptions of being valued and respected from other ethnic ingroup members can serve as a source of psychological support. Thus, it is important not only to promote respect between the institution and its individual members and ethnic subgroups, but also to consider the quality of relationships within each ethnic group.

Implications for managing ethnically diverse institutions in the twenty-first century

Our goal in this chapter was to review research that demonstrates how varying levels and sources of respect (personal, subgroup, and ethnic intragroup) can shape the viability of ethnically diverse institutions. The research presented illustrates the potential benefits of experiences with respect for building a sense of inclusion, but also highlights certain limitations. Below, we discuss how insights derived from the findings presented can inform efforts by managers, policymakers, and other stakeholders to create inclusive environments. We describe two pathways through which institutions can promote inclusion and, consequently, reap benefits in the form of greater commitment and loyalty among its members and higher levels of psychological well-being. The first focuses on efforts to foster interpersonal interactions in institutions that convey personal respect. The second focuses on the construction of systematic diversity policies that promote subgroup and ethnic intragroup respect.

Table 4.2 Perceived discrimination and ethnic intragroup respect as predictors of indicators of psychological well-being

Self-esteem

	Whites	*Asians*	*Blacks*	*Latinos*
Perceived discrimination	−0.317**	−0.122+	−0.152*	−0.415**
Intragroup respect	0.544**	0.622**	0.457**	0.454**
R^2	0.419**	0.385**	0.323**	0.397**

Psychological stress

	Whites	*Asians*	*Blacks*	*Latinos*
Perceived discrimination	0.283**	0.182*	0.159*	0.392**
Intragroup respect	−0.491**	−0.546**	−0.322**	−0.441**
R^2	0.342**	0.338**	0.235**	0.369**

Anxiety

	Whites	*Asians*	*Blacks*	*Latinos*
Perceived discrimination	0.216**	0.158*	0.096	0.387**
Intragroup respect	−0.546**	−0.528**	−0.446**	−0.475**
R^2	0.347**	0.294**	0.273**	0.387*

Physical health

	Whites	*Asians*	*Blacks*	*Latinos*
Perceived discrimination	−0.398**	−0.394**	−0.338**	−0.538**
Intragroup respect	0.147+	0.115	0.222**	0.146*
R^2	0.201**	0.190**	0.177*	0.332**

Notes:
+ $p < 0.10$, * $p < 0.05$, ** $p < 0.01$.
Numerical entries are standardized regression coefficients.
Background variables (age, sex, education) were entered as control variables in all models.

Developing institutional norms for conveying personal respect

Institutional cultures that communicate respect to individual members (personal respect) can engender not only attachment and loyalty to the institution but also higher levels of psychological well-being. A large body of research shows that one of the most effective ways to communicate respect is by treating individuals in a relationally fair way (see Smith et al., 2003 for a review). In particular, institutional leaders (e.g. administrators, managers), empowered to make decisions and set policies, are particularly potent sources of information about the extent to which individual members are valued by the group (Tyler & Lind, 1992). Decision-makers who listen to their constituents, behave in a polite manner, and show that they are unbiased are perceived as behaving in a fair way and, in turn, communicate respect for the affected individual (Tyler & Blader, 2000; Tyler et al., 1996). In addition, there is growing evidence that group members, acting in concert in a fair or unfair way, can also effectively convey the value of the individual to the group (Ellemers et al., 2004; Huo et al., 2010b; Simon & Stürmer, 2003). Efforts to draw awareness to the importance of interpersonal interactions and their consequences would allow institutions to create inclusion through the communication of respect for individuals. Such efforts can be carried out through the selection and training of institutional leaders (e.g. work supervisors) as well as developing a climate that underscores the importance of behaving in a relationally fair way.

Developing diversity policies that promote subgroup and ethnic intragroup respect

Since the 1960s the United States and many other Western nations have debated the merits of various diversity policies. While some advocate for a colorblind policy that de-emphasizes group-based divisions, others argue for the benefits of a more multicultural approach that acknowledges the importance of ethnic attachments (see Van der Zee and Otten chapter, this volume). Our research, while lending general support to multicultural policies, also draws attention to potential limitations and challenges of this approach. In particular, our findings suggest that policies of ethnic recognition can create inclusion by communicating respect for valued ethnic identities (subgroup respect). We find that ethnic minority members respond to the communication of subgroup respect with more positive feelings toward and engagement in the institution. In contrast, we did not find evidence of any effects (positive or negative) of ethnic recognition on Whites.

As the U.S. moves toward becoming a plurality nation and the White subpopulation continues to decline, institutions may be faced with two contrasting scenarios. On the one hand, as Whites transition from their status as a majority ethnic group to one of several minority groups, the benefits of policies that reflect the multicultural principle of inclusion may extend to all ethnic groups, including Whites. On the other hand, the threat of losing their status as the dominant ethnic group may prompt negative reactions among Whites. Emerging evidence shows that multicultural policies at the workplace lead to feelings of exclusion among Whites (Plaut et al., 2011). Moreover, Whites may resist efforts to create ethnic group-based equality and respond in ways that work to maintain or restore the prevailing social hierarchy (Binning & Unzueta, 2012; Outten et al., 2012). Thus, for now, our findings lean toward support of a multicultural approach. The communication of respect for ethnic groups has positive institutional outcomes for ethnic minorities with no adverse outcomes for Whites. However, as the U.S. population shifts and the status of Whites is called into question, such an approach can potentially create a backlash that is not currently evident.

In addition to communicating a symbolic message of ethnic recognition, multicultural policies can be manifested, more instrumentally, in support for establishing ethnically based networks within institutions. Resistance against such efforts is rooted in concerns that these networks might undermine the goal of building institutional commitment and morale by creating social divisions. However, what a colorblind approach overlooks, and what our findings suggest, is that ethnic networks can be an important source of social evaluative feedback. Discouraging or prohibiting such networks eliminates an important mechanism for promoting individual well-being, especially for members of ethnic minority groups. And, whether or not institutions actively support ethnically based networks, it is important to recognize that individuals do not check their ethnic identity at the door when they arrive at work or school. Furthermore, related research suggests that colorblind policies that downplay or obscure ethnic group identities can lead individuals to react in such a way as to further embrace the group-based attachments that the policies were intended to eradicate (Hornsey & Hogg, 2000; Huo et al., 2005). Thus, in addition to facilitating more positive inter-ethnic relations, support for ethnically based networks may have the additional benefit of promoting psychological well-being.

Conclusion

The experience of respect is central to the functioning of institutions. In workplaces, schools, and other institutions characterized by ethnic, cultural, and racial diversity, feeling valued by members of important self-relevant groups shapes attitudes and behaviors that affect the viability of the institution and the welfare of individuals within it. Such feelings of respect can be manifested in multiple ways—directed from the institution toward the individual (personal respect), directed from the institution toward ethnic subgroups (subgroup respect), and finally directed from the ethnic group toward the individual (ethnic intragroup respect). Our findings suggest that individuals, regardless of their ethnic group membership, respond positively to the communication of personal respect directed toward them as members of the institution. While the influence of subgroup respect and ethnic intragroup respect are most relevant to members of ethnic minority groups within institutions, our research suggests that, as a whole, institutions, have more to gain than to lose in adopting systemic policies that acknowledge and give support to valued ethnic attachments. In sum, the communication of respect, at multiple levels, can work in concert to promote inclusion and organizational viability in ethnically diverse institutions.

Note

1 Correspondence concerning this chapter should be addressed to Yuen J. Huo, Department of Psychology, University of California, Los Angeles, 4625 Franz Hall, Box 941563, Los Angeles, CA 90095-1563 or by email to huo@psych.ucla.edu.

References

Begeny, C. T. & Huo, Y. J. (2013, January). How intragroup respect shapes the psychological well-being of ethnic minority versus majority group members in the U.S. Poster presented at the Fourteenth Annual Meeting of the Society for Personality and Social Psychology, New Orleans, LA.

Binning, K. R. & Huo, Y. J. (2012). Understanding status as a social resource. In K. Y. Törnblom & A. Kazemi (Eds.), *Handbook of social resource theory* (pp. 133–147). New York: Springer.

Binning, K. R. & Unzueta, M. M. (2012). Perceiving ethnic diversity on campus: Group differences in attention to hierarchical representation. *Social Psychological and Personality Science, 4*(4), 500–507.

Crocker, J. & Major, B. (1989). Social stigma and self-esteem: The self-protective properties of stigma. *Psychological Review, 96*, 608–630.

Crocker, J., Luhtanen, R., Blaine, B., & Broadnax, S. (1994). Collective self-esteem and psychological well-being among White, Black, and Asian college students. *Personality and Social Psychology Bulletin, 20*, 503–513.

Dovidio, J. F., Gaertner, S. L., & Saguy, T. (2009). Commonality and the complexity of "we": Social attitudes and social change. *Personality and Social Psychology Review, 13*(3), 3–20.

Ellemers, N., Doosje, B., & Spears, R. (2004). Sources of respect: The effects of being liked by ingroups and outgroups. *European Journal of Social Psychology, 34*, 155–172.

Elovainio, M., Van den Bos, K., Linna, A., Kivimaki, M., ALa-Mursula, L., & Pentti, J. (2005). Combined effects of uncertainty and organizational justice on employee health: Testing the uncertainty management model of fairness judgments among Finnish public sector employees. *Social Science & Medicine, 61*(12), 2501–2512.

Emler, N. & Reicher, S. D. (1995). The social psychology of adolescent delinquency. Oxford, UK: Basil Blackwell.

Giamo, L. S., Schmitt, M. T., & Outten, H. R. (2012). Perceived discrimination, group identification, and life satisfaction among multiracial people: A test of the rejection-identification model. *Cultural Diversity and Ethnic Minority Psychology, 18*, 319–328.

Greenberg, J. (2006). Losing sleep over organizational injustice: attenuating insomniac reactions to underpayment inequity with supervisory training in interactional justice. *Journal of Applied Psychology, 91*, 58–69.

Gruenewald, T. L., Kemeny, M. E., & Aziz, N. (2006). Subjective social status moderates cortisol responses to social threat. *Brain Behavior and Immunity, 20*, 410–419.

Hehman, E., Gaertner, S. L., Dovidio, J. F., Mania, E. W., Guerra, R., Wilson, D. C., & Friel, B. M. (2012). Group status drives majority and minority integration preferences. *Psychological Science, 26*, 46–52.

Hornsey, M. J. & Hogg, M. A. (2000). Assimilation and diversity: An integrative model of subgroup relations. *Personality and Social Psychology Review, 4*(2), 143–156.

Huo, Y. J. & Tyler, T. R. (2001). Diversity and the viability of organizations: The role of procedural justice in bridging differences. In J. Greenberg & R. Cropanzano (Eds.), *Advances in organizational justice* (pp. 213–244). Palo Alto, CA: Stanford University Press.

Huo, Y. J. & Molina L. E. (2006). Is pluralism a viable model of diversity? The benefits and limits of subgroup respect. *Group Processes & Intergroup Relations*, *9*(3), 359–376.

Huo, Y. J., Binning, K. R., & Molina, L. E. (2010a). The interplay between fairness and the experience of respect: Implications for group life. In E. A. Mannix, M. A. Neale, & E. Mullen (Eds.), *Research on managing groups and teams: Fairness and groups* (Vol. 13, pp. 95–120). Bingley, UK: Emerald Group Publishing Limited.

Huo, Y. J., Binning, K. R., & Molina, L. E. (2010b). Testing an integrative model of respect: Implications for social engagement and well-being. *Personality and Social Psychology Bulletin*, *36*, 200–212.

Huo, Y. J., Molina, L. E., Sawahata, R., & Deang, J. M. (2005). Leadership and the management of conflicts in diverse groups: Why acknowledging versus neglecting subgroup identity matters. *European Journal of Social Psychology*, *35*(2), 237–254.

Huo, Y. J., Molina, L. E., Binning, K. R., & Funge, S. P. (2010). Subgroup respect, social engagement, and well-being: A field study of an ethnically diverse high school. *Cultural Diversity and Ethnic Minority Psychology*, *16*, 427–436.

Huo, Y. J., Binning, K. R., Molina, L. E., Danbold, F., & Yee, C. (2012). *The diversity challenge: The asymmetrical influence of personal and group respect among dominant and subordinate group members*. Manuscript submitted for publication.

Jetten, J., Branscombe, N. R., & Spears, R. (2002). On being peripheral: Effects of identity insecurity on personal and collective self-esteem. *European Journal of Social Psychology*, *32*, 105–123.

Jones, J. M. (2003). TRIOS: A psychological theory of the African legacy in American culture. *Journal of Social Issues. Special Issue: Youth Perspectives on Violence and Injustice*, *59*(1), 217–242.

Knowles, E. D. & Marshburn, C. K. (2010). Understanding White identity politics will be crucial to diversity science. *Psychological Inquiry*, *21*, 134–139.

Koper, G., Van Knippenberg, D. V., Bouhuijs, F., Vermunt, R., & Wilke, H. (1993). Procedural fairness and self-esteem. *European Journal of Social Psychology*, *23*, 313–325.

Leach, C. W., Van Zomeren, M., Zebel, S., Vliek, M. L. W., Pennekamp, S. F., Doosje, B., . . . Spears, R. (2008). Group-level self-definition and self-investment: A hierarchical (multicomponent) model of in-group identification. *Journal of Personality and Social Psychology*, *95*, 144–165.

Leary, J. D., Brennan, E. M., & Briggs, H. E. (2005). The African American adolescent respect scale: A measure of a prosocial attitude. *Research on Social Work Practice*, *15*, 462–469.

Lind, E. A. & Tyler, T. R. (1988). *The social psychology of procedural justice*. New York, NY: Plenum Press.

Marmot, M. (2004). *The status syndrome*. New York, NY: Henry Holt and Company.

Murphy, M. L. M., Slavich, G. M., Rohleder, N., & Miller, G. E. (2013). Targeted rejection triggers differential pro- and anti-inflammatory gene expression in adolescents as a function of social status. *Clinical Psychological Science*, *1*, 30–40.

Osborne, D., Smith, H. J., & Huo, Y. J. (2012). More than a feeling: Discrete emotions mediate the relationship between relative deprivation and reactions to workplace furloughs. *Personality and Social Psychology Bulletin*, *38*, 628–641.

Outten, H. R., Schmitt, M. T., Miller, D. A., & Garcia, A. L. (2012). Feeling threatened about the future: Whites' emotional reactions to anticipated ethnic demographic changes. *Personality and Social Psychology Bulletin*, *38*, 14–25.

Phinney, J. S. (1996). When we talk about American ethnic groups, what do we mean? *American Psychologist, 51,* 918–927.

Plaut, V. C., Garnett, F. G., Buffardi, L. E., & Sanchez-Burks, J. (2011). What about me? Perceptions of exclusion and Whites' reactions to multiculturalism. *Journal of Personality and Social Psychology, 101,* 337–353.

Postmes, T. & Branscombe, N. R. (2002). Influences of long-term racial environmental composition on subjective well-being in African Americans. *Journal of Personality and Social Psychology, 83,* 735–751.

Schmitt, M. & Dörfel, M. (1999). Procedural injustice at work, justice sensitivity, job satisfaction and psychosomatic well-being. *European Journal of Social Psychology, 29,* 443–453.

Sidanius, J., Feshbach, S., Levin, S., & Pratto, F. (1997). The interface between ethnic and national attachment: Ethnic pluralism or ethnic dominance. *Public Opinion Quarterly, 61,* 103–133.

Simon, B. & Stürmer, S. (2003). Respect for group members: Intragroup determinants of collective identification and group-serving behavior. *Personality and Social Psychology Bulletin, 29,* 183–193.

Smith, H. J., Tyler, T. R., & Huo, Y. J. (2003). Interpersonal treatment, social identity and organizational behavior. In S. A. Haslam, D. van Knippenberg, M. J. Platow, & N. Ellemers (Eds.), *Social identity at work: Developing theory for organizational practice* (pp. 155–171). Philadelphia, PA: Psychology Press.

Smith, H. J., Tyler, T. R., Huo, Y. J., Ortiz, D., & Lind, E. A. (1998). The self-relevant implications of the group-value model: Group membership, self-worth, and treatment quality. *Journal of Experimental and Social Psychology, 34,* 470–493.

Spears, R., Ellemers, N., Doosje, B., & Branscombe, N. (2006). *The individual within the group: Respect!* Thousand Oaks, CA: Sage Publications, Inc.

Toossi, M. (2002). A century of change: The U.S. labor force, 1950–2050. *Monthly Labor Review, 125* (5), 15–28.

Turner, J. C. (1987). A self-categorization theory. *Rediscovering the social group: A self-categorization theory, 42,* 67.

Tyler, T. R. & Lind, E. A. (1992). A relational model of authority in groups. *Advances in Experimental Social Psychology, 25,* 115–191.

Tyler, T. R. & Blader, S. (2000). *Cooperation in groups. Procedural justice, social identity, and behavioral engagement.* Philadelphia, PA: Psychology Press.

Tyler, T. R., Degoey, P., & Smith, H. (1996). Understanding why the justice of group procedures matters: A test of the psychological dynamics of the group-value model. *Journal of Personality and Social Psychology, 70*(5), 913–930. doi:10.1037/0022-3514.70.5.913.

U.S. Census Bureau (2012). *U.S. census bureau projections show a slower growing, older, more diverse nation half a century from now.* In U.S. Census Bureau [database online]. www.census.gov/newsroom/releases/archives/population/cb12-243.html.

Van Kleef, G. A., Steinel, W., & Homan, A. C. (2012). On being peripheral and paying attention: Prototypicality and information processing in intergroup conflict.

Waters, M. C. (1990). *Ethnic options: Choosing identities in America.* Berkeley, CA: University of California Press.

Wiley, S., Perkins, K., & Deaux, K. (2008). Through the looking glass: Ethnic and generational patterns of immigrant identity. *International Journal of Intercultural Relations, 32,* 385–398.

5 Predictors and consequences of exclusion and inclusion at the culturally diverse workplace

Sabine Otten and Wiebren S. Jansen

Over the past decades, organizations throughout both Europe and the U.S. have become increasingly culturally diverse (Eurostat, 2010; Hooghe et al., 2008). Objectively, this demographic change in the composition of modern workforces goes together with a higher probability of contact between different cultural groups, which, according to classic social-psychological theories (Allport, 1954; Pettigrew, 1998) should lead to more positive intergroup relations. Yet, the implementation or further increase of diversity in organizations is oftentimes problematic, and may not always lead to positive interactions between the subgroups involved (Stark et al., 2013). Meta-analytic results indicate, for example, that—compared to homogeneous teams—diverse work groups seem to struggle with decreased interpersonal trust and with a higher probability of interpersonal conflict (e.g. Joshi & Roh, 2009; Williams & O'Reilly, 1998).

Problems in diverse teams arise when members of different subgroups differ in their status position in the group and/or when members of a specific subgroup feel excluded from contact opportunities. For example, a Turkish-Dutch employee might struggle with the impression that his superior shows disproportionately little interest in his work, or that his colleagues do not include him in their chats during coffee breaks. Such subjective experiences of relative disadvantage or social exclusion at work may not only seriously hamper the functioning of the respective employee, but also of the work team as a whole. Accordingly, diagnosing the type and the prominent targets of discrimination and social exclusion at work is a relevant issue both theoretically and practically (e.g. Hitlan et al., 2006). The present chapter therefore starts with providing an overview of the prevalence of social exclusion and unfair treatment for especially minority, but also majority, members in the labor market and at work.

After having discussed possible negative experiences that employees may face in culturally diverse organizations, we will then turn to the positive potential of intercultural contact in organizations. More specifically, we will analyze the *characteristics of an inclusive organization*. Here we will again focus on employees' subjective experiences. Importantly, in our analysis we assume that inclusion in culturally diverse institutions implies more than the mere absence of exclusion. Even though employees may experience very little incidence of actual exclusion or discrimination, they may still doubt whether they do safely belong to and are appreciated by their organization. We will therefore argue that an inclusive organization is one in which diversity is not only tolerated, but rather seen as a defining and valuable aspect of the organizational identity.

Exclusion and discrimination in diverse work environments

It is well documented in the literature (e.g. Baumeister et al., 2013; Williams, 2007; Williams & Nida, 2011) that social exclusion is an aversive experience with many negative consequences attached to it, be it on the intrapersonal level (e.g. diminished self-regulation, distress and even physical pain), the interpersonal level (e.g. decreased prosocial behavior, aggressiveness) or on the intergroup level (e.g. enhanced probability of conflict).

But how likely are experiences of exclusion in *the context of work*? In the following, we will focus on this question and are especially interested in comparing the prevalence of these experiences of cultural minority employees, on the one hand, and cultural majority employees, on the other hand. According to the attraction-selection-attrition (ASA) framework of Schneider (1987), organizations have a natural tendency towards homogeneity. This is due to a cycle of three processes: (a) potential job applicants are more attracted to organizations for which they perceive congruence between characteristics of themselves and values of the organization (attraction), (b) organizations are likely to select those candidates that (demographically) resemble the current organizational population (selection), and (c) employees who do not fit choose or are forced to leave the organization, with the people remaining being less diverse than those who were initially hired (attrition). Taken together, these processes generate high levels of homogeneity within organizations, and they lead to the prediction that cultural minority members, as a result of being different, are more likely to experience exclusion than cultural majority members.

In line with this expectation, in the Netherlands, monitors of discrimination based on cultural background signal that minority members are facing more disadvantages in entering the workforce as compared to the Dutch majority group. In 2011, the unemployment rate of non-Western immigrants in the Netherlands was 14 percent, which was more than three times higher than what was reported for the ethnic majority (i.e. 4 percent; Andriessen et al., 2012). At least in part, social exclusion might be a reason for this asymmetry. More specifically, Andriessen and collaborators found that non-Western immigrants had a significantly lower chance to be invited for a job interview than equally qualified ethnic majority members (Andriessen et al., 2010; Andriessen et al., 2012). These data suggest that, at least in the stage of looking for a job, being a member of an ethnic minority, and especially being a member of a non-Western ethnic minority, goes together with a substantially higher chance of exclusion and discrimination in the job market. This observation is not only valid in the Netherlands, but also in other industrialized Western countries such as the United States (e.g. Avery, McKay, & Wilson, 2008), Sweden (e.g. Carlsson & Rooth, 2006), and the United Kingdom (e.g. Brynin & Güveli, 2012).

There are both theoretical and empirical arguments supporting the assumption that the situation of these cultural minority group members may improve as a consequence of integration[1] at the workplace. According to Intergroup Contact Theory (Pettigrew, 1998), creating repeated opportunities for intergroup contact, and encouraging intergroup cooperation, has a high probability to reduce discrimination and to enhance harmony between the groups involved. From this viewpoint, introducing cultural diversity at work should be a powerful tool to facilitate social integration of cultural minorities. Evidence in line with this idea was recently provided by De Vroome and collaborators (De Vroome et al., 2011). In a large survey among Dutch immigrants from Turkish or Moroccan descent, their studies indicated that having work was reliably linked to indicators of social trust in immigrants. And, indeed, the amount of contact with majority members was a significant mediator of the link between employment status and social trust. Hence, at least for the Netherlands, this study indicates that providing work opportunities for immigrants, that is, their inclusion in work settings, can play a decisive role in the functioning of culturally diverse societies (De Vroome et al., 2011; see also De Vroome and Verkuyten, this volume).

Yet, as outlined above when summarizing the ASA-framework (Schneider, 1987), the odds for minority members to get a job are, in general, lower than for majority members. But also for those minority members who do get in, and who, as a consequence, may develop more identification with and trust in the host society, there may still be an enhanced chance to become the target of prejudice, discrimination, and social exclusion. In the past, national surveys in the Netherlands have indicated that still a sizable number of non-Western minority employees do experience discrimination based on their ethnicity or religion (e.g. Andriessen et al., 2010). However, these surveys often lack a comparison with the majority group who may just as well feel that they are a target of social exclusion or unfair treatment at work. In addition, these studies very strongly focus on experiences of exclusion and discrimination that are blatantly related to cultural background (e.g. a female employee with Turkish background being criticized for wearing a headscarf) or at least assumed to be related to cultural background (e.g. a minority employee recognizing that (s)he is not promoted while an equally or even less qualified employee is).

It must be noted that experiences of exclusion and disadvantage need not necessarily relate to cultural background, but can also refer to other categorical characteristics (such as gender or age) or can refer to interpersonal rather than intergroup distinctions. In this case, belonging to the cultural majority versus the minority should be less predictive for experiencing disadvantage at work. Indeed, a study by Otten and Van der Zee (2011), in which the frequency of experiences of disadvantage at work was assessed without explicitly referring to cultural background, revealed surprisingly little differences between Dutch majority employees and both Western and Non-Western minority members. In this online survey, participants from all ethnic backgrounds reported relatively few situations in which they felt unfairly treated or excluded at work. Looking at the described instances of negative situations at work, exclusion from relevant information at work was most frequently mentioned, besides instances of procedural injustice (such as being excluded from relevant decision processes) or distributive injustice (such as being not promoted, while a similarly qualified fellow employee is). As a reflection of this absence of differences between majority and minority members in experiences of exclusion and disadvantage, social trust (in colleagues, the superior, and the organization as a whole) was similarly high in all three ethnic groups. These findings also fit results by De Vroome and collaborators (De Vroome et al., 2012), who found that, when controlling for the impact of employment status, social trust is comparable for ethnic minority and majority members.

A somewhat less optimistic picture, however, was provided by a study conducted in 2007 in a large governmental organization in the Netherlands, showing that cultural minority employees had a higher probability of leaving their job (voluntary turnover) than majority employees. Moreover, although overall work satisfaction did not differ significantly, satisfaction in various domains, mostly relating to job recognition (e.g. salary, work content, career development), was significantly lower (see Hofhuis et al., 2012). Patterns of findings revealing unfavorable work outcomes for minority members are not specific to the Netherlands, but also apply to other industrialized Western countries. For example, Brynin and Güveli (2012) recently concluded that in Britain inequalities between ethnic minorities relative to Whites in education and occupational position have decreased, but less so in earnings.

In sum, the findings reported in this section show that social exclusion and unfair treatment still occur at the culturally diverse workplace. Yet, for most employees, they are not defining their daily reality, nor are the odds of experiencing such negative experiences necessarily much higher for ethnic minority and majority members. As the results by De Vroome and collaborators (2011; see also De Vroome and Verkuyten, this volume) reveal, majority-minority differences in social trust decrease or vanish when controlling for employment status. Yet, other findings indicate that especially when it comes to job recognition, minority employees may still struggle with disadvantages as compared to their majority colleagues. Hence, structural integration at the workplace, that is, merely bringing cultural minority and majority members together within the same work context, might not suffice. Rather, as is also argued in several other chapters in this volume, cultural diversity in organizations needs to be managed in order to minimize negative, and especially to maximize positive, outcomes.

How much does this review of findings regarding social exclusion in (mostly Dutch) organizations tell us about how far these organizations can be classified as being inclusive? As already stated, we assume that inclusion is more than the absence of exclusion, and it will be of especial interest to those organizations who do not just want to avoid any trouble that may be associated with cultural diversity, but who rather strive for getting added value out of it. In our view, the reduction or even absence of social exclusion is probably a necessary but certainly not a sufficient condition to become an inclusive organization. As will be outlined in the following section, organizations need to provide their employees, both minority and majority members, not only with the objective experience of inclusion (as manifested in having a job), but also with the *psychological* experience of inclusion to capitalize on the benefits of cultural diversity. Such experience, we assume, is based on employees' perceptions that they safely belong and that they may exhibit their unique and authentic self.

Inclusive organizations

In the previous section we demonstrated that cultural diversity within the workplace may have both positive and negative consequences for employee well-being (e.g. work satisfaction) and organizational performance (e.g. turn-over rates). As a result, organizations are increasingly striving to create work environments in which employees from diverse backgrounds feel included (Bilimoria et al., 2008; Roberson, 2006; Shore et al., 2011; Thomas & Ely, 1996). Accordingly, the concept of inclusion has received considerable attention in both the organizational diversity literature (e.g. Lirio et al., 2008; Miller, 1998; Pelled et al., 1999; Pless & Maak, 2004; Roberson, 2006; Shore et al., 2011) and in related disciplines such as social work (Mor Barak, 2000), social psychology (Brewer, 1991; Ellemers & Jetten, 2012), educational research (Koster et al., 2009), and sports psychology (Allen, 2006). However, while there is consensus that the concept of inclusion is relevant, its concep-tualization is not unambiguous (Shore et al., 2011). Thus, in the present section, we first analyze and classify existing inclusion conceptualizations and subsequently formulate our own theoretically derived definition. Next, we explore how both individuals and organizations can establish perceptions of inclusion and how this, in turn, affects relevant work outcomes.

Theoretical perspectives on inclusion

We conducted an extensive literature review and found that existing con-ceptualizations of inclusion differ on at least two dimensions. First, while some definitions capture the *inclusion of individual employees* within an organization (which is the counterpart of the concept of exclusion that we focused on in the first part of this chapter), other definitions take the organization as their focal point and thus capture the overall *inclusiveness*

	Employee inclusion in the organization	Organizational inclusiveness
Perceptions	*Do I perceive that I am included in the organization?* Janssens & Zanoni (2008) Lirio et al. (2008) Shore et al. (2011)	*Do I perceive the organization to be inclusive?* Harquail & Cox (1993) Pless & Maak (2004) Wasserman et al. (2008)
Practices	*Am I included in organizational practices?* Mor Barak & Cherin (1998) Pelled et al. (1999) Shore et al. (2011)	*Is the organization inclusive in its practices?* Avery et al. (2008) Holvino et al. (2004) Lirio et al. (2008)

Figure 5.1 Taxonomy of existing definitions of inclusion.

of an organization. Second, some definitions define inclusion in terms of employees' *perceptions* of inclusion, while others view inclusion in terms of organizational *practices* of inclusion (such as information sharing and providing employees with influence in decision making). Combining these two dimensions allows us to distinguish four perspectives on inclusion (see Figure 5.1).

We illustrate each of these perspectives in turn. First, the definitions in the upper left cell conceptualize inclusion as the extent to which employees perceive themselves to be included within the organization. This is reflected in the definition of Janssens and Zanoni (2008), who defined inclusion as "the degree to which employees feel part of the organization" (p. 4). Here, the question of organizational inclusion is determined through the eyes of individual employees and refers specifically to their own experience of inclusion in the organization. Second, the definitions in the upper right cell take the perspective of perceived organizational inclusiveness. Here, an example is provided by Pless and Maak (2004), who relate inclusion to the work environment, stating that an inclusive work environment is one where individuals from diverse backgrounds feel valued, respected, and recognized. In these conceptualizations, the organization as a whole is the unit of analysis, and its inclusiveness is determined by the aggregated perceptions of its employees. Third, the definitions placed in the bottom left cell focus on employee inclusion in organizational practices. As an example, Mor Barak and Cherin (1998) define inclusion as the extent to which employees feel part of critical organizational processes, such as having access to information and resources, and having the ability to influence decision-making processes. Fourth, the definitions categorized in the bottom right cell conceptualize inclusion as the belief that an organization deploys specific practices to include all of its employees. This is illustrated by the definition of Avery, McKay,

Wilson, and Volpone (2008): "[inclusion is] the extent to which employees believe their organizations engage in efforts to involve all employees in the mission and operation of the organization with respect to their individual talents" (p. 6). Note that, while these four types of definitions clearly differ in their focus and level of abstraction, they are similar in the sense that they all refer to individual perceptions, beliefs, and feelings regarding inclusion rather than to objective criteria of inclusion.

Components of inclusion

Besides revealing different perspectives on organizational inclusion, our conceptual analysis of definitions provided in the literature also illustrates that existing conceptualizations distinguish different components of inclusion. As a next step, we therefore focused on identifying the common elements in these definitions. In particular, we found two recurring components. First, inclusion entails a *sense of belonging to* the organization (Janssens & Zanoni, 2008; Lirio et al., 2008; Pelled et al., 1999; Pless & Maak, 2004; Wasserman et al., 2008). The need to belong is the human motivation to form and maintain strong, stable relationships with other people. To satisfy this need, people need to have frequent and affectively pleasant interactions in a temporally stable group (Baumeister & Leary, 1995). Research suggests that, when the need for belongingness is thwarted, individuals may experience cognitive, emotional, behavioral, and health problems (Baumeister et al., 2005; DeWal et al., 2011).

Second, the conceptualizations of organizational inclusion implicitly (Janssens & Zanoni, 2008; Pelled et al., 1999) or explicitly (Avery, McKay, Wilson, & Volpone, 2008; Harquail & Cox, 1993; Holvino et al., 2004; Pless & Maak, 2004; Wasserman et al., 2008) refer to employees' sense of recognition and appreciation of their idiosyncratic personality, opinions, and skills. We label this component *authenticity*, which reflects the extent to which an individual perceives themself to be allowed and encouraged by the organization to remain true to themself (cf. Ito & Kodama, 2005). Satisfying one's need for authenticity has been shown to be positively associated with individual well-being (Deci & Ryan, 2000; Ito & Kodama, 2005; Sheldon et al., 1997; Wood et al., 2008) and organizational performance (Sheldon et al., 1997).

Inclusion versus identification

Importantly, the above analysis not only allows us to identify the key components of inclusion, but also underlines that inclusion is different from the related concepts of social and organizational identification (Edwards & Peccei, 2007; Leach et al., 2008; Mael & Ashforth, 1992). This distinction is important because it helps to further clarify who the target and who the

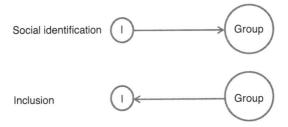

Figure 5.2 The individual–group relationship in social identification and inclusion.
Source: Jansen et al., 2014.

source is in the process of inclusion. Whereas identification reflects the extent to which an individual connects to and values the group (Edwards & Peccei, 2007; Ellemers et al., 1999; Leach et al., 2008; Mael & Ashforth, 1992; Postmes et al., 2012), in the process of inclusion it is the group that primarily determines whether an individual is included or not. This conceptualization of inclusion is in line with sociometer theory (Leary & Baumeister, 2000), which poses that people constantly monitor their social environment for cues or signals that pertain to one's inclusionary status, and with experimental manipulations of inclusion (and exclusion) in which it is the group that includes (or excludes) the individual (e.g. Baumeister et al., 2005; DeWall et al., 2011). Figure 5.2 portrays these different foci of identification and inclusion schematically.

Defining inclusion

Combining our two-dimensional conceptualization of inclusion as consisting of perceptions of belonging and authenticity with the notion that in the process of inclusion it is the group that is the primary actor, we define inclusion as *the degree to which an individual perceives that the group provides him or her with a sense of belonging and authenticity*. This particular definition of inclusion is broadly in line with the model suggested by Shore and collaborators (2011), who defined inclusion as "the degree to which individuals experience treatment from the group that satisfies their need for belongingness and uniqueness" (Shore et al., 2011: 1265). Importantly, however, we deviate from this conceptualization in one principal aspect. Whereas Shore and collaborators consider value in *uniqueness* an important second dimension of inclusion, we substituted this with the value in *authenticity*.

This adaptation of the conceptualization by Shore and collaborators is important, as valuing uniqueness may imply a threat for majority members, who are, by definition, less unique within the organization than minority members. Indeed, research has shown that cultural majority group members are likely to experience exclusion in groups that emphasize the benefits of uniqueness (Plaut et al., 2011). In contrast to uniqueness, authenticity does

	Low belongingness	High belongingness
Low authenticity	*Exclusion*	*Assimilation*
High authenticity	*Differentiation*	*Inclusion*

Figure 5.3 Typology of inclusion.
Source: Adapted from Shore et al., 2011.

not per se imply *being different*, but refers to *being true to oneself* irrespective of whether the self fits the mainstream or not. Thus, similar to valuing uniqueness, valuing authenticity implies that group members are allowed to be different from each other. Unlike valuing uniqueness, however, valuing authenticity *also* implies that group members are just as well allowed to be similar to each other. In this sense, valuing authenticity is a broader concept than valuing uniqueness, and may appeal to both atypical (e.g. minority) and prototypical (e.g. majority) group members. In this respect, our adaptation to the model by Shore and collaborators resembles the concept of all-inclusive multiculturalism as introduced by Stevens et al. (2008) (see Van der Zee and Otten, this volume). In sum, defining inclusion as a two-dimensional construct, consisting of perceptions of belonging and authenticity, theoretically creates four different types of inclusion (see Figure 5.3).

An individual perceives *exclusion* to the extent that he or she is not treated as an insider and also receives signals from the organization that he or she is not allowed to be him- or herself. An individual facing exclusion is neither able to satisfy his or her need for belongingness nor the need for authenticity. As we discussed in the first part of this chapter, this should reduce work satisfaction and well-being, but most probably also the productivity of employees. Exclusion therefore seems to have the least favorable consequences for both individuals and organizations.

The *assimilation* cell reflects situations in which an individual does perceive him- or herself as belonging to the group, but where this sense of belonging is only warranted if the individual leaves part of his or her (unique) identity behind to assimilate to the rest of the organization. In diverse organizations, this usually implies that cultural minority members should conform to the norms of the cultural majority group. Majority members, conversely, should typically have less trouble with this type of organization. Their majority status implies that—at least psychologically—there is a large overlap between the perception of who they are, and of what is typical and normative for the organization as a whole (ingroup projection, Wenzel et al., 2007).

The *differentiation* cell, with low belonging and high authenticity, reflects cases in which the individual is treated as a marginal member by the organization, but at the same time is allowed and encouraged to be authentic. Although marginal group members who can remain themselves may potentially offer the organization the opportunity of enlarging their external social capital (Ellemers & Jetten, 2012; Granovetter, 1973), there is the risk that they are not motivated to do so, because they lack a sense of belonging to the organization.

Finally, an individual will perceive *inclusion* if the organization provides him or her with a sense of belonging and allows and encourages him or her to be authentic. This implies that inclusion is not simply the opposite of exclusion; at least not on a single dimension. Rather, following from the conceptual framework of Figure 5.3, inclusion differs from exclusion on two dimensions: belonging and authenticity. That is, in order to move from exclusion to inclusion, a group member both needs to perceive an enhanced level of belonging within the group and needs to feel that he or she is more valued by the group for being him or herself. Inclusion seems to be the most beneficial state for both individuals and organizations. We will address the determinants and consequences of inclusion in more detail in subsequent sections.

Determinants of organizational inclusion

Now, an important question for both organizations and diversity scholars is *how* inclusion can be established among both minority and majority employees. A well-documented insight from the fields of relational demography and social psychology is that people generally prefer to seek connection with groups whose members are relatively similar to themselves (Byrne, 1971; Guillaume et al., 2012; Kristof-Brown et al., 2005; Tsui et al., 1992; Tsui & Gutek, 1999). However, as mentioned before, homogeneous work groups are the exception rather than the rule, as organizations have progressively diversified over the last decades (Van Knippenberg & Schippers, 2007). As a result, employees are often confronted with diverse work environments in which the simultaneous satisfaction of the needs for belonging and authenticity might be difficult to achieve. In the following, we will address how individual employees may deal with this particular challenge.

Phrased in terms of theories on social categorization (such as Self-Categorization Theory, SCT; Turner et al., 1987), inclusion can be understood as the maintenance of one's personal identity within a larger social identity. In this logic, employees are more likely to feel included in an organization if they pursue certain strategies that enable them to retain their individuality within the organization. For example, individuals can take a specific, distinct role within the organization (Bettencourt et al., 2006), or join an organization that encourages employees to express their individuality (Hornsey & Jetten, 2004; Lorenzi-Cioldi, 2006). Another line of research hints at the opportunity for individuals to secure a sense of group inclusion by employing cognitive strategies. Here, it is assumed that people's bond with a diverse group can either be inferred from their perceived own prototypicality within the group (i.e. self-stereotyping) or by the projection of one's own individual characteristics onto the group (i.e. self-anchoring, Cadinu & Rothbart, 1996). Particularly this latter process seems beneficial for identification processes in diverse groups. To illustrate, recent research by Van Veelen and collaborators showed that minority members who were invited to focus on their individual self, first, and then reflect on how far what characterizes them as an individual might also apply to the group as a whole (self-anchoring), identified stronger with the diverse group than those who were reflecting to what extent group features might also apply to themselves as an individual (self-stereotyping). For majority members, who are by definition more prototypical for the overarching group, it did not matter from which angle the link between self and group was constructed (Van Veelen et al., in press). Interestingly, however, with self-anchoring, majority members were more convinced that diversity might be of added value for the diverse group then after having engaged in self-stereotyping (Van Veelen et al., manuscript under review).

These findings suggest that not just a focus on the level of cultural subgroups, as is characteristic for the multiculturalism ideology, but also a focus on the individual in the group may be beneficial for the functioning of diverse groups. The latter idea is also central in the concept of *inductive identity formation* as introduced by Postmes et al. (2005). They argue that groups can form both top-down, such that individual group members adapt to an already existing group prototype, or bottom-up, such that the group prototype is defined over time, and is shaped by the contributions of *all* individual members. Both processes may lead to well-functioning groups, but in heterogeneous groups, inductive group formation seems to be most beneficial (Jans et al., 2011, 2012). Taken together, these lines of research suggest that it should be feasible that employees in a diverse work setting perceive themselves as belonging to the organization while at the same time remaining true to their individual self (Sheldon & Bettencourt, 2002).

Realizing inclusion, however, does not only imply challenges for the individual, but also requires effort from organizations. In order to create perceptions of inclusion among both cultural minority and majority employees, organizations have adopted certain diversity approaches (see Van der Zee and Otten, this volume, for an extensive discussion of diversity approaches). Diversity approaches reflect the organizations' normative beliefs and expectations about the reason to diversify, the value of cultural diversity, and its connection to work processes (Stevens et al., 2008). The two most commonly adopted diversity approaches are colorblindness and multiculturalism. Whereas the colorblind perspective advocates that group membership should be ignored and that employees should be primarily seen as individuals, the multicultural perspective acknowledges that people from different groups possess different perspectives and skills, which are valuable resources for organizational learning. Preliminary evidence (see later) suggests that these diversity approaches not only affect employees' well-being and functioning, but also their perceived inclusion in the organization.

In our own research we found that the extent to which an organization adopts a colorblind diversity approach predicted perceptions of inclusion for cultural majority employees, but not for cultural minority employees. In contrast, the extent to which an organization adopted a multicultural approach predicted feelings of inclusion for cultural minority employees, but not for cultural majority employees. For both groups however, feeling included in their organization, in turn, predicted the extent to which they were satisfied with their job and to what extent they believed their organization to be innovative (Vos et al., 2013). Further evidence of the difference between majority and minority members in their response to diversity statements and the importance of inclusion was provided by Plaut and colleagues (2011). They investigated whether cultural majority and cultural minority employees from a large U.S. healthcare organization differed in their support for organizational diversity programs. Results showed that cultural majority employees (White males) were less likely than their colleagues from a cultural minority background to support organizational diversity policies and initiatives. Importantly, this difference was attenuated by taking into account how included employees felt in their organization's diversity statement, such that majority employees who felt more included in their organization's diversity statement endorsed organizational diversity to a greater extent.

In sum, these findings suggest that approaches that are either purely based on the colorblind ideology, or that solely take a multicultural approach, are likely to result in low levels of perceived inclusion among at least one of the cultural subgroups present in the organization. Alternatively, an approach which emphasizes the value of diversity, but, at the same time, stresses that this diversity constitutes both minorities *and* majorities, might be received more positively by both groups (see also Van der Zee and Otten, this volume). Successful diversity management thus rests on finding a fine balance between fulfilling the inclusion needs of both minority and majority groups.

Consequences of experiencing inclusion

Up to now, we have focused on exploring what inclusion is and how individual employees and organizations strive to attain organizational inclusion. However, the question of why inclusion is important still needs to be addressed. On a very general level, one could assert that being included in groups offers many advantages to individuals (Correll & Park, 2005). Groups serve our material interests (Caporael & Baron, 1997; LeVine & Campbell, 1972), enhance our self-esteem (Abrams & Hogg, 1988; Leary & Baumeister, 2000; Luhtanen & Crocker, 1992), validate our beliefs (Hogg & Abrams, 1993; Swann et al., 2004), provide us with the notion of symbolic immortality (Greenberg et al., 1990), and offer us distinctiveness and acceptance (Brewer, 1991). However, inclusion in some groups is more important to us than inclusion in others. In particular, the group of our coworkers is arguably one of the groups that is most central to us (Van Knippenberg & Van Schie, 2000). We spend most of our working life in the presence of our direct colleagues and depend on our work to provide us with an income, to give us status, and to offer us a sense of connectedness. Therefore, it is highly likely that organizational inclusion is positively associated with individual well-being.

Indeed, in one of the studies we conducted we found that the extent to which employees felt included in their organization positively predicted the satisfaction with their job and their self-esteem (Jansen et al., 2014). Importantly, each of the two components of inclusion, belonging and authenticity, predicted a unique portion of variance of these outcome measures. Thus, consistent with our conceptual framework as depicted in Figure 5.3, employees benefited from both perceptions of belonging to the organization and perceptions of authenticity within the organization.

Interestingly, other findings by Jansen and collaborators (2012) also pointed to a relevant moderator variable for the link between perceived inclusion and work outcomes. More specifically, the effects were slightly different depending on the extent to which employees had an interdependent and an independent self-construal. The interdependent self-construal is defined as a "flexible, variable self that emphasizes (a) external, public features such as statuses, roles, and relationships, (b) belonging and fitting in, (c) occupying one's proper place and engaging in appropriate action, and (d) being indirect in communication and reading others' minds" (Singelis, 1994: 581). People with a strong interdependent self-construal think about themselves in terms of their connectedness to others. Thus, it is predicted that those with a well-developed interdependent self-construal will gain self-esteem through establishing and maintaining positive relations with others. In contrast, the independent self-construal is defined as a "bounded, unitary, stable self that is separate from social context" (Singelis, 1994: 581). People with a strong independent self-construal think of themselves in terms of their own abilities, attributes, characteristics or goals rather than in terms of those of others. As a result, it is predicted that those with a strong independent self-construal should gain self-esteem through expressing the self and validating their internal attributes. The findings are in line with these expectations: The more employees had an interdependent self-construal, the better their perceived belongingness to the organization predicted their job satisfaction and self-esteem. Likewise, the more employees had an independent self-construal, the stronger the effect of authenticity was on these two outcome variables (Jansen et al., 2012).

Inclusion may not only benefit the individual employee, but can also be advantageous for organizations as a whole (cf. Haslam et al., 2003). It has been argued that as group members perceive themselves to be more included in their group, they become more likely to act in accordance with group goals (Ellemers & Jetten, 2012). Importantly, both perceptions of belonging and perceptions of authenticity may play a crucial role in this process. While perceptions of belonging are key in ensuring that group members are *motivated* to use their knowledge and skills for the benefit of the group (by creating a bond between the group and the individual), perceptions of authenticity may *enable* them to actually do so (by creating a scope for individual contributions). First empirical evidence for such positive effects of inclusion on organizational outcomes was provided by our own research. We found that the extent to which employees perceived themselves to be included in their organization positively predicted the degree to which they perceived their organization to be innovative. Again, these effects were similar for both belonging and authenticity, indicating that both inclusion components are important for organizational functioning (Vos et al., 2013). Note that, although these beneficial effects for the organization have so far only been measured based on employee's self-reports, these findings suggest that securing employees' perceptions of inclusion might be a relevant factor towards a smooth and efficient functioning of diverse work teams.

Conclusions and implications

In this chapter, after having discussed the prevalence of actual experiences of exclusion and unfair treatment at the culturally diverse workplace, we have turned to conceptualizing and exploring the features of an inclusive organization. A relevant starting point in this conceptualization is that getting positive outcomes from cultural diversity at work necessitates more than the mere absence of structural disadvantage and social exclusion for—especially—ethnic minority members. Rather, employees need a context in which they feel that they safely belong, but also in which their authenticity and individuality is accepted and valued. In this respect, the concept of inclusion touches upon the role of *the individual in the group*, and the interplay between personal and social self.

Inferring from social-psychological research investigating how individuality, diversity, and group identification can be reconciled (e.g. Jans et al., 2011; Van Veelen et al., in press), we can conclude that, both at the individual and at the group level, it may be worthwhile to encourage employees in culturally diverse work environments to retain their individuality. Such interventions most probably will not only increase levels of identification, but also may result in heightened perceptions of inclusion. Finally, and related, on the organizational level, psychological inclusion may be facilitated by communicating diversity ideologies that are 'colorful' rather than colorblind (see Van der Zee and Otten, this volume). These ideologies are particularly likely to encourage self-anchoring and inductive group processes by recognizing and valuing differences, rather than promoting a fixed overarching organizational identity to which everybody should subscribe. Indeed, data summarized in this chapter already reveal that perceived inclusion relates to employees' work satisfaction, self-esteem, but also the perceived innovativeness of the organization.

Finally, we would like to stress that the goal of having inclusive organizations implies that *both* majority and minority members should feel that they safely belong and that they are valued for who they are. As is also implied by the concept of all-inclusive multiculturalism (Stevens et al., 2008), and by the focus on authenticity rather than uniqueness in our conceptualization of psychological inclusion, it is relevant—and possible—to appreciate differences without downgrading similarities and sharedness. In contrast, if diversity is embraced in a way that implies that being mainstream is negative, then including minorities might imply a threat to the inclusion needs of majority members. Accordingly, both differences *and* similarities need to be respected and valued in culturally diverse organizations to serve the needs of *all* groups involved. Yet, research findings are promising that diversity and individuality may blend nicely with commitment, identification, and perceived inclusion.

By offering a conceptualization of the components of perceived inclusion in organization, and by developing a scale that measures all relevant aspects of the psychological experience of inclusion (Jansen et al., 2014), our work should not only enhance theory but should be of practical value to organizations. By distinguishing various aspects of feeling included, and by distinguishing this concept from organizational identification, organizations striving for more inclusiveness have better opportunities to identify both weak and strong points, be it for individual employees, be it for teams and work groups, or for the organization as a whole. Based on such analysis, more tailored interventions may be developed.

Note

1 With integration, we mean *structural* integration (i.e. the mere fact that employees from both the cultural majority and cultural minorities are part of the same work setting).

References

Abrams, D. & Hogg, M. A. (1988). Comments on the motivational status of self-esteem in social identity and intergroup discrimination. *European Journal of Social Psychology*, *18*(4), 317–334. doi:10.1002/ejsp.2420180403.

Allen, J. B. (2006). The perceived belonging in sport scale: Examining validity. *Psychology of Sport and Exercise*, *7*(4), 387–405. doi:10.1016/j.psychsport.2005.09.004.

Allport, G. W. (1954). *The nature of prejudice*. Oxford, UK: Addison-Wesley.

Andriessen, I., Nievers, E., & Dagevos, J. (2012). *Facing disadvantage. Discrimination of non-Western immigrants on the labor market*. [Op achterstand. Discriminatie van niet-westerse migranten op de arbeidsmarkt.]. Den Haag: Sociaal en Cultureel Planbureau.

Andriessen, I., Nievers, E., Faulk, L., & Dagevos, J. (2010). *Better Mark than Mohammed? Research on discrimination of non-Western immigrants on the labor market via practical tests*. [Liever Mark dan Mohammed? Onderzoek naar arbeidsmarktdiscriminatie van niet-westerse migranten via praktijktests.]. Den Haag: Sociaal en Cultureel Planbureau.

Avery, D. R., McKay, P. F., & Wilson, D. C. (2008). What are the odds? How demographic similarity affects the prevalence of perceived employment discrimination. *Journal of Applied Psychology, 93*(2), 235–249. doi:10.1037/0021-9010.93.2.235.

Avery, D. R., McKay, P. F., Wilson, D. C., & Volpone, S. D. (2008). Attenuating the effect of seniority on intent to remain: The role of perceived inclusiveness. Paper presented at the meeting of the Academy of Management, Anaheim, CA.

Baumeister, R. F. & Leary, M. R. (1995). The need to belong: Desire for interpersonal attachments as a fundamental human motivation. *Psychological Bulletin, 117*(3), 497–529. doi:10.1037/0033-2909.117.3.497.

Baumeister, R. F., Masicampo, E. J., & Twenge, J. M. (2013). The social self. In H. Tennen, J. Suls, and I. B. Weiner (Eds.), *Handbook of psychology, vol. 5: Personality and social psychology* (pp. 247–273). Hoboken, NJ: John Wiley & Sons, Inc.

Baumeister, R. F., DeWall, C. N., Ciarocco, N. J., & Twenge, J. M. (2005). Social exclusion impairs self-regulation. *Journal of Personality and Social Psychology, 88*(4), 589–604. doi:10.1037/0022-3514.88.4.589.

Bettencourt, B. A., Molix, L., Talley, A. E., & Sheldon, K. M. (2006). Psychological need satisfaction through social roles. In T. Postmes & J. Jetten (Eds.), *Individuality and the group: Advances in social identity* (pp. 196–214). Thousand Oaks, CA: Sage Publications, Inc.

Bilimoria, D., Joy, S., & Liang, X. (2008). Breaking barriers and creating inclusiveness: Lessons of organizational transformation to advance women faculty in academic science and engineering. *Human Resource Management, 47*(3), 423–441. doi:10.1002/hrm.20225.

Brewer, M. B. (1991). The social self: On being the same and different at the same time. *Personality and Social Psychology Bulletin, 17*(5), 475–482. doi:10.1177/0146167291175001.

Brynin, M. & Güveli, A. (2012). Understanding the ethnic pay gap in Britain. *Work Employment & Society, 26*, 574–587. doi:10.1177/0950017012445095.

Byrne, D. (1971). *The attraction paradigm.* New York: Academic Press.

Cadinu, M. R. & Rothbart, M. (1996). Self-anchoring and differentiation processes in the minimal group setting. *Journal of Personality and Social Psychology, 70*(4), 661–677. doi:10.1037/0022-3514.70.4.661.

Caporael, L. R. & Baron, R. M. (1997). Groups as the mind's natural environment. In J. A. Simpson & D. T. Kenrick (Eds.), *Evolutionary social psychology* (pp. 317–344). Hillsdale, NJ: Lawrence Erlbaum Associates, Inc.

Carlsson, M. & Rooth, D. (2006). *Evidence of ethnic discrimination in the Swedish labor market using experimental data.* (No. 2281). Bonn: Institute for the Study of Labor.

Correll, J. & Park, B. (2005). A model of the ingroup as a social resource. *Personality and Social Psychology Review, 9*(4), 341–359. doi:10.1207/s15327957pspr0904_4.

De Vroome, T., Coenders, M., Van Tubergen, F. A., & Verkuyten, M. J. A. M. (2011). Economic participation and national self-identification of refugees in the Netherlands. *The International Migration Review, 45*(3), 615–638.

De Vroome, T., Coenders, M., Van Tubergen, F. A., & Verkuyten, M. J. A. M. (2012). Werk, diversiteit en sociaal vertrouwen [Work, diversity, and social trust]. In S. Otten & W. S. Jansen (Eds.), *Wanneer werkt diversiteit?* [When does diversity work?]. Groningen, The Netherlands: Instituut ISW [Institute for Integration and Social Efficacy].

Deci, E. L. & Ryan, R. M. (2000). The "what" and "why" of goal pursuits: Human needs and the self-determination of behavior. *Psychological Inquiry, 11*(4), 227–268. doi:10.1207/S15327965PLI1104_01.

DeWall, C. N., Deckman, T., Pond, R. S. J., & Bonser, I. (2011). Belongingness as a core personality trait: How social exclusion influences social functioning and personality expression. *Journal of Personality*, *79*(6), 979–1012. doi:10.1111/j.1467-6494.2010.00695.x.

Edwards, M. R. & Peccei, R. (2007). Organizational identification: Development and testing of a conceptually grounded measure. *European Journal of Work & Organizational Psychology*, *16*(1), 25–57. doi:10.1080/13594320601088195.

Ellemers, N. & Jetten, J. (2012). The many ways to be marginal in a group. *Personality and Social Psychology Review*. doi:10.1177/1088868312453086.

Ellemers, N., Kortekaas, P., & Ouwerkerk, J. W. (1999). Self-categorisation, commitment to the group and group self-esteem as related but distinct aspects of social identity. *European Journal of Social Psychology*, *29*(2–3), 371–389. doi:10.1002/(SICI)1099-0992(199903/05)29:2/3<371::AID-EJSP932>3.0.CO;2-U.

Eurostat. (2010). Labour market participation by sex and age. Retrieved 01 09 2011, from http://epp.eurostat.ec.europa.eu/statistics_explained/index.php/Labour_market_participation_by_sex_and_age.

Granovetter, M. S. (1973). The strength of weak ties. *American Journal of Sociology*, *78*(6), 1360–1380.

Greenberg, J., Pyszczynski, T., Solomon, S., Rosenblatt, A., Veeder, M., Kirkland, S., & Lyon, D. (1990). Evidence for terror management theory II: The effects of mortality salience on reactions to those who threaten or bolster the cultural worldview. *Journal of Personality and Social Psychology*, *58*(2), 308–318. doi:10.1037/0022-3514.58.2.308.

Guillaume, Y. R. F., Brodbeck, F. C., & Riketta, M. (2012). Surface- and deep-level dissimilarity effects on social integration and individual effectiveness related outcomes in work groups: A meta-analytic integration. *Journal of Occupational and Organizational Psychology*, *85*(1), 80–115. doi:10.1111/j.2044-8325.2010.02005.x.

Harquail, C. V. & Cox, T. C. (1993). Organizational culture and acculturation. *Cultural diversity in organizations: Theory, research and practice* (pp. 161–176). San Francisco: Berret-Koehler Publishers.

Haslam, S. A., Eggins, R. A., & Reynolds, K. J. (2003). The ASPIRe model: Actualizing social and personal identity resources to enhance organizational outcomes. *Journal of Occupational and Organizational Psychology*, *76*(1), 83–113. doi:10.1348/096317903321208907.

Hitlan, R. T., Kelly, K. M., Schepman, S., Schneider, K. T., & Zárate, M. A. (2006). Language exclusion and the consequences of perceived ostracism in the workplace. *Group Dynamics: Theory, Research, and Practice*, *10*(1), 56–70. doi:10.1037/1089-2699.10.1.56.

Hofhuis, J., Van der Zee, K. I., & Otten, S. (2012). Social identity patterns in culturally diverse organizations: The role of diversity climate. *Journal of Applied Social Psychology*, *42*(4), 964–989. doi:10.1111/j.1559-1816.2011.00848.x.

Hogg, M. A. & Abrams, D. (1993). Towards a single-process uncertainty-reduction model of social motivation in groups. In M. A. Hogg & D. Abrams (Eds.), *Group motivation: Social psychological perspectives* (pp. 173–190). Hertfordshire, UK: Harvester Wheatsheaf.

Holvino, E., Ferdman, B. M., & Merrill-Sands, D. (2004). Creating and sustaining diversity and inclusion in organizations: Strategies and approaches. In M. S. Stockdale & F. J. Crosby (Eds.), *The psychology and management of workplace diversity* (pp. 245–276). Malden: Blackwell Publishing.

Hooghe, M., Trappers, A., Meuleman, B., & Reeskens, T. (2008). Migration to European countries: A structural explanation of patterns, 1980–2004. *International Migration Review*, *42*(2), 476–504. doi:10.1111/j.1747-7379.2008.00132.x.

Hornsey, M. J. & Jetten, J. (2004). The individual within the group: Balancing the need to belong with the need to be different. *Personality and Social Psychology Review, 8*(3), 248–264. doi:10.1207/s15327957pspr0803_2.

Ito, M. & Kodama, M. (2005). Sense of authenticity, self-esteem, and subjective and psychological well-being. *Japanese Journal of Educational Psychology, 53*(1), 74–85.

Jans, L., Postmes, T., & Van der Zee, K. I. (2011). The induction of shared identity: The positive role of individual distinctiveness for groups. *Personality and Social Psychology Bulletin, 37*(8), 1130–1141. doi:10.1177/0146167211407342.

Jans, L., Postmes, T., & Van der Zee, K. I. (2012). Sharing differences: The inductive route to social identity formation. *Journal of Experimental Social Psychology, 48*(5), 1145–1149. doi:10.1016/j.jesp.2012.04.013.

Jansen, W. S., Vos, M. W., Otten, S., & Van der Zee, K. I. (2012). Diversity perspectives. What works when and for whom? In S. Otten, A. Dotinga & W. S. Jansen (Eds.), *When does diversity work?* [Diversiteitsperspectieven. Wat werkt wanneer en voor wie?] (pp. 5–13). Groningen: Instituut ISW.

Jansen, W. S., Otten, S., Van der Zee, K. I. & Jans, L. (2014). Inclusion: Conceptualization and measurement. *European Journal of Social Psychology.* doi:10.1002/ejsp.2011.

Janssens, M. & Zanoni, P. (2008). *What makes an organization inclusive? Organizational practices favoring the relational inclusion of ethnic minorities in operative jobs.* Unpublished manuscript.

Joshi, A. & Roh, H. (2009). The role of context in work team diversity research: A meta-analytic review. *Academy of Management Journal, 52*(3), 599–627.

Koster, M., Nakken, H., Pijl, S. J., & Van Houten, E. (2009). Being part of the peer group: A literature study focusing on the social dimension of inclusion in education. *International Journal of Inclusive Education, 13*(2), 117–140.

Kristof-Brown, A., Zimmerman, R. D., & Johnson, E. C. (2005). Consequences of individuals' fit at work: A meta-analysis of person–job, person–organization, person–group, and person–supervisor fit. *Personnel Psychology, 58*(2), 281–342. doi:10.1111/j.1744-6570.2005.00672.x.

Leach, C. W., Van Zomeren, M., Zebel, S., Vliek, M. L. W., Pennekamp, S. F., Doosje, B., Ouwerkerk, J. P., & Spears, R. (2008). Group-level self-definition and self-investment: A hierarchical (multicomponent) model of in-group identification. *Journal of Personality and Social Psychology, 95*(1), 144–165. doi:10.1037/0022-3514.95.1.144.

Leary, M. R. & Baumeister, R. F. (2000). The nature and function of self-esteem: Sociometer theory. In M. P. Zanna (Ed.), *Advances in experimental social psychology, vol. 32.* (pp. 1–62). San Diego, CA: Academic Press.

LeVine, R. A. & Campbell, D. T. (1972). *Ethnocentrism: Theories of conflict, ethnic attitudes, and group behavior.* Oxford, UK: John Wiley & Sons.

Lirio, P., Lee, M. D., Williams, M. L., Haugen, L. K., & Kossek, E. E. (2008). The inclusion challenge with reduced-load professionals: The role of the manager. *Human Resource Management, 47*(3), 443–461. doi:10.1002/hrm.20226.

Lorenzi-Cioldi, F. (2006). Group status and individual differentiation. In T. Postmes & J. Jetten (Eds.), *Individuality and the group: Advances in social identity.* (pp. 93–115). Thousand Oaks, CA: Sage Publications, Inc.

Luhtanen, R. & Crocker, J. (1992). A collective self-esteem scale: Self-evaluation of one's social identity. *Personality and Social Psychology Bulletin, 18*(3), 302–318. doi:10.1177/0146167292183006.

Mael, F. & Ashforth, B. E. (1992). Alumni and their alma mater: A partial test of the reformulated model of organizational identification. *Journal of Organizational Behavior, 13*(2), 103–123. doi:10.1002/job.4030130202.

Miller, F. A. (1998). Strategic culture change: The door to achieving high performance and inclusion. *Public Personnel Management, 27*(2), 151–160.

Mor Barak, M. E. (2000). Beyond affirmative action: Toward a model of diversity and organizational inclusion. *Administration in Social Work, 23*, 47–68.

Mor Barak, M. E. & Cherin, D. A. (1998). A tool to expand organizational understanding of workforce diversity: Exploring a measure of inclusion-exclusion. *Administration in Social Work, 22*(1), 47–64.

Otten, S. & Van der Zee, K. I. (2011). Experiencing exclusion and disadvantage at work. In S. Otten & K. I. Van der Zee (Eds.), *Werkt diversiteit? Inclusie en exclusie op de werkvloer.* [Uitsluiting en benadeling op de werkvloer] Groningen: Instituut ISW.

Pelled, L. H., Ledford, G. E., & Mohrman, S. A. (1999). Demographic dissimilarity and workplace inclusion. *Journal of Management Studies, 36*(7), 1013–1031.

Pettigrew, T. F. (1998). Intergroup contact theory. *Annual Review of Psychology, 49,* 65–85. doi:10.1146/annurev.psych.49.1.65.

Plaut, V. C., Garnett, F. G., Buffardi, L. E., & Sanchez-Burks, J. (2011). "What about me?" Perceptions of exclusion and whites' reactions to multiculturalism. *Journal of Personality and Social Psychology, 101*(2), 337–353. doi:10.1037/a0022832.

Pless, N. M. & Maak, T. (2004). Building an inclusive diversity culture: Principles, processes and practice. *Journal of Business Ethics, 54*(2), 129–148.

Postmes, T., Haslam, S. A., & Jans, L. (2012). A single-item measure of social identification: Reliability, validity, and utility. *British Journal of Social Psychology.* doi:10.1111/bjso.12006.

Postmes, T., Spears, R., Lee, A. T., & Novak, R. J. (2005). Individuality and social influence in groups: Inductive and deductive routes to group identity. *Journal of Personality and Social Psychology, 89*(5), 747–763. doi:10.1037/0022-3514.89.5.747.

Roberson, Q. M. (2006). Disentangling the meanings of diversity and inclusion in organizations. *Group & Organization Management, 31*(2), 212–236. doi:10.1177/1059601104273064.

Schneider, B. (1987). The people make the place. *Personnel Psychology, 40*(3), 437–453. doi:10.1111/j.1744-6570.1987.tb00609.x.

Sheldon, K. M. & Bettencourt, B. A. (2002). Psychological need-satisfaction and subjective well-being within social groups. *British Journal of Social Psychology, 41*(1), 25–38. doi:10.1348/014466602165036.

Sheldon, K. M., Ryan, R. M., Rawsthorne, L. J., & Ilardi, B. (1997). Trait self and true self: Cross-role variation in the big-five personality traits and its relations with psychological authenticity and subjective well-being. *Journal of Personality and Social Psychology, 73*(6), 1380–1393. doi:10.1037/0022-3514.73.6.1380.

Shore, L. M., Randel, A. E., Chung, B. G., Dean, M. A., Holcombe Ehrhart, K., & Singh, G. (2011). Inclusion and diversity in work groups: A review and model for future research. *Journal of Management, 37*(4), 1262–1289. doi:10.1177/0149206310385943.

Singelis, T. M. (1994). The measurement of independent and interdependent self-construals. *Personality and Social Psychology Bulletin, 20*(5), 580–591. doi:10.1177/0146167294205014.

Stark, T. H., Flache, A., & Veenstra, R. (2013). Generalization of positive and negative attitudes toward individuals to outgroup attitudes. *Personality & Social Psychology Bulletin, 39*(5), 608–622. doi: 10.1177/0146167213480890.

Stevens, F. G., Plaut, V. C., & Sanchez-Burks, J. (2008). Unlocking the benefits of diversity: All-inclusive multiculturalism and positive organizational change. *Journal of Applied Behavioral Science, 44*(1), 116–133. doi:10.1177/0021886308314460.

Swann, W. B., Polzer, J. T., Seyle, D. C., & Ko, S. J. (2004). Finding value in diversity: Verification of personal and social self-views in diverse groups. *Academy of Management Review, 29*(1), 9–27.

Thomas, D. A. & Ely, R. J. (1996). Making differences matter: A new paradigm for managing diversity. *Harvard Business Review, 74*(5), 79–90.

Tsui, A. S. & Gutek, B. A. (1999). *Demographic differences in organizations: Current research and future directions.* New York, NY: Lexington Books/Macmillan.

Tsui, A. S., Egan, T. D., & O'Reilly, C. A. (1992). Being different: Relational demography and organizational attachment. *Administrative Science Quarterly, 37*(4), 549–579. doi:10.2307/2393472.

Turner, J. C., Hogg, M. A., Oakes, P. J., Reicher, S. D., & Wetherell, M. S. (1987). *Rediscovering the social group: A self-categorization theory.* Cambridge, MA: Basil Blackwell.

Van Knippenberg, D. & Van Schie, E. C. M. (2000). Foci and correlates of organizational identification. *Journal of Occupational and Organizational Psychology, 73*(2), 137–147. doi:10.1348/096317900166949.

Van Knippenberg, D. & Schippers, M. C. (2007). Work group diversity. *Annual Review of Psychology, 58*, 515–541. doi:10.1146/annurev.psych.58.110405.085546.

Van Veelen, R., Otten, S., & Hansen, N. (in press). A personal touch to diversity: Self-anchoring increases minority members' identification in a diverse group. *Group Processes & Intergroup Relations.*

Van Veelen, R., Otten, S., & Hansen, N. Enhancing majority members' pro-diversity beliefs: The facilitating effect of self-anchoring. Manuscript under review.

Vos, M. W., Jansen, W. S., Otten, S., Podsiadlowski, A., & Van der Zee, K. I. (2013). Colorblind or colorful? The impact of diversity approaches on inclusion and work outcomes among majority and minority employees. Manuscript under review.

Wasserman, I. C., Gallegos, P. V., & Ferdman, B. M. (2008). Dancing with resistance: Leadership challenges in fostering a culture of inclusion. In K. M. Thomas (Ed.), *Diversity resistance in organizations* (pp. 175–200). New York: Taylor & Francis Group/Lawrence Erlbaum Associates.

Wenzel, M., Mummendey, A., & Waldzus, S. (2007). Superordinate identities and intergroup conflict: The ingroup projection model. *European Review of Social Psychology, 18*, 331–372. doi:10.1080/10463280701728302.

Williams, K. D. (2007). Ostracism. *Annual Review of Psychology, 58*, 425–452.

Williams, K. D. & Nida, S. A. (2011). Ostracism: Consequences and coping. *Current Directions in Psychological Science, 20*, 71–75.

Williams, K. Y. & O'Reilly, C. A. (1998). Demography and diversity in organizations: A review of 40 years of research. *Research in Organizational Behavior, Vol 20, 1998, 20*, 77–140.

Wood, A. M., Linley, P. A., Maltby, J., Baliousis, M., & Joseph, S. (2008). The authentic personality: A theoretical and empirical conceptualization and the development of the authenticity scale. *Journal of Counseling Psychology, 55*(3), 385–399. doi:10.1037/0022-0167.55.3.385.

6   To lead, ASPIRe

Building organic organizational identity

Kim Peters, S. Alexander Haslam,
Michelle K. Ryan, and Niklas K. Steffens

According to the social identity perspective, successful leaders are those who are able to create, advance, represent, and embed a sense of social identity that is shared with those they want to influence (Haslam et al., 2011). This is because, according to this perspective, which encompasses both social identity theory (Tajfel & Turner, 1979) and self-categorization theory (Turner, 1985; Turner et al., 1987; Turner et al., 1994), when people identify with a group they incorporate that group into their self-concept and use it to inform both their attitudes and behaviour. Consequently, as well as having a sense of self that derives from who they think they are as unique individuals (their personal identity as "I"), employees in an organization also have a sense of social identity that reflects their membership of the organization and/or specific units within it (their organizational identity as "us"). A wealth of research has shown that, when organizational identity is salient, highly identified employees will prioritize the organization's goals above their own personal goals and engage in the constructive forms of interaction and influence that underpin effective organizations (e.g. Haslam et al., 2011; Millward et al., 2007; Morton et al., 2012; Riketta & Van Dick, 2005; Van Knippenberg, 2000).

It follows, then, that a key task—perhaps *the* key task—facing any organizational leader is one of *identity management*: needing to promote a sense of group identity that is shared with followers (e.g. Haslam et al., 2011). However, in today's globalized workplace, this is far from a simple task. As we will discuss in greater detail, employees generally tend to identify more highly with subgroups within an organization—such as a team or department, or some other demographic or cultural category—than they do with the organization as a whole (Van Knippenberg & Van Schie, 2000). For this reason (and others), employees are often highly resistant to leaders' efforts to increase their levels of identification with the superordinate organizational group (e.g. Riketta & Van Dick, 2005). As Putnam (2007, p. 139) puts it "the central challenge, for modern, diversifying societies is to create a new, broader sense of 'we.'"

This, then, is the central challenge that this chapter addresses: seeking to understand exactly what leaders can do to manage social identities in ways that cultivate (rather than compromise) an integrated sense of the collective 'us'. In the remainder of this chapter, we will discuss the issues facing leaders who seek to embed a shared sense of organizational identity and provide an overview of one practical framework for guiding these efforts— the Actualizing Social and Personal Identity Resources (*or* ASPIRe) model. We will review recent literature that suggests that the ASPIRe model provides the most promising approach to building organizational identity, because— uniquely among models of this type—it seeks to draw on employees' existing social identity resources in order to build an organic organizational identity that provides a meaningful and subjectively valid representation of employees' goals and aspirations. At the same time, our overview will make clear that the ASPIRe process is not without risks: it is an expensive and effortful process, requiring engagement from employees at all levels of the organization. Moreover, the success of ASPIRe as a leadership tool relies very much on the wielder. Only those leaders who are willing to relinquish some control and involve employees in the shaping of organizational identity and the setting of organizational goals are likely to reap rewards from this process.

Identity complexity in a globalized workplace

One of the obvious challenges facing a leader who is trying to create and embed a sense of shared organizational identity among an organization's employees is the fact that within any organization there are a multitude of groups with which any individual can identify, and that the organization as a whole is just one of these options. Indeed, as self-categorization theory (Turner, 1985; Turner et al., 1987, 1994) observes, individuals can categorize themselves as belonging to multiple groups, and the salience of these group memberships (or identities) can vary considerably as a function of the context within which individuals find themselves (Oakes et al., 1994).

In today's globalized and rapidly changing world, organizational life presents individuals with many different foci for identification. For instance, organizations are, by their nature, internally differentiated. Employees may be grouped into teams, departments, occupations, geographical regions, and so on and consequently may see any of these groupings as a basis for identification (e.g. Ashforth & Johnson, 2001; Van Knippenberg & Van Schie, 2000). In addition, mass migration and societal change has meant that in many organizations there will be a sizeable proportion of employees who embrace identities as members of salient minority groups (and, in contrast to these, majority groups), such as those based on ethnicity, gender, and sexuality. Furthermore, with increasing levels of contact between individuals of different cultures (either at a societal level, or within multinational organizations) has come an increased awareness of cultural and value-based differences, and evidence suggests that these are increasingly providing a source of social identification (Schwartz et al., 2008). Indeed, research suggests that, over time, this kind of deep-level diversity (i.e. that associated with differences in psychological characteristics, such as values, personality traits, and cognitive styles) becomes more important for team functioning than high-visibility surface-level diversity (e.g. demographic characteristics; Harrison et al., 1998).

Adding to this complexity, not only is the organization just one of many possible sources of identification for employees, but there is also evidence that many employees identify most highly with those organizational subgroups (e.g. project teams or office mates) that serve as the most meaningful basis for their daily work activity (Riketta & Van Dick, 2005). As a demonstration of the way in which the structure of employees' daily workplace interactions can shape their organizational identification, Millward et al., (2007) found that employees who were allocated fixed desks in close proximity to other members of their work teams identified more highly with that team than they did with the organization. However, the opposite pattern of identification was observed among employees who did not have fixed desks (i.e. who were 'hot-desking'). The researchers found evidence that this could be attributed to the different patterns of communication within each group. Specifically, because employees with fixed desks were located near to their teammates, these employees tended to prioritize face-to-face communication, and this in turn served to build team identity. In contrast, because those employees whose desk location shifted from day to day were often some distance from their teammates, they prioritized electronic communication. And the fact that this medium in turn rendered every member of the organization equally accessible served to build organizational identity.

Where employees' most valued organizational identity is a subgroup identity, additional challenges can arise from the fact that employees may fail to perceive an alignment between the goals of their subgroup and those of the organization. Indeed, in the extreme, employees may perceive that their subgroup identity conflicts with that of the organization as a whole (see Fiol et al., 2009). In particular, during the process of organizational restructuring and merger, research has observed such sentiments among members of lower-status groups (e.g. acquired organizations). Members of these groups tend to feel that their pre-change organizational identity is not reflected in the merged organization, and this leads them to regard their valued pre-merger identity as in conflict with the new organizational identity (e.g. Jetten & Hutchison, 2011).

For all these reasons, leaders who wish to strengthen levels of organizational identification within a given workforce may have to contend with employees who do not perceive the organization to be a meaningful self-defining group in their working lives. On the one hand it may simply be seen as irrelevant, but more potently it may also be seen as posing some threat to a valued subgroup identity.

Nevertheless, the literature does provide leaders with some suggestions as to the strategies that they might employ in order to build organizational identification. In the next section, we will discuss two that have received strong empirical support. The first involves seeking to enhance the status of the organization as a whole; the second involves attempts to recategorize relevant organizational identities in ways that draw attention to commonalities rather than differences. However, as we shall see, there is also evidence that these strategies may be of limited use in diverse organizations, especially among employees who perceive the superordinate organizational identity as threatening to a valued subgroup identity. For instance, one of the factors that has been identified in the demise of the DaimlerChrysler merger is the resistance of Chrysler employees to a perceived imposition of Daimler's disciplined and bureaucratic culture (Finkelstein, 2002). In these organizations, leaders who wish to direct employees' energies towards ensuring the success of the organization as a whole need to draw on employees' existing identities in order to construct an overarching organizational identity that speaks both to and for employees' subgroup-related concerns and aspirations. The ASPIRe model provides a structured communication-based framework for building this kind of organic organizational identity.

Strategies for building organizational identification

Increasing the perceived status of the organization

For leaders who are seeking to build organizational identification, the social identity perspective suggests at least two key strategies that might be successful. First, drawing on social identity theory, leaders can seek to increase the perceived status of the organization on the basis of an assumption that employees will be more willing to identify with an entity that contributes positively to their self-concept (e.g. Albert & Whetten, 1985; Haslam et al., 2011). In self-categorization theory's terms, this strategy seeks to foster superordinate identification by increasing the *normative fit* of organizational identity (Oakes et al., 1994).

This claim has received considerable empirical support. For instance, Ellemers et al. (1988) found that participants who were randomly assigned to a higher-status group (as a function of the group's supposed performance on a task) identified more highly with their group than those who were assigned to the lower-status group. This was especially the case when group boundaries were perceived to be permeable such that there was a possibility for individuals to move between groups (as is the case in some organizations). In the same way, perceptions of organizational status have been shown to positively predict organizational identification in a number of contexts (e.g. Mael & Ashforth, 1992).

Such research suggests that one way for leaders to boost organizational identification is to attempt to create the impression that the organization is a positive and distinct entity. While this may prove challenging in many organizational circumstances (e.g. where organizations champion a low-cost or budget business model; Peters et al., 2010), it is important to remember that the definition of ingroup identity, including group members' understanding of its status, is potentially flexible, and will depend, among other things, on the intergroup comparisons that are made in a given context. In this regard, leaders can play a significant role in shaping ingroup definition—and hence ingroup identification—by focusing on particular comparison groups (e.g. lower-status competitors) and on particular dimensions of comparison (e.g. those on which the ingroup performs relatively well).

As one example of this, Elsbach and Kramer (1996) show how business school leaders in the US selectively reproduce particular league tables that provide rankings of the quality of business school programs in order to make their program look good and hence foster the loyalty and commitment of its members. As Reicher and colleagues observe, in this they can be seen to be acting as 'entrepreneurs of identity' who define the meaning of the group and engage members (followers) in the process of enacting it (e.g. Reicher et al., 2005).

Recategorizing relevant organization identities

Leaders who find the prospect of attempting to shape their organization's identity in these ways daunting (perhaps because the reality constraints are too limiting) are likely to find the second strategy rather more appealing. This draws on self-categorization theory's claim that, when a given social category provides a salient basis for self-definition, individuals will tend to view the social world through the lens of this identity and behave in line with its norms (Turner, 1985). On this basis, the *common ingroup identity model* (Gaertner & Dovidio, 2000; Dovidio et al., 1998) argues that, if leaders encourage members of distinct subgroups to recategorize themselves as members of a more inclusive superordinate group which incorporates and subsumes previously conflictual subgroups, then they should help to reduce previously observed levels of intergroup bias and hostility. In self-categorization theory's terms, this strategy seeks to foster superordinate identification by increasing the *comparative fit* of organizational identity (Oakes et al., 1994).

Consistent with these claims, there is some evidence that factors which increase the salience and meaningfulness of a shared organizational identity for employees—including a leader's willingness to use inclusive language (Platow et al., 2006)—do indeed serve to boost levels of organizational identification (Van Dick et al., 2005). However, while this recategorization strategy has undoubted appeal, most of the evidence that shows it to be effective comes from laboratory studies using minimal groups which hold little meaning for participants. Research conducted using real identities has found that employees are often very resistant to any attempts to shift their identification from a valued subgroup to the superordinate organization (Jetten & Hutchison, 2011), especially when they perceive the values of the two entities to be incompatible (Brehm, 1966; Kelly & Kelly, 1991; O'Brien et al., 2004) or where the initiatives undertaken by an organization's leaders are perceived to threaten the integrity or positive distinctiveness (Brewer, 1991) of a valued subgroup identity.

Illustrative of this point, Gómez et al. (2008) found that whether students responded positively to a message claiming that they shared a superordinate 'student' identity with students from a different school depended on who the message originated from. When this message came from an ingroup member (someone from their own school), the vast majority of participants adopted this inclusive identity. However, when the message came from an outgroup member (someone from the other school), fewer than half of participants were willing to adopt this inclusive identity. It thus appears that calls to see the world in terms of an inclusive organizational identity will tend to succeed only where they make sense in terms of individuals' lived experience and when individuals are receptive to the source of this influence attempt.

Additional research has demonstrated the importance of respecting individuals' chosen identities in organizational restructuring processes and also called into question the political imperatives that underpin the common ingroup identity model (Dixon et al., 2012). For instance, Barreto and Ellemers (2002) found that, when students' chosen identities were neglected by others in an assigned work group (that is, group members ignored the fact that these students had been assigned to a subgroup with which they did not identify), then they were less likely to work in line with group norms and towards the goals of that group. In this way, it is apparent that misalignment between the way that a person wants to see him- or herself (his or her internalized self-categorization) and the way that they are perceived by others (external categorizations) can induce both reactance and resistance (Brehm, 1966) and therefore scupper efforts to work towards collective goals.

Respecting relevant subgroups within the organization

On the basis of findings such as these, most researchers now recognize the importance of respecting employees' existing sources of self-definition as these valued subgroup memberships provide the most promising basis for productive engagement with members of other organizational subgroups (e.g. Fiol et al., 2009). In line with these ideas, Eggins et al. (2002, Study 1) found that permitting (versus not permitting) individuals to draw on valued subgroup memberships in a negotiation about an issue that was relevant to this subgroup identity led to more positive perceptions of the negotiation, even though these participants initially expressed less willingness to compromise. Moreover, a second study found that these positive perceptions of negotiation arose because, ultimately, allowing participants to act in terms of subgroup identities served to increase their identification with the superordinate group.

The *dual identity model* (Brewer & Miller, 1984; Brewer et al., 1987) builds on this research by arguing that, while increasing the salience of the superordinate category alone may have negative consequences, these can be ameliorated by simultaneously increasing the salience of individuals' valued subgroups.

In line with this idea, Hornsey and Hogg (2000; see also Gaertner & Dovidio, 2000) varied the salience of a subgroup and superordinate identities and found that students in different faculties displayed the greatest intergroup bias when only the superordinate (student) group was made salient, but the least when both superordinate and subgroup (i.e. dual) identities were salient.

While the dual-identification approach probably provides the most promising strategy for leaders who wish to boost employees' organizational identification by manipulating salience (e.g. in their organizational communication), there is nevertheless evidence that this strategy still relies on employees' sense that their valued subgroups actually align with the organizational identity as a whole. For instance, Riketta and Nienaber (2007) found that pharmaceutical employees' identification with the store in which they worked was a positive predictor of their identification with the cooperative network that their store belonged to, but that this was moderated by perceptions that the values of their store aligned with those of the network as a whole. Among those employees who perceived a lack of alignment between store and network, the positive association was much weaker.

This suggests that, where employees embrace valued subgroup identities that they perceive to be out of alignment with the identity of the organization as a whole, efforts by leaders to build identification with the organization (whether by increasing perceptions of the status of the organization or by increasing the salience of this identity) are unlikely to meet with much success. Indeed, more troublingly, there is a danger that they will actually backfire. As Fiol et al. (2009) argue, in many situations of identity conflict a first step towards resolving this is often to decouple these identities, so that subgroup and superordinate group identities are not perceived to be in opposition to each other.

A further issue with the dual identity model is that it does not provide any method by which leaders can identify employees' valued subgroup identities. Instead, researchers tend to assume that the subgroup identities that are operating in a given situation are surface-level, visible identities (such as team membership or gender). This is problematic because, as noted, there is evidence that among individuals who have long-lasting relationships it is the less visible, deep-level identities (e.g. those that concern cultural values) that drive perceptions of diversity and group functioning (Harrison et al., 1998). Finally, in light of the fact that employees' identities often reflect the substantive realities of their organizational experience (e.g. related to differences in resources, privileges, power, and status), it is questionable whether rhetorical or purely cognitive strategies will ever be sufficient to deliver and sustain the tangible outcomes that leaders are looking for. To achieve this, we would argue, leaders need to engage with the material reality of employees' experiences.

With this in mind, in what follows, we outline a practical communication-based activity that specifies how leaders can work to build organizational identification in a bottom-up manner: the *ASPIRe model*. Unlike the mostly cognitive strategies discussed earlier, this model seeks to specify activities that can be used to bring subgroup and superordinate identities into alignment with a view to building organizational identification. We will also discuss a growing body of literature that speaks to the utility of this model but which at the same time points to the challenges associated with its implementation.

The ASPIRe model of diversity management

The *ASPIRe* model (where ASPIRe stands for Actualizing Social and Personal Identity Resources; Haslam et al., 2003; see also Eggins et al., 2002, 2008) describes four phases of structured organizational activities (depicted in Figure 6.1) through which leaders can work with employees to build (or consolidate) an organic organizational identity—that is, one whose content is constructed from the bottom-up in a way that recognizes subgroup differ-ence (Haslam, 2001; see also Jans et al., 2011). Specifically, in the first two *subgroup* phases (AIRing[1] and Sub-Casing[2], respectively), the model aims (a) to build a consensual understanding of the identities at play in the organiza-tion and, subsequently, (b) to facilitate understanding of the perspectives of each subgroup. This is followed by two *superordinate* phases (Super-Casing[3] and ORGanizing[4]) that aim to (a) identify commonalities in the experiences and aspirations of these groups and then (b) ensure that the organization's strategic objectives recognize, incorporate, and harness these aspirations.

In this way, the model delineates a structured pathway for identifying, and capitalizing upon, the potentialities afforded by salient subgroup identi-ties (as outlined in the previous section) by feeding these into the emergent goals of the organization as a whole. The assumption underlying this model is that benefits will accrue to the organization more readily when its leaders work with (rather than against) the grain of the social identities that provide meaning in employees' working lives (Haslam et al., 2011).

We will now provide a brief overview of each phase in the ASPIRe model, before discussing empirical research that can speak to its efficacy. It is worth noting that, while this research suggests that the ASPIRe model provides

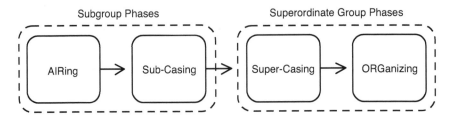

Figure 6.1 The ASPIRe model.
Notes: AIRing = Ascertaining Identity Resources.
　　　　Sub-Casing = Subgroup Consensualising.
　　　　Super-Casing = Superordinate Consensualising.
　　　　ORGanizing = Organic Goal Setting.
Source: Haslam et al., 2003.

leaders with a useful, if effortful, tool for the promotion of organizational identification among employees, it also reveals that the key to its success lies with leaders themselves. The ASPIRe process embodies a truly distributive approach to leadership (Spillane, 2012), which assumes that leadership can be done—and, indeed, needs to be done—by all members of all groups. In other words, the ASPIRe model provides the tools through which leaders can enact the "3Rs" of leadership (as identified by Haslam et al., 2011): to *reflect* on the nature of the group that they seek to lead, to *represent* the group (Haslam & Platow, 2001; Hogg, 2001), and to help its members to *realize* their collective ambitions (Reicher et al., 2005). Leaders who are not willing to translate ASPIRe outcomes (which are by their very nature, unpredictable) into an organizational reality face the risk of disengagement, resistance or reactance among employees who contributed to the process. We will, therefore, complete this review with a discussion of the leader's role in the successful implementation of the ASPIRe model.

Phase 1: ascertaining identity resources (AIRing)

This first phase of the ASPIRe process seeks to uncover the identities that provide meaning for employees by asking them to identify the group that is most important to them in their work and to describe the relationships between this ingroup and other important organizational subgroups. A key outcome of this first phase is the creation of an *identity map* that delineates the contours of employees' salient subgroup identities (for examples see Eggins et al., 2008). This phase is intended to provide insight into the nature of the identity-based diversity that exists within their organization and is therefore a practical way of enacting the first of the "3Rs" of leadership— *reflecting* on the nature of the group (Haslam et al., 2011).

Phase 2: subgroup consensualizing (Sub-Casing)

In this second phase employees are presented with the identity map and asked to assign themselves to the subgroup that corresponds most closely to their sense of who they think they are in the workplace. The members of each subgroup are then brought together and asked to identify their group's key goals as well as the barriers that stand in the way of their achievement. This phase is intended to make subgroup identities salient and to increase subgroup identification by providing a basis for constructive interaction among group members.

Phase 3: superordinate consensualizing (Super-Casing)

This third phase mirrors the previous one, but occurs at a higher level of abstraction. Here subgroups (or their representatives) are brought together and asked to present the outcomes of the previous Sub-Casing phase to each other. Having done this, they work together to identify shared obstacles that need to be overcome as well as shared goals that would enhance organizational functioning. These higher-order organizational goals are intended to incorporate and build upon those identified by different subgroups; in this way Super-Casing is intended to maximize opportunities for the goals of those subgroups to be brought into alignment. This process should increase the salience of an organic organizational identity that explicitly recognizes relevant forms of internal differentiation (Haslam, 2001) and consequently increase employees' willingness to internalize that identity.

Phase 4: organic goal setting (ORGanizing)

In the fourth and final phase of the ASPIRe process, subgroups (or their representatives) are again brought together, but this time to develop a formal plan that builds upon the collective goals that have been identified in the preceding phases. This plan then provides a strategic framework around which ongoing organizational activity can be structured. The fact that both goals and plans are the outcome of a participatory process increases the likelihood that employees will internalize them and work towards their realization.

A key point here too is that in this final phase, as in those that precede it, leadership takes the form of working with groups to develop strategy rather than merely imposing that strategy upon them. In this, the ASPIRe model speaks to the second and third of the "3Rs of leadership" identified by Haslam et al. (2011): the need for leaders to *represent* the group and also to help its members *realize* their collective ambitions. Critically, though, it sees these processes as ones that involve "walking the walk" of organic organizational identity, rather than just "talking the talk."

The ASPIRe model in action

While the ASPIRe process seems, on the surface, fairly straightforward, the reality of implementing this model in organizations is in many cases rather more complicated. However, as we will show in one recent example, it is nonetheless workable. We will describe this specific case in more detail to illustrate how the various phases of the ASPIRe model can be realized. Here, we will pay specific attention to the AIRing and Sub-Casing phases, which have proved to be the most challenging in implementation. This is because these stages require the identification of a *manageable* number of subgroup identities; they also require that a reasonable number of individuals (i.e. more than three, but ideally roughly proportional to the number of participants) are willing to assign themselves to each subgroup. Satisfying these requirements often involves making difficult choices about which subgroups to take forward, and therefore necessitates a consultative and flexible approach.

Background: The authors (Peters et al., in prep.) were recently approached by the leadership team of one division of a UK scientific organization who were concerned about levels of division identification among employees following a restructure. In particular, in this restructure, pre-existing research departments had been grouped into one of five superordinate divisions, and budget and support functions were centralized within each division. The division in question was especially diverse, with employees working in three main roles (research, technical support, professional services), in five departments (including division headquarters) and across three geographical locations. The leadership team felt that the restructure had failed to yield the desired efficiencies because employees' behaviour appeared to reflect pre-existing departmental identities, which created silos within the division. The leadership team was keen to implement the ASPIRe model in order to promote identification with the division as a whole and in this way promote engagement and collaboration across departmental boundaries.

AIRing: In order to ascertain employees' identity resources, we administered an online AIRing survey via e-mail to division staff. One hundred and seventy-one employees (or approximately 31 percent of division staff) completed this survey, which (among other things) asked employees to nominate the group that was most important to them in their work and to indicate their levels of identification with (a) this nominated group, (b) the department, and (c) the division as a whole (as reported below).

In line with previous findings (e.g. Van Knippenberg & Van Schie, 2000), when selecting their most valued work-related group membership, respondents primarily selected subgroups that reflected their closest day-to-day working relationships, with only a very small minority ($N = 24$, 14 percent) nominating their department or the division. In total, more than 60 unique ingroups were nominated, the majority of which ($N = 44$) were nominated by two or more individuals. The nature of these valued subgroups varied systematically as a function of role and department. So, while technical and professional staff tended to nominate groups that reflected their particular support function, researchers tended to nominate groups that reflected relevant research streams. Further, the inclusiveness of these research-stream groups varied widely, so that in two departments they reflected small research labs, but in the remaining departments they reflected broader research themes. The identity map that was generated from this exercise was disseminated via e-mail to all division staff in order to promote the development of a more consensual understanding of the valued identities within this division.

Sub-Casing: Reconciling the diverse identities that emerged from the AIRing phase into a manageable but representative set that could be used in the subsequent stages of the ASPIRe process was one of the major challenges of the process. When selecting which identities to take forward to the Sub-Casing phase in the process, we were guided by the following goals: (a) to incorporate identities that are mentioned most frequently in the AIRing phase (even where these formed overlapping subgroups), (b) to show sensitivity towards lower-status identities and identities that may not have emerged in the AIRing phase, and (c) to make these decisions in an open and consultative manner (e.g. by communicating with relevant staff about the subgroup selection processes and by asking for their input into these).

In line with these guidelines, we engaged in an extensive consultative process in order to reduce the number of groups within each department and within the headquarters to a maximum of eight, but preferably six. In light of the fact that two-thirds of staff did not complete the AIRing questionnaire, we provided staff with the opportunity to identify missing groups or to propose new groupings in an effort to encourage these staff to engage with the process at this stage. Nevertheless, this process was somewhat fraught, with some individuals and groups proving highly resistant to the request that they select one group for the Sub-Casing phase. This meant that, in some instances, groups with as few as three individuals went forward to the Sub-Casing phase. One department insisted that individuals should be able to sign up to more than one Sub-Casing meeting. We acceded to these requests, and they did not seem to adversely impact on the process.

Superordinate phases: Once the allocation of individuals to subgroups had been achieved, the rest of the ASPIRe process proceeded reasonably smoothly. Division administrators took responsibility for bringing subgroup staff together to discuss each subgroup's goals and barriers. Two representatives were selected from each subgroup to take part in a second Sub-Casing phase at the departmental level (this was done, in part, because the department was a very meaningful subgroup in most employees' working lives, and because the number of subgroups involved precluded moving directly to the Super-Casing phase at the level of the division). Division administrators again took responsibility for bringing subgroup representatives within each department together, where they were tasked with summarising the outcomes of the previous Sub-Casing before identifying barriers and goals that were shared across the department.

Representatives were selected from each department, and these individuals then took part in the final Super-Casing and ORGanizing meeting that was attended by the division's leadership team (in our experience, the Super-Casing phase leads naturally to problem solving and the identification of shared goals, which means that it is very feasible to draw these two phases together). These meetings revealed a remarkable commonality of experience, and the leadership team was able to identify a number of shared goals and barriers to address in their strategy formulation. Informal discussions with participants in the process suggested that they found it worthwhile, and a number of changes that were a direct outcome of the process were instituted within individual departments and across the organization.

As this example shows, implementing the ASPIRe model in a large, complex organization is expensive and effortful, but it is possible. The really big question that remains, of course, is "Does it work?"

Tests of the ASPIRe model

Tests of Ascertaining Identity Resources (AIRing)

A growing body of evidence speaks to the effectiveness of the AIRing phase of the ASPIRe model. In particular, studies indicate that AIRing reveals patterns of identification that diverge (sometimes quite dramatically) from those that might be anticipated on the basis of formal organizational maps (e.g. workflow charts, line-reporting protocols). As with less visible deep diversity characteristics more generally, such patterns were therefore liable to be inadvertently ignored by organizational leaders, which could have negative consequences for their capacity to increase engagement or enact productive change.

In one demonstration of this, O'Brien and colleagues conducted AIRing in a UK hospital in order to identify key subgroup identities and examine patterns of subgroup and organizational identification (see O'Brien et al., 2004; Eggins et al., 2008). Again in line with previous research (e.g. Van Knippenberg & Van Schie, 2000), participants generally had higher levels of identification with their subgroup (e.g. nurses, porters, kitchen staff) than with the broader organization, although this tendency was moderated by subgroup status. Specifically, higher-status groups were more likely than lower-status groups to engage with the hospital in relatively inclusive, super-ordinate terms (e.g. thinking of themselves as a hospital employee).

Importantly, this process pointed to divergences between the formal organizational structure and the emergent hospital identity map. So, for instance, although both porters and catering staff were formally recognized as two distinct subgroups, only the porters self-categorized as such (with approximately three-quarters nominating this subgroup as their most valued group membership). In contrast, fewer than half of the catering staff self-categorized as caterers, with the majority of these employees instead nominating kitchen or dining room staff as their most valued group membership. Importantly, these subgroup distinctions were (a) consensually recognized by the caterers and (b) predicted employees' perceptions of the key staff groups with whom they had important relationships (e.g. the kitchen staff nominated porters and nurses as important groups in their daily work, but the dining staff did not).

A further example of the utility of the AIRing process as a means of gaining an understanding of the key identities at play in an organization is provided by Peters et al., (in prep.). As described above, in this research we measured the subgroup and superordinate perceptions of employees working for one division of a UK scientific organization. On average, as Figure 6.2 indicates, employees reported higher levels of identification with their valued subgroup and with the department than they did with the division (measured on a 7-point Likert scale where 1 = strongly disagree, 7 = strongly agree). However, this pattern of identification varied as a function of staff role, such

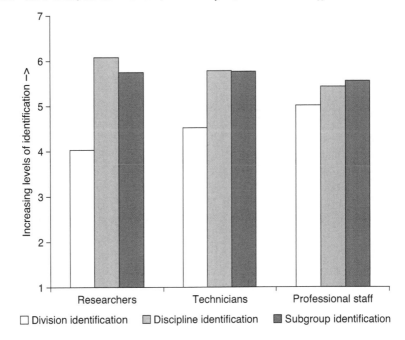

Figure 6.2 Employees' levels of group identification as a function of employee role and identity focus.

that this pattern was most pronounced for researchers and weakest for professional staff (about half of whom worked in the division headquarters). More fine-grained analysis revealed further evidence of differences in patterns of identification between groups. Specifically, among technicians and professional staff, levels of subgroup identification were positively associated with division identification, which in turn predicted levels of strategy support. In contrast, among researchers, a perception of greater subgroup alignment was the only predictor of increased division identification as well as strategy support. In sum, this AIRing exercise suggested that leaders interested in building superordinate identification and strategy support within this organization needed to concern themselves with respectful acknowledgement and alignment of subgroup identities rather more when dealing with researchers than when dealing with support staff.

There is also evidence that respecting the valued subgroups that emerge through AIRing when engaging with employees is likely to have positive implications for those employees' responsiveness to leaders' initiatives. Specifically, Eggins et al. (2008) examined the extent to which students responded positively to a university engagement exercise that aimed to gain a deeper appreciation of students' perspectives on a contentious issue as a function of whether the participants were either (a) allowed to generate an identity map of their own which captured their own interests and those of other students or (b) instead presented with a map devised by the university to represent important student groups (one that in fact aggregated information presented by students themselves). As predicted by the ASPIRe model, those students who were able to generate their own identity map expressed higher levels of identification with their ingroup and also rated the exercise as more useful than did those who were asked to function within an imposed identity map.

A starker example of the dangers that can follow from the imposition of subgroup identities is provided by Batalha and Reynolds' (2012) analysis of the largely unsuccessful 2009 United Nations Climate Change Conference in Copenhagen. Specifically, these authors argue convincingly that, while the subgroups through which nations were required to engage in these negotiations may have effectively reflected historically important national perspectives, the social and economic changes that had recently been experienced by individual nations together with the relatively new threat of climate change meant that these subgroups were no longer fit for purpose. For instance, the G77/China block, which was formed five decades ago to promote the economic interests of developing countries, incorporates countries that have very diverse concerns, from island states that are especially vulnerable to rising sea levels (e.g. Cape Verde) to OPEC nations who are motivated to protect trade in oil (e.g. Saudi Arabia). Batalha and Reynolds (2012) conclude that it is not until nations are able to interact in blocks that are seen by their members to genuinely represent their interests that there will be potential for building the cross-national superordinate identity that facilitates successful resolution of social dilemmas of this kind.

Test of the full ASPIRe model

It is only recently that empirical tests have moved beyond a focus on the importance of AIRing to examine the effectiveness of the ASPIRe model as a whole. The first of these tests was provided by Peters et al. (2013). This utilized the model in a two-day organizational strategy workshop that was held for 20 leading members of a sizeable and highly diverse Military Health Services Organization in the UK. The two subgroup phases (AIRing and Sub-Casing) were implemented on Day 1 and the two superordinate phases (Super-Casing and ORGanizing) on Day 2. The authors administered questionnaires measuring attendees' subgroup and organizational perceptions at the beginning of the workshop (providing a baseline measure) and on completion of activities at the end of Day 1 and then the end of Day 2.

Figure 6.3 provides a summary of attendees' perceptions following the subgroup and superordinate phases of the workshop (respondents measured perceptions of change on a 7-point Likert scale, from −3 = much less than before, to +3 = much more than before). From this it is clear that attendees reported increasingly positive *subgroup* perceptions as a consequence of taking part in the workshop, such that at the workshop's end there was an

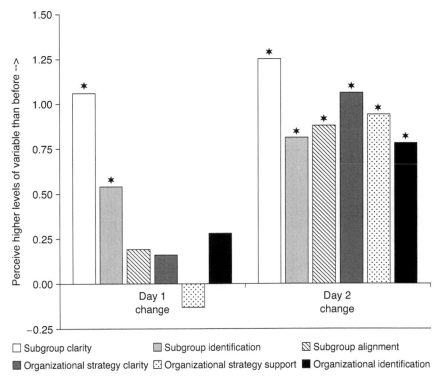

Figure 6.3 Employees' perceptions that ASPIRe activities (Day 1's subgroup phases, Day 2's superordinate phases) led to a change in subgroup and organizational perceptions.

Note: ✱ = level of perceived change differed from scale mid-point (0 = no change), $p < 0.05$.

increased sense of subgroup clarity, subgroup identification, and alignment. They also reported increasingly positive perceptions of the *organization* in the form of increased organizational identification together with an enhanced sense of strategy clarity and enhanced support for that strategy. Second, in line with the claim that organizations benefit from respecting valued subgroup identities and then using these as a resource that supports improved organizational engagement, it is also apparent that the subgroup and organizational perceptions were differentially responsive to the different phases of the workshop. So, while Day 1 of the workshop had positive consequences for subgroup clarity and identification, Day 2 had positive consequences for perceptions of subgroup alignment, organizational identification, and strategy support.

Interestingly, subgroup identification continued to rise in the latter—Super-Casing and ORGanizing—phases of the workshop and indeed in these phases seemed to rise at least as much as superordinate identity. While not anticipated, there are a number of plausible explanations for these findings which are consistent with ASPIRe-based reasoning. In particular, they can be seen to reflect the fact that the Super-Casing phase still involved participants engaging with the process on the basis of their subgroup identities. In particular, in this phase, subgroup representatives presented the outcomes of the Sub-Casing phase to the entire group before participants worked to identify shared goals and obstacles. Alternatively, it is possible that, with the increased alignment between subgroup and superordinate group identities, increases in superordinate group identification had a reciprocal impact on levels of subgroup identification.

Finally, an examination of the relationships between these subgroup and organizational perceptions revealed that participants perceived their subgroup and superordinate identities to become more aligned over the course of the workshop. Indeed, in combination with improvements in participants' identification with the organization, this accounted for most of the improvement in attendees' perceptions of the clarity of organizational strategy and in their support for this strategy.

Although this workshop leaves unanswered questions about the relative efficacy of the ASPIRe model when compared with other team-building activities, and about the durability of the observed positive effects, it is nevertheless the case that it provides a promising demonstration of the model's potential as a tool for developing organizational social capital. However, from the perspective of generalizability, it is worth being mindful of the fact that this test was a relatively simple one, involving a small number of participants who occupied positions of broadly equivalent status. In addition, the organization's leader demonstrated his commitment to the democratic bottom-up approach to strategy formation that is central to the ASPIRe model by acting more as a facilitator than as a driver of the ORGanizing phase and by readily endorsing the plan that emerged. As we will discuss more in the next section, these conditions represent major challenges that leaders face when seeking to build an organic organizational identity using this process.

Leading a successful ASPIRe process

The successful test of the ASPIRe model, discussed above, was arguably conducted in particularly favourable conditions: it involved a manageable number of participants of roughly equivalent status, and their leader was fully committed to the democratic approach at the heart of the process. In what follows, we argue that the latter factor (leaders' willingness to support the construction of an organic organizational identity on the basis of subgroup concerns) will often present as a particularly demanding hurdle to overcome.

This is the case because for the ASPIRe process to have beneficial consequences for employees' organizational engagement beyond the immediate process itself requires a full commitment on the part of leaders to take action. Specifically, leaders need to bring the material reality of the organization into alignment with the organic organizational identity and associated organizational strategy that emerges from the process. Leaders who engage with this process from the perspective of most traditional managerial models—which prioritize the organization's financial bottom line over concern for employee welfare and which want to create the appearance of giving employees voice while still insisting on preserving the managerial prerogative (i.e. managers' right to manage; Taylor, 1911)—will not reap long-term benefits from this process (e.g. Haslam, 2001; Kelly & Kelly, 1991). This is because, as we discussed earlier, employees' levels of identification reflects the material reality of organizational life as encountered through their daily workplace experiences. Accordingly, if leaders who implement the ASPIRe process have no real interest in using the process for its intended purpose—to bring about material change that reflects the aspirations of all subgroups—then the process is likely to fail and may even prove counterproductive (Tame, 2007).

Conclusion

Our experience suggests that the ASPIRe process is demanding in every sense. It takes time, costs money, and relies on the will of employees at every level of the organization. However, the data (both quantitative and qualitative) that we and others have accumulated over the last decade suggests that, for those who are interested in the outcomes it promises to deliver, these demands are worth making.

Nevertheless, it is clear too that the ASPIRe process can serve as something of an organizational litmus test in itself—serving to establish whether an organization (and more particularly its leaders) *really is* interested in participation, empowerment, democracy, and diversity. For, unlike other models of social and organizational contact, its goal is very definitely not simply to make managers and workers 'feel good' about each other in ways that then allow the status quo (or managers' plans for change) to move forward without meaningful resistance (see Dixon et al., 2012). Rather, the goal is to produce forms of policy, strategy, and change that have the backing, and are in the interests, of *all* groups, not just those with power and privilege. This, we contend, is what—properly construed—organizational (and societal) diversity is all about.

Hence, the ASPIRe model provides a concrete example of the perspective that it is only possible to manage diversity successfully if people are willing to engage in mutual learning and then to enact the requisite organizational changes (see Van der Zee and Otten, this volume). Yet, for most contemporary organizations, this is a tough ask. For many it may simply be too tough.

At core, this is because the ASPIRe process asks what is perhaps the most difficult and pressing question of all, not just for practitioners and managers but for academics too: do we really want to embrace diversity or do we simply want to think about it? Are we happy just to do the talk or are we ready to do the walk?

Notes

1 AIRing = Ascertaining identity resources.
2 Sub-Casing = Subgoup consensualising
3 Super-Casing = Superordinate consensualising
4 ORGanizing = Organic goal setting

References

Albert, S. & Whetten, D. A. (1985). Organizational identity. *Research in Organizational Behavior, 7*, 263–295.
Ashforth, B. E. & Johnson, S. A. (2001). Which hat to wear? The relative salience of multiple identities in organizational contexts. In M. Hogg & D. J. Terry (Eds.) *Social identity processes in organizational contexts* (pp. 31–48). Psychology Press: Philadelphia, PA.
Barreto, M. & Ellemers, N. (2002). The impact of respect versus neglect of self-identities on identification and group loyalty. *Personality and Social Psychology Bulletin, 28*(5), 629–639.
Batalha, L. & Reynolds, K. J. (2012). ASPIRing to mitigate climate change: Superordinate identity in global climate negotiations. *Political Psychology, 33*(5), 743–760.
Brehm, J. W. (1966). A *theory of psychological reactance*. General Learning Press: New York.
Brewer, M. B. (1991). The social self: On being the same and different at the same time. *Personality and Social Psychology Bulletin, 17*(5), 475–482.
Brewer, M. B. & Miller, N. (1984). Beyond the contact hypothesis: Theoretical perspectives of desegregation. In N. Miller & M. B. Brewer (Eds.) *Groups in contact: The psychology of desegregation*. Academic Press: Orlando, FL.
Brewer, M. B., Ho, H., Lee, J., & Miller, M. (1987). Social identity and social distance among Hong Kong school children. *Personality and Social Psychology Bulletin, 13*, 156–165.
Dixon, J., Levine, M., Reicher, S., & Durrheim, K. (2012). Beyond prejudice: Relational inequality, collective action, and social change revisited. *Behavioral and Brain Sciences, 1*(1), 411–266.
Dovidio, J. F., Gaertner, S. L., & Validzic, A. (1998). Intergroup bias: Status, differentiation, and a common in-group identity. *Journal of Personality and Social Psychology, 75*(1), 109.
Eggins, R. A., Haslam, S. A., & Reynolds, K. J. (2002). Social identity and negotiation: Subgroup representation and superordinate consensus. *Personality and Social Psychology Bulletin, 28*(7), 887–899.
Eggins, R. A., O'Brien, A. T., Reynolds, K. J., Haslam, S. A., & Crocker, A. S. (2008). Refocusing the focus group: AIRing as a basis for effective workplace planning. *British Journal of Management, 19*(3), 277–293.
Ellemers, N., Van Knippenberg, A., De Vries, N., & Wilke, H. (1988). Social identification and permeability of group boundaries. *European Journal of Social Psychology, 18*(6), 497–513.
Elsbach, K. D. & Kramer, R. M. (1996). Members' responses to organizational identity threats: Encountering and countering the *Business Week* rankings. *Administrative Science Quarterly*, 442–476.
Finkelstein, S. (2002). *The Daimler Chrysler Merger*. Tuck School of Business, retrieved on 28 June, 2013, from http://mba.tuck.dartmouth.edu/pdf/2002-1-0071.pdf.

Fiol, C. M., Pratt, M. G., & O'Connor, E. J. (2009). Managing intractable identity conflicts. *Academy of Management Review, 34*(1), 32–55.

Gaertner, S. L. & Dovidio, J. F. (2000). *Reducing intergroup bias: The common ingroup identity model.* Psychology Press: Philadelphia, PA.

Gómez, Á., Dovidio, J. F., Huici, C., Gaertner, S. L., & Cuadrado, I. (2008). The other side of we: When outgroup members express common identity. *Personality and Social Psychology Bulletin, 34*(12), 1613–1626.

Harrison, D. A., Price, K. H., & Bell, M. P. (1998). Beyond relational demography: Time and the effects of surface- and deep-level diversity on work group cohesion. *Academy of Management Journal, 41*(1), 96–107.

Haslam, S. A. (2001). *Psychology in organizations.* Sage Publications Limited: London.

Haslam, S. A. & Platow, M. J. (2001). The link between leadership and followership: How affirming social identity translates vision into action. *Personality and Social Psychology Bulletin, 27*(11), 1469–1479.

Haslam, S. A., Eggins, R. A., & Reynolds, K. J. (2003). The ASPIRe model: Actualizing social and personal identity resources to enhance organizational outcomes. *Journal of Occupational and Organizational Psychology, 76*(1), 83–113.

Haslam, S. A., Reicher, S. D., & Platow, M. J. (2011). *The new psychology of leadership: Identity, influence and power.* Psychology Press: New York.

Hogg, M. A. (2001). A social identity theory of leadership. *Personality and Social Psychology Review, 5*(3), 184–200.

Hornsey, M. J. & Hogg, M. A. (2000). Subgroup relations: A comparison of mutual intergroup differentiation and common ingroup identity models of prejudice reduction. *Personality and Social Psychology Bulletin, 26*(2), 242–256.

Jans, L., Postmes, T., & Van der Zee, K. I. (2011). The induction of shared identity: The positive role of individual distinctiveness for groups. *Personality and Social Psychology Bulletin, 37*(8), 1130–1141.

Jetten, J. & Hutchison, P. (2011). When groups have a lot to lose: Historical continuity enhances resistance to a merger. *European Journal of Social Psychology, 41*(3), 335–343.

Kelly, C. & Kelly, J. (1991). "Them and us": Social psychology and "the new industrial relations." *British Journal of Industrial Relations, 29*, 25–48.

Mael, F. & Ashforth, B. E. (1992). Alumni and their alma mater: A partial test of the reformulated model of organizational identification. *Journal of Organizational Behavior, 13*(2), 103–123.

Millward, L. J., Haslam, S. A., & Postmes, T. (2007). Putting employees in their place: The impact of hot desking on organizational and team identification. *Organization Science, 18*(4), 547–559.

Morton, T. A., Wright, R. G., Peters, K., Reynolds, K. J., & Haslam, S. A. (2012). Social identity and the dynamics of organizational communication. In H. Giles (Ed.) *The handbook of intergroup communication.* Routledge: New York and Oxford.

Oakes, P. J., Haslam, S. A., & Turner, J. C. (1994). *Stereotyping and social reality.* Blackwell Publishing: Oxford.

O'Brien, A. T., Haslam, S. A., Jetten, J., Humphrey, L., O'Sullivan, L., Postmes, T., Eggins, R., & Reynolds, K. J. (2004). Cynicism and disengagement among devalued employee groups: The need to ASPIRe. *Career Development International, 9*(1), 28–44.

Peters, K., Tevichapong, P., Haslam, S. A., & Postmes, T. (2010). Making the organization fly: Organizational identification and citizenship in full-service and low-cost airlines. *Journal of Personnel Psychology, 9*(3), 145–148.

Peters, K., Haslam, S. A., Ryan, M. K., & Fonseca, M. (2013). Working with sub-group identities to build organizational identification and support for organizational strategy: A test of the ASPIRe model. *Group and Organization Management, 38*(1), 128–144.

Peters, K., Haslam, S. A., Ryan, M., & Steffens, N. (in prep.). Building organizational engagement: Challenges in the implementation of the ASPIRe model. University of Exeter.

Platow, M. J., Van Knippenberg, D., Haslam, S. A., Van Knippenberg, B., & Spears, R. (2006). A special gift we bestow on you for being representative of us: Considering leader charisma from a self-categorization perspective. *British Journal of Social Psychology, 45*(2), 303–320.

Putnam, R. D. (2007). E pluribus unum: Diveristy and community in the twenty-first century. The 2006 Johan Skytte Prize Lecture. *Scandinavian Political Studies, 30*(2), 137–174.

Reicher, S., Haslam, S. A., & Hopkins, N. (2005). Social identity and the dynamics of leadership: Leaders and followers as collaborative agents in the transformation of social reality. *The Leadership Quarterly, 16*(4), 547–568.

Riketta, M. & Van Dick, R. (2005). Foci of attachment in organizations: A meta-analytic comparison of the strength and correlates of workgroup versus organizational identification and commitment. *Journal of Vocational Behavior, 67*(3), 490–510.

Riketta, M. & Nienaber, S. (2007). Multiple identities and work motivation: The role of perceived compatibility between nested organizational units. *British Journal of Management, 18*(s1), S61–S77.

Schwartz, S. J., Zamboanga, B. L., & Weisskirch, R. S. (2008). Broadening the study of the self: Integrating the study of personal identity and cultural identity. *Social and Personality Psychology Compass, 2*(2), 635–651.

Spillane, J. P. (2012). *Distributed leadership* (vol. 4). Jossey-Bass: San Francisco.

Tajfel, H. & Turner, J. C. (1979). An integrative theory of intergroup conflict. In W. G. Austin & S. Worchel (Eds). *The social psychology of intergroup relations.* Brooks/Cole: Monterey, CA.

Tame, R. (2007). *Leadership programs: do they make a difference?* Paper presented at the Learnx International Training conference and expo. Sydney, July 27.

Taylor, F. W. (1911). *Shop management.* Harper & Brothers: New York.

Turner, J. C. (1985). Social categorization and the self-concept: A social cognitive theory of group behavior. *Advances in Group Processes: Theory and Research, 2,* 77–122.

Turner, J. C., Oakes, P. J., Haslam, S. A., & McGarty, C. (1994). Self and collective: Cognition and social context. *Personality and Social Psychology Bulletin, 20,* 454–463. doi:10.1177/0146167294205002.

Turner, J. C., Hogg, M. A., Oakes, P. J., Reicher, S. D., & Wetherell, M. S. (1987). *Rediscovering the social group: A self-categorization theory.* Basil Blackwell: Oxford.

Van Dick, R., Wagner, U., Stellmacher, J., & Christ, O. (2005). Category salience and organizational identification. *Journal of Occupational and Organizational Psychology, 78*(2), 273–285.

Van Knippenberg, D. (2000). Group norms, prototypicality, and persuasion. In D. J. Terry & M. A. Hogg (Eds.). *Attitudes, behavior, and social context: The role of norms and group membership.* Lawrence Erlbaum Associates Publishers: Mahwah, NJ.

Van Knippenberg, D. & Van Schie, E. C. M. (2000). Foci and correlates of organizational identification. *Journal of Occupational and Organizational Psychology, 73,* 137–147.

7 Creative processes in culturally diverse teams[1]

Paul B. Paulus and Karen van der Zee

Diversity, creativity, and teamwork are a combination much hyped today as the key to innovative success (cf. Milliken et al., 2003). Given the increasing complexity of science, engineering, technology, and societal problems, novel solutions to problems presumably require collaboration in diverse teams that represent a broad range of skills and knowledge among their members. Furthermore, given the increasing social and cultural diversity of many Western societies and workplaces, the demographic diversity in work teams is also on the increase. Because people with different backgrounds and experiences can bring unique perspectives to a problem, one might expect demographically diverse teams to be more innovative than homogeneous ones (e.g. Egan, 2005; Holtzman & Anderberg, 2011; Lubart, 2010). However, thus far the simple story of the advantages of diverse teams for creativity does not have a simple ending. Reviews of the literature suggest that the evidence for the benefits of diversity for teamwork and creativity is limited (Han et al., 2011; Roberge & Van Dick, 2010; Van Knippenberg & Schippers, 2007). In this chapter, we will discuss the link between diversity and creativity both from a theoretical and an empirical perspective. In doing so, we will try to uncover the reasons for the limited effects and to shed light on the conditions under which positive effects can be obtained. We will highlight some of the key issues, provide some implications for practice and suggest some new directions for research.

Group and team creativity

Creativity is typically defined as the generation of novel ideas that have some degree of utility or acceptance (Amabile, 1996). Relying on this definition, a recommended measure of creativity is the number of good ideas, defined as ideas that are both novel and useful (Reinig et al., 2007). The number of ideas and number of good ideas tend to be highly correlated (Paulus, Kohn et al., 2011; Reinig et al., 2007). However, novelty and utility are often negatively related, and average novelty is typically not related to number of good ideas (Baruah & Paulus, 2008).

Many people presume that group interaction will enhance creativity (Paulus et al., 1995). However, studies of face-to-face interactive groups have typically found that such groups generate fewer ideas and fewer good ideas than the pooled performance of the same number of individuals generating ideas alone (nominal groups: Diehl & Stroebe, 1987; Mullen et al., 1991). In spite of their poor performance, interactive group members tend to rate their performance more positively than nominal groups (Paulus et al., 1993). The productivity loss in groups has been attributed to a wide variety of factors such as social loafing, evaluation apprehension, production blocking (the inability to generate ideas as they occur), and social matching of low performance among group members (Diehl & Stroebe, 1987; Paulus & Brown, 2003). In spite of these negative factors in groups, it has been proposed that groups have much creativity potential because of the stimulating value of diverse perspectives exchanged (Nijstad & Stroebe, 2006; Paulus & Brown, 2007). There has indeed been evidence that groups can demonstrate enhanced creativity relative to nominal groups under certain conditions (Dugosh et al., 2000; Paulus & Yang, 2000).

The basic prescription for enhanced creativity in groups is fairly simple. Share ideas efficiently and process the shared ideas carefully. Moreover, it helps to be highly motivated to perform well on the task (Putman & Paulus, 2009; De Dreu et al., 2011; Kohn et al., 2011). The benefits of idea generation should be particularly evident in groups that have potentially diverse perspectives, although evidence supporting this idea is scarce (Mannix & Neale, 2005). Even scarcer is the evidence for the representation of cultural diversity in groups as a factor that increases their creative potential. We will focus on the cultural dimension in this chapter. Extensive reviews of the general effects of diversity on team performance already exist (e.g. Bell et al., 2011; Roberge & Van Dick, 2010; Van Dijk et al., 2012). However, prior reviews have not focused on cultural diversity and creativity in teams.

Phases of the creative process

The impact of diversity on creativity is likely to differ depending on phase in the creative process. Although idea generation and divergent thinking are an important aspect of the creative process, various scholars have emphasized that innovation involves multiple phases (Basadur et al., 2012; Puccio & Cabra, 2012). For example the Creative Problem Solving approach by Parnes and Osborn (Parnes, 1975) emphasized the five phases of fact finding, problem definition, idea generation, solution finding, and acceptance. The different stages of the innovation process involve different degrees of convergent and divergent thinking. The idea generation process is one which emphasizes divergent thinking in that the focus is on generating a wide range of ideas. However, in the selection phase the process is a convergent one in that group members try to select the most promising ideas for possible action or implementation. These two different phases require rather different orientations (Basadur et al., 2012; Van der Zee & Paulus, 2008). During the divergent stage it is typically important to generate a large number of ideas. So there should be an emphasis on quantity and low evaluation (no criticism). Group cohesion may not be particularly important or may even inhibit the free expression of ideas. In the idea evaluation phase the focus will be on quality and will involve critical evaluation of ideas and potential, combining some features of the best ideas. In this process some degree of group cohesion may be important in order for individuals to be able to work together effectively on a common goal and to be receptive to each other's evaluative comments. It seems that the benefits of diversity will be most evident in the phases of idea generation, where *variety* is the primary aim. In the idea evaluation phase, lower cohesion in diverse groups may inhibit the process of reaching agreement. Since most of the relevant creativity research has focused on the idea generation phase, we will focus on that phase in this chapter.

A framework for diversity and creativity

Figure 7.1 provides a summary of the major factors that play a role in the creative process in multicultural teams and determine the extent to which diverse groups and teams effectively tap their creative potential. One obvious factor is the type of diversity and how it is expressed and perceived. A second factor involves the processes that are critical for creative building process in groups. This includes the degree of effective sharing or communication, cognitive stimulation and elaboration, and collective motivation for creativity. The extent to which diverse characteristics and related processes lead to creative outcomes is also influenced by a number of moderator variables such as group climate/cohesion, collective experience, and attitude toward diversity.

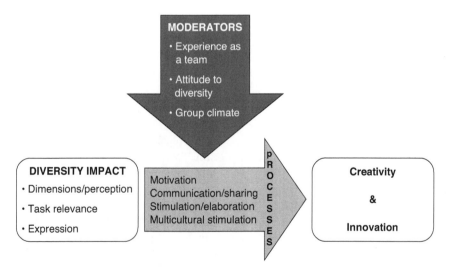

Figure 7.1 Major factors involved in the creative process in multicultural teams.

Diversity in groups

Studying the effects of diversity in groups is not an easy task. A team is potentially a complex social unit, and the particular composition of the team may be critical in determining the outcome of variations in diversity (Bouncken, 2004; Reiter-Palmon et al., 2012). For example, the effects of a team composed of a young Protestant black female, an older agnostic white male, a middle-aged Catholic Latino gay male, and middle-aged female Muslim Jordanian immigrant will vary depending on a wide variety of factors, such as the level of outcome variables (individual versus team), types of measures employed, the type of task, the past team experience, and shared attitudes to diversity (e.g. Hülsheger et al., 2009). At an initial meeting of such a team there may be some level of discomfort in social interactions and a reticence to open sharing of perspectives (Camacho & Paulus, 1995). After some experience as a team and the development of some level of trust, cohesion and mutual respect, interactions may be more facile and open and team performance should be enhanced. However, that does not mean that this team will necessarily be optimal for creativity tasks. This will depend on the extent to which the task taps the unique skills and experiences of the different team members. On a science or math task, this demographically and culturally diverse group has no basis for outperforming a more homogeneous group. However, on a task that is focused on the development of a more inclusive and tolerant society, this team is likely to come up with more unique ideas than a homogeneous group. Yet, would that diverse group be more creative overall than the average of four groups that span the same diversity dimensions as the members in our diverse group but are composed of all the same type of individuals (e.g. either four young Protestant black females, four older agnostic white males, etc.)? That is, is there any synergistic benefit of being in a diverse team on creativity so that the combination leads to more positive outcomes that the average of the non-diverse teams? We will attempt to unravel this puzzle on how to get the most creativity out of culturally diverse teams using our summary framework.

Diversity dimensions and perception of diversity

As suggested by our above example, teams can be diverse along many dimensions. In their review of the literature, Harrison and Klein (2007) organize diversity along three dimensions—separation (e.g. values), variety (e.g. differences in knowledge) and disparity (differences in status or resources). Cultural diversity can imply variations in values, knowledge/experience and status. One of the major challenges of diversity in teams is the simple problem of the perception of social differences. In terms of Harrison and Klein (2007) this refers to diversity as a variable that may *separate* group members from each other. People tend to like those who are similar to themselves and select those individuals for socialization and friendship (Berscheid

& Reis, 1998). There is also an extensive literature on problems related to intergroup bias (Crisp & Hewstone, 2007). Members of distinct groups have generally negative reactions to each other. Social identity theory explains this in terms of in-group bias and the need for self-enhancement. By identifying with one's own group and elevating its status relative to other groups, one can increase one's feelings of self-esteem (Hogg, 2006). The similarity bias and in-group bias help explain the observation that diverse groups can lead to a number of negative social outcomes such as lower levels of communication and cohesion (Reiter-Palmon et al., 2012). These negative social effects should hinder an open and motivated exchange of ideas or perspectives in teams and lead to a low level of creativity, as observed in several studies (cf. Hoever et al., 2012).

A number of scholars (e.g. Bell et al., 2011; Milliken et al., 2003) have noted that first impressions and categorization are often based on easily observed surface characteristics such as age, sex, and race (e.g. Fiske & Neuberg, 1990; Stangor et al., 1992), with some evidence that race diversity may be the most salient characteristic (Harrison et al., 2002). Cultural diversity may often involve differences in ethnicity or race, but variations in cultural diversity will also be salient when we consider people who come from different countries or regions of a country. In many countries there are distinct differences between people who live in the north and southern regions. However, differences among some regions and countries are much more extreme than among others along such dimensions as religion, traditions, economic level, language etc. It is of course difficult to empirically assess the relevance of all those dimensions systematically. Many studies of diversity use some kind of index of diversity that represents the degree of diversity along multiple dimensions among team members (O'Reilly et al., 1998). Others simply compare teams that are diverse on several demographic dimensions with teams that do not vary on these dimensions (e.g. Nakui et al., 2011).

In general, it appears that negative effects of diversity are most evident with demographic diversity such as age, gender, and ethnicity (e.g. Basset-Jones, 2005; Cady & Valentine, 1999; Hülsheger et al., 2009). Bell et al. (2011) reviewed the literature on demographic diversity and team performance and found racial diversity had a small negative effect on team performance, but only in field settings. However, a careful examination of the team studies that have used objective measures of creativity (based on the review and related results provided by Van Dijk et al., 2012), the pattern is somewhat different. Although age and gender diversity do not appear to be consistently related to team creativity, racial and ethnic diversity appear to have a positive effect. McLeod et al. (1996) found that ethnically heterogenous groups generated ideas that were more effective and feasible than those from homogeneous groups on a brainstorming task. Cady and Valentine (1999) found that racial diversity in groups increased the number of ideas but not the quality of ideas on a task requiring solutions to a business problem. Interestingly, age and function had no effect on either measure, but gender diversity had a negative effect on idea quality. In both of these studies, racial/ethnic diversity was related to negative perceptions of the group. In a study with MBA students over the course of a semester it was found that culturally diverse teams generated fewer alternatives and a more limited range of perspectives on two business cases than homogeneous teams in the first half of the semester (Watson et al., 1993). However, this pattern was reversed for the two business cases in the second half of the semester. Perceptions of group process were initially more negative in the diverse group, but by the end of the semester there was no difference in perception.

Task relevance

Negative effects of demographic diversity are easy to understand from the in-group bias perspective and the fact that there may be some increased discomfort in demographically diverse teams. When differences in demographic dimensions are related to different experiences and knowledge relevant to a specific task, a positive effect of demographic diversity on performance and creativity should be observed. This is suggested by the fact that, when group members differ in task expertise (functional diversity), positive effects of this type of diversity can be found. For example, Bell et al. (2011) reviewed the literature on diversity and team performance and found that functional diversity had a small positive effect on team performance, including team creativity and innovation. Similarly, Hülsheger et al. (2009) found a positive effect of job-relevant diversity on team innovation.

It has been suggested that effects of cultural diversity will be obtained more easily with culturally relevant tasks (McLeod et al., 1996; Williams & O'Reilly, 1998). Obviously such tasks would more effectively tap differences in perspectives related to cultural differences among group members. That is, do the diverse characteristics and abilities of the group members provide a basis for generating creative ideas for a particular problem? One reason why studies of the effects of demographic diversity on team performance have not shown much effect is that often this diversity may not have been particularly relevant to the tasks employed. We know of no study in which the knowledge and experience relevant to a problem was measured for participants who varied along demographic dimensions. Thus, there may often be no deep-level diversity in such studies. However, if the task is relevant to a demographic variation, deep-level differences may be tapped and effects on group creativity may be obtained. Deep-level differences related to cultural diversity can include language, knowledge of landscapes, and features of culture. These types of differences are likely to lead to very different perspectives on social issues but not on problem-solving tasks that involve general cognitive skills.

Interestingly, in the studies cited earlier in which cultural diversity had positive effects on creativity, the tasks employed appear to be relevant to variation in perspectives based on different cultural experiences (business tasks, Cady & Valentine, 1999, Watson et al., 1993; tourist task, McLeod et al., 1996). Nakui et al. (2011) used a culturally relevant task in a study in which students who varied in ethnicity and native language were asked to generate ideas to enhance the cultural diversity experience at the university (Nakui et al., 2011). Positive effects of diversity were obtained for participants who also had a positive attitude toward diversity and were thus presumably motivated to process the shared (diversity-relevant) ideas. However, several studies have found that even with tasks that appear to have little relevance, effects can be obtained (Giambatista & Bhappu, 2010; Tadmor, Satterstrom et al., 2012). For example, Tadmor, Satterstrom et al. (2012) found that a pair of brainstormers generated more ideas and more novel ideas on the task of uses for a brick when the pair consisted of an Asian and a Caucasian who both had a high level of multicultural experience than in other pair combinations. It is possible that the diverse experiences of this pair allowed them to imagine more unique uses on a task that was not particularly culturally relevant. Giambatista and Bhappu (2010) found a negative effect of ethnic diversity on generating ideas for a commercial in face-to-face groups but enhanced creativity related to diversity when using a nominal group technique or a computer mediated interaction technique. Apparently these latter techniques were more effective in tapping task-relevant differences related to ethnicity while minimizing any discomfort that might have been experienced in the face-to-face condition. In other words, conditions were created that caused differences to be perceived in terms of useful variation rather than in terms of separation (Harrison & Klein, 2007). A clear determination of the role of task relevance in effects of cultural diversity on creativity in teams will require a systematic assessment of culturally related differences in perspectives in participants and their relationship to team performance on tasks varying in cultural relevance.

Expression of diversity in groups

Although much of our discussion has focused on the negative factors related to the perception and expression of diversity, others have argued that it is important for diverse group members to maintain and express their uniqueness. Swan and colleagues have emphasized the importance of maintaining one's uniqueness in a diverse group as part of their self-verification perspective (cf. Swann et al., 2004). They argue that individuals have a strong desire to affirm their unique identity. Verification of one's identity increases the feeling of being understood by other group members, increases identification with the group, and increases the willingness to share creative or unique ideas. They found that in groups which had a high level of self-verification, demographic diversity was related to enhanced performance on a creative task. In groups in which there was not a significant degree of self-verification, diversity was negatively related to creative performance (Polzer et al., 2002). This perspective is of course contrary to one that focuses on minimizing perception of differences in diverse groups or emphasizing commonalities (cf. Mannix & Neale, 2005).

Other scholars departing from the tradition of social identity theory have also stressed the value of unique identities in groups. For example, it has been argued that people's bond with a diverse group can either be inferred from their perceived own prototypicality within the group (i.e. self-stereotyping) or by the projection of one's own individual characteristics onto the group (i.e. self-anchoring; Cadinu & Rothbart, 1996). Particularly this latter process seems beneficial for identification processes in diverse groups. To illustrate, recent research by Van Veelen and collaborators showed that minority members who were invited to focus on their individual self and then reflect on how far what characterizes them as an individual might also apply to the group as a whole (self-anchoring), identified more strongly with the diverse group than those who were reflecting on to what extent group features might also apply to themselves as an individual (self-stereotyping). Although for majority members identification was not facilitated by self-anchoring, self-anchoring did promote beliefs that diversity might be of added value for a diverse group (Van Veelen et al., 2013; see also Chapter 9).

A comparable perspective is reflected in the concept of *inductive identity formation* as introduced by Postmes et al. (2005). These authors argue that groups can form both top-down, such that individual group members adapt to an already existing group prototype, or bottom-up, such that the group prototype is shaped by the contributions of individual members. Both processes may lead to cohesive groups, but in heterogeneous groups, inductive group formation may be more successful in doing so. Moreover, inductive processes are more successful in facilitating the expression of individuality in groups (Jans et al., 2011, 2012; Chapter 9) which may in turn promote creativity. It must be noted that, to date, little evidence is available to support this latter claim.

The importance of maintaining awareness of one's unique identity has also been noted in the group literature. For example, Phillips et al. (2006) found that ethnically diverse groups performed better on a hidden profile task than homogeneous groups. However, discovering deep-level similarities hindered performance for heterogeneous groups but not homogeneous groups. Apparently, even though discovery of similarities among group members may enhance attraction or cohesion, it may inhibit the sharing of unique information. The researchers suggest that surface-level diversity may have a positive effect on group performance not only because of related differences in perspectives but also because the recognition that group members are different on some very salient dimensions may make the sharing of unique perspectives more expected and accepted. The importance of maintaining cultural differences in teams in order to enhance their creativity potential has also been emphasized in the fusion model of Janssens and Brett (2006) which will be discussed in more detail later.

Key processes in creative teams

We have highlighted a number of factors that may inhibit communication and the sharing of unique perspectives in diverse groups. To counteract this tendency, teams need to be highly motivated to take advantage of their diversity, openly share their unique perspectives, and effectively build on the stimulation value of this exchange process. We will highlight how these key processes relate to effective creative functioning in teams.

Motivation

One problem with diverse teams is that team members may not be highly motivated to take advantage of the diverse perspectives in the team because of social barriers or differences. Some creativity models emphasize the importance of intrinsic motivation (e.g. Amabile & Mueller, 2007), presuming that intrinsic motivation for a particular activity is important for creative outcomes. Research on group and team creativity has not examined the role of this factor but has found that extrinsic motivational factors (cf. Eisenberger & Aselage, 2009) can be influential. Research has suggested that, when team members are motivated to share their perspectives and build on those perspectives, a high level of creativity may occur (De Dreu et al., 2011; Paulus & Dzindolet, 2008; Hoever et al., 2012). Paulus and his colleagues (cf. Paulus et al., 2002; Paulus, Dzindolet et al., 2011) have emphasized the importance of motivational factors such as goal setting, feedback, social competition, accountability and upward comparison. These factors can increase the extent to which team members attend to each other, build on each other's ideas, and persist in the search for more creative ideas.

Sharing unique perspectives

Research on group creativity has found that a key factor in creativity is the cognitive stimulation and related associations derived from shared ideas (Nijstad & Stroebe, 2006; Paulus & Brown, 2007). A culturally diverse team can share potential diverse perspectives about many aspects of life. This may enrich conversations and potentially performance on creativity tasks that can benefit from cross-cultural perspectives. This is the focus of the fusion model of Janssens and Brett (2006). Janssens and Brett rely on two influences to ensure synergistic functioning of diverse groups. The first is the concept of pluralistic democracy that allows for the coexistence of differences among team members; the second is fusion cooking. Fusion cooking is a method that relies on combining different styles of cooking and cooking ingredients in such a way that the elements remain identifiable, but their juxtaposition is unique. In this regard, recognition and respect of cultural differences among team members should facilitate unique conceptual or idea combinations based on differences in values and perspectives. In extending this perspective,

Crotty and Brett (2012) proposed that it is important for team participation to be meaningful and that team members have meta-cognitive skills. Meaningful participation involves group members being responsible for sharing their unique perspectives when they are relevant.

Meaningful participation presumes that the team is open to such sharing and would depend on the extent to which participants feel a sense of psychological safety about sharing those ideas (Roberge & Van Dick, 2010; West & Richter, 2008; see also Otten and Jansen, this volume). Consistent with this idea are findings by Nakui (2006) who compared the creative performance of homogeneous versus culturally heterogeneous brainstorming groups. He found that groups whose members believed they shared positive attitudes toward diversity produced higher numbers of creative ideas. Crotty and Brett (2012) also emphasize the importance of cultural metacognition, or cultural awareness, or sensitivity during team interaction. They found evidence for their predictions in a study of multicultural work teams that varied in nationality and primary language. Teams that reported higher levels of fusion also reported higher levels of creative applications. Higher levels of metacognition in team members were related to higher reported creativity.

In a similar vein Kooij-de Bode et al. (2008) found that ethnic diversity hindered the effective exchange and integration of information of participants in decision-making groups unless they received special instructions on the exchange and integration of the shared information. It is most likely that some balance between similarity or cohesion and focus on unique demographic dimensions may be optimal (Van der Zee & Paulus, 2008). It may be particularly important to have a focus on commonality in the early phases of team interaction. The resulting cohesion can then make group members more comfortable with sharing unique perspectives.

Stimulation and elaboration

Once ideas are shared by a diverse group, it is important for participants to build or elaborate on them to develop creative ideas that would not have been possible in a homogeneous group. So multicultural teams need to be highly motivated to do a full sharing of their divergent perspectives and then effectively process and build on them. The semantic network model of Paulus and Brown (2003, 2007) emphasizes the importance of attention to the shared ideas so they can be cognitively processed, related to each group member's network of ideas and lead to additional associations. Under such conditions shared ideas can stimulate group members to think of ideas or categories of ideas they might have otherwise not considered. This creative potential of building on the ideas of others was clearly shown in a study by Kohn and colleagues (2011). Students were presented with ideas and asked to use those ideas to generate new ones. They were to indicate which ideas were used to build the new ideas. This ensured that participants were attentive to the presented ideas and the task of building on those ideas. Participants were provided with either common or unique ideas to build on either alone or as part of a group. They found that group sharing of ideas during the building process enhanced the originality and feasibility of ideas relative to the alone condition (Kohn et al., 2011).

Van Knippenberg et al. (2004) proposed a categorization elaboration model (CEM) of diversity which also emphasizes the importance of cognitive processing of shared ideas. In diverse groups the categorization and in-group bias factors may inhibit elaboration (discussion, exchange, and integration of ideas). However, if group members are internally or externally motivated, they may engage in the elaboration processes that allow them to benefit from their unique perspectives and knowledge. Similarly, De Dreu et al. (2011) have proposed a motivated information processing model (MIPG) that suggests that teams need both epistemic motivation (systematic processing and sharing of information) and prosocial motivation (positive group orientation by means of shared identity or cooperative group arrangements) in order to tap their creative or innovative potential. In terms of Harrison and Klein (2007), these motives refer to reducing tendencies toward separation versus enhancing tendencies to explore variation, respectively.

Mulicultural stimulation

Our discussion of the stimulating effects of shared ideas suggests that the creative potential of teams can also be enhanced by the shared multicultural experiences of the group members. That is, the exchange of cultural perspectives in general as part of social interaction among team members may affect the cognitive perspectives of the team members in a way that may enhance their individual and collaborative creativity. Recent studies on the impact of experiences in other cultures have indeed found that such experiences can increase individual creativity (Leung et al., 2008). A critical factor in whether such experiences lead to enhanced creativity is whether or not the experience is cognitively challenging. That is, does the experience require the individuals to reevaluate their own perspectives because of their experiences in another culture (e.g. Crisp & Turner, 2011; Leung et al., 2008)? This experience does not have to be extensive in terms of time, and in fact even exposure to multicultural information in a short-term setting can have similar benefits (Leung & Chiu, 2008). A key factor appears to be the multicultural learning experiences that come from living in another country (Maddux et al., 2010).

Although this literature has focused on individuals, it has potential relevance to multicultural teams. Interactions among culturally diverse team members can provide mutual challenges to team members' personal perspectives on a range of issues. Such challenges may enhance the creative potential of the team. One reason that changes in perspective may lead to enhanced creativity is that such experiences increase team member cognitive complexity. That is, team members may view the world in more nuanced and complex ways, and this may be reflected in their creative products (Tadmor, Galinsky et al., 2012). It is also possible that such experiences increase the ability to empathize with or understand the perspectives of others. Such empathy may be an important factor in enhancing the creativity of diverse teams (Hoever et al., 2012; Roberge & Van Dick, 2010). For example, Hoever et al. (2012) found that, when diverse groups are instructed to take the perspectives of other group members, the creativity of these groups is enhanced relative to homogeneous groups. This effect was mediated by information elaboration. Another relevant factor may be that exposure to different or minority perspectives can enhance subsequent divergent thinking or creativity (De Dreu & West, 2001; Nemeth & Kwan, 1985; Nemeth & Nemeth-Brown, 2003; Schulz-Hardt et al., 2008). Presumably exposure to a minority perspective may require reappraisal of one's own views in comparison to other perspectives. This type of experience may increase the tendency toward divergent thinking on a subsequent unrelated task.

In sum, there is great potential for creativity in multicultural groups or teams, but it is also possible that too much cognitive complexity and surprise related to diversity can have negative effects (Austin, 1997). Too much complexity may be threatening, as individuals can no longer make sense out of their environment, with rigid automatic-responding patterns as a consequence. A moderate degree of diversity may be optimal in teams (Richard et al., 2004). However, individuals who are bicultural may be able to handle the complexity of high levels of diversity more effectively (Tadmor, Satterstrom et al., 2012). Biculturally integrated individuals may also show enhanced creativity when they are provided with cues related to a more dominantly creative culture. For example, biculturally integrated Asian Americans generated more ideas when they were exposed to cues related to American rather than Asian culture during the idea generation process (Mok & Morris, 2010). It also appears to be optimal if multiple team members have multicultural experiences. Tadmor, Satterstrom and colleagues (2012) found that pairs of brainstormers in which both partners had multicultural experience was optimal in terms of generation of creative ideas.

Moderators of the diversity-creativity link

We have discussed the importance of motivational and cognitive processes involved in creativity of multicultural teams. However, there are a broad range of factors that are likely to influence the extent to which such creative outcomes are realized (cf. Hülsheger et al., 2009; Paulus & Dzindolet, 2008). We will highlight three such factors or moderators that appear to be particularly important for multicultural teams.

Experience as a team

There are a number of other factors that appear to be important for the diversity potential in teams to be realized. One factor may be the experience as a team. For example, Cummings and Kiesler (2008) have found that shared experience as a team is important for the success of interdisciplinary teams. Experience as a team allows team members to overcome some of their initial social reservations, share in positive experiences, discover common or shared perspectives, develop group cohesion, and learn about each others' unique skills and abilities (e.g. Watson et al., 1993). Even though diversity may have great creative potential, it is also important for the team to have some degree of "social sharedness" or common ground (Greve, 2009; Tindale & Kameda, 2000). This common ground allows the group to bond along the dimensions they have in common while enjoying differences in other dimensions. Increased experience as a team also helps develop shared mental models so that group members have a shared understanding of the goals of the group and the ways to achieve them (Salas et al., 2009).

Attitude towards diversity

A second important moderating factor is the attitude of team members to one another. Much literature on intergroup bias and prejudice has found that, if the group members have some common cooperative goal, the negative feelings can be greatly reduced (Dovidio et al., 2013). Interestingly, among college students there can actually be a bias in favor of ethnically diverse groups (Van der Zee et al., 2009). This is particularly true in the case of performance settings rather than social settings and if students have a strong positive attitude toward diversity. Several studies have demonstrated moderating effects of diversity beliefs on team performance and identification. Teams that value diversity are more likely to demonstrate positive relationships between ethnic diversity and various outcomes (Van Dick et al., 2008) and a more positive relationship between diversity and group identification (Van Knippenberg et al., 2007).

Similar effects have also been found for group creativity. If team members have a positive attitude toward working in diverse groups, the performance of the diverse team is enhanced in terms of quality of ideas (Nakui et al., 2011; see also Chapter 9 in this volume). Similarly, Swan et al. (2003) found that initial positive impressions are important for positive effects of diversity (combined functional and demographic) on group projects for MBA students. In addition to the impact of positive attitudes on performance in diverse groups, the extent to which individuals value diversity also influences their perception of diversity. Those who value diversity perceive the diversity of group members in terms of individual difference rather than as a basis for subgrouping (Homan et al., 2010). This perceptual disposition is likely to enhance the positive impact of group diversity on creativity. Interestingly, simply instructing individuals about the value of diversity seems to be sufficient to lead to positive effects of informational diversity on generating ideas on a desert survival task (Homan et al., 2007).

Although one can measure attitude to diversity directly, a number of other personal factors are likely to influence one's disposition to diversity in teams.

Openness to experience (Homan et al., 2008) and need for cognition (Kearney et al., 2009) are two personal difference factors that have been found to relate to performance in diverse workgroups. Furthermore, the Multicultural Personality Questionnaire appears to be a useful predictor of performance in culturally diverse teams (cf. van der Zee et al., 2003; van der Zee et al., 2004).

Group climate

The social climate of the group also appears to be an important factor in moderating the impact of diversity on creativity. That is, to what extent are there mutually positive feelings, common interests, a sense of trust, and psychological safety in the group (Paulus, Dzindolet et al., 2011)? This type of cohesion has been shown to be important for group and team performance in general, but is particularly important for culturally diverse groups working on a creative task. In diverse groups, individuals may have a high level of uncertainty about how other group members will react to novel or "non-normative ideas." If the group members have strong positive feelings toward one another (high cohesion), they should be more comfortable in sharing their ideas and thus be more creative (e.g. Craig & Kelly, 1999). Studies have also demonstrated that team cohesion is a strong predictor of team innovation (Hülsheger et al., 2009). When participants have had some time to get to know each other, they may develop feelings of trust. That is, they may expect their fellow group members to be honest and supportive. Such feelings of trust have been related to innovation and may be particularly beneficial in diverse groups (cf. Carmeli & Speitzer, 2009).

Research has also found that common interests may enhance the benefits of demographic diversity in organizations (e.g. Chatman et al., 1998; Mannix & Neale, 2005). That is, it may be important for members of a diverse group to have some "common ground" which enables them to feel a positive connection to their fellow group members. However, a focus on similarity in cultural values could hinder identification with one's work group and hence its performance or creativity (Luijters et al., 2008). However, when there is a strong intercultural group climate in the organization (positive perception of diversity), there is a strong identification with the team and the organization. Such a climate has also been related to enhanced job outcome for both minority and majority members (Hofhuis et al., 2012). Finally, a number of studies have emphasized the role of psychological safety—the extent to which group or team members feel free to express their ideas without concern for negative consequences. West and Richter (2008) and Edmondson and Mogelof (2006) have emphasized the importance of this factor in team innovation. The review by Hülsheger et al. (2009) has shown that this is indeed the case.

Conclusions

Much literature on the effects of demographic/cultural diversity in teams has highlighted the negative factors associated with diversity that can inhibit team performance. Thus it is not surprising that reviews of the literature find little evidence for an overall benefit of this type of diversity on team performance. In contrast, diversity based on functional or expertise differences appears to have some beneficial effect on team performance. Unfortunately, most studies of team innovation or creativity have used subjective reports as measures. Studies that have employed both objective data and subjective reports have often found little correspondence between them. However, from the small number of studies of demographic diversity on creativity it appears that racial and ethnic diversity (but not age and gender) can be related to an increase in the number and quality of ideas generated. Creativity tasks may be particularly sensitive to differences in perspective related to cultural differences implied by race and gender (and presumably cultural background). On the basis of the literature on cultural diversity and creativity and the broader literature on demographic diversity and team performance, we have outlined a number of factors that are likely to influence the impact of cultural diversity on creativity. The specific dimension of diversity, the relevance of the task to the perspectives and knowledge that underlie the a specific type of diversity, and the extent to which participants in a team feel free to express their unique perspectives will determine whether or not an effect of cultural diversity on creativity will be observed. The creative potential of diverse groups will be realized only if the group members effectively share their unique perspectives and build on or elaborate the shared ideas. This presumes that the team members are highly motivated to work together and are open to the cognitive stimulation that can result from exposure to diverse cultural perspectives. Whether or not effective creative processes occur in teams will depend on at least three moderating factors— the experience as team, the attitude to diversity, and the group climate. The relationships highlighted on our review and model should help practitioners and leaders who are concerned with enhancing the innovative potential of their teams.

Future directions

The research on creativity in multicultural teams is in its infancy and there are many empirical gaps that remain to be addressed. Although there is a fairly solid basis for understanding ideational creativity in multicultural teams, there has been little consideration of the impact of cultural differences on the other phases of the innovation process. How does multicultural diversity influence problem selection, idea evaluation and implementation—the more convergent aspects of innovation? Each of these phases requires some degree of consensus. Although divergent thinking might be enhanced by cultural diversity, gaining consensus may be more difficult with high levels of diversity in a team. Research on multicultural teams has focused almost exclusively on young adults. Would similar effects be found in young children or older adults? Young children may be less influenced by their cultural context than adults. Older adults may have a stronger cultural identity, and therefore the impact of cultural diversity in teams with older adults may be magnified. Differences in culture and language may often be highly correlated. Thus it may be difficult to disentangle their distinct effects. Research by Ji et al. (2004) suggests that both may be important in influencing the nature of the creative process. There are many culturally relevant dimensions along which team members may differ (e.g. race, ethnicity, sexual orientation, religion, politics). Studies which simultaneously examine a variety of such cultural factors in teams would be valuable in determining additive or interactive effects of these factors.

Investigators should also carefully consider the nature of the team task for degree of relevance to the cultural diversity being examined. It will be important for future studies to develop ways to assess cultural and diversity relevance of tasks and to examine the importance of this dimension for demonstrating benefits of cultural diversity on team creativity.

Another important consideration is that most studies of innovation have used self-report measures of performance. In a meta-analytic review by Van Dijk et al. (2012) it was found that negative effects of ethnic diversity on team performance were found only for subjective ratings. When objective performance measures were used, there was not a significant effect of ethnic diversity. Apparently, biases related to ethnicity and other culturally relevant dimensions may negatively influence perception of performance. It will be important for future studies to use objective measures whenever feasible. There is much evidence for inconsistency between self-report measures and objective measures, so obtaining both measures will continue to be critical for advancing our understanding of the creative process in multicultural teams.

One way in which teams can increase their diversity is to use virtual interaction modalities. This allows teams to work with individuals through-out the world without the requirement of working in the same place. Although it is assumed that multicultural diversity enhances virtual team performance, thus far there is no definitive evidence (Dzindolet et al., 2012; Gibson & Gibbs, 2006). Research on social networks has emphasized the benefits of diversity (Greve, 2009). However, this work has focused primarily on the role of functional diversity and mutual need. There is no research on multicultural networks and innovation or creativity. Since social networks are often based on similarity of interests or background, the level of multi-cultural diversity may be fairly low in most naturally formed networks (DiPrete et al., 2011).

Research on the different phases of the innovative process has been limited. Most studies have focused on idea generation. There have been a number of studies that have examined the idea selection process after group brain-storming. These studies have found that individuals and group members have a difficult time in selecting the best ideas (Putman & Paulus, 2009; Rietzschel et al., 2006). The top ideas selected are typically not more novel than the average of all the ideas generated. There is a bias to selecting ideas that are feasible. Rietzschel et al. (2010) tried a number of techniques to increase the selection of novel ideas and found that instructing participants to select original ideas did increase the selection of those ideas. One problem may be that, once a group has generated a large number of ideas, the task of picking the best ideas becomes a bit overwhelming. A more efficient process may be to alternate short divergent and convergent thinking sessions. However, it is possible that beginning convergent selection sessions before groups have generated a high number ideas may fixate the group on the ideas that gained acceptance early in the process. Since original ideas tend to come later in the divergent thinking session (Paulus et al., 2013), this may limit the group's creative potential. Thus, research is needed to determine the optimal balancing of convergent and divergent thinking on a creativity task. Furthermore, thus far no study has examined the impact of diversity on this process.

No studies have examined asynchronous interaction in diverse teams. When a diverse range of unique ideas are shared, it may be beneficial to have some time to reflect on them and build on them with one's own ideas or expertise. Studies have shown that much benefit of shared ideation can be tapped in such sessions (Paulus et al., 2006). Such sessions can be mixed with interactive sessions. We don't know the optimal mix for such sessions in terms of time and frequency, but, based on semantic network theory, it may be beneficial to have these sessions in close proximity to optimize the tapping of associations stimulated during the interactive session (Brown & Paulus, 2002). The use of an effective asynchronous idea-sharing process may increase the benefits of exposure to diverse perspectives.

Even though research on cultural diversity and team creativity has been limited, we have gained some important insights about the basic processes and moderators that are important in understanding how to effectively tap the creative potential of culturally diverse groups. These insights should be helpful to organizations that want to effectively utilize their diverse population in creative endeavors. However, many interesting questions remain to be examined to develop a more complete picture of the relevant factors involved in the full range of activities involved in innovation in multicultural teams.

Note

1 Some of the research reported in this chapter was supported by collaborative grant BCS 0729305 to the first author from the National Science Foundation, which included support from the Deputy Director of National Intelligence for Analysis and a collaborative CreativeIT grant 0855825 from the National Science Foundation. Any opinions, findings, and conclusions or recommendations expressed in this material are those of the authors and do not necessarily reflect the views of the National Science Foundation.

References

Amabile, T. M. (1996). *Creativity in context*. Boulder, CO: West-view Press.

Amabile, T. M. & Mueller, J. S. (2007). Studying creativity, its processes, and its antecedents: An exploration of the componential theory of creativity. In J. Zhou & C. Shalley (Eds.), *Handbook of organizational creativity*. Mahwah, NJ: Lawrence Erlbaum Associates.

Austin, J. R. (1997). A cognitive framework for understanding demographic influences in groups. *The International Journal of Organizational Analysis, 5*(4), 342–359.

Baruah, J. & Paulus, P. B. (2008). Effects of training on idea generation in groups. *Small Group Research, 39*, 523–541.

Basadur, M., Basadur, T., & Licina, G. (2012). Organizational development. In M. D. Mumford (Ed.), *Handbook of organizational creativity* (pp. 668–703). Amsterdam: Elsevier.

Bassett-Jones, N. (2005). The paradox of diversity management, creativity and innovation. *Creativity and Innovation Management, 14*(2), 169–175.

Bell, S. T., Villado, A. J., Lukasik, M. A., Belau, L. & Briggs, A. (2011). Getting specific about demographic diversity variable and team performance relationships: A meta-analysis. *Journal of Management, 37*, 709–743.

Berscheid E. & Reis, H. T. (1998). Attraction and close relationships. In D. T. Gilbert, S. T. Fiske, & G. Lindzey (Eds.), *The handbook of social psychology* (pp. 193–281). New York: McGraw-Hill.

Bouncken, R. B. (2004). Cultural diversity in entrepreneurial teams: Findings of new ventures in Germany. *Creativity and Innovation Management, 13*(4), 240–253.

Brown, V. R. & Paulus, P. B. (2002). Making group brainstorming more effective: Recommendations from an associative memory perspective. *Current Directions in Psychological Science, 11*, 208–212.

Cadinu, M. & Rothbart, M. (1996). Self-anchoring and differentiation processes in the minimal group setting. *Journal of Personality and Social Psychology, 70*(4), 661–677. doi:10.1037/0022-3514.70.4.661.

Cady, S. H. & Valentine, J. (1999). Team innovation and perceptions of consideration: What difference does diversity make? *Small Group Research, 30*(6), 730–750.

Camacho, L. M. & Paulus, P. B. (1995). The role of social anxiousness in group brainstorming. *Journal of Personality and Social Psychology, 68*, 1071–1080.

Carmeli, A. & Spreitzer, G. M. (2009). Trust, connectivity, and thriving: Implications for innovative behaviors at work. *Journal of Creative Behavior, 43*, 169–199.

Chatman, J. A., Polzer, J. T., Barsade, S. G., & Neale, M. A. (1998). Being different yet feeling similar: The influence of demographic composition and organizational culture on work processes and outcomes. *Administrative Science Quarterly, 43*, 749–780.

Craig, T. Y. & Kelly, J. R. (1999). Group cohesiveness and creative performance. *Group Dynamics: Theory, Research, and Practice, 3*(4), 243–256.

Crisp, R. J. & Hewstone, M. (2007). Multiple social categorization. In M. P. Zanna (Ed.), *Advances in experimental social psychology* (Vol. 39, pp. 163–254). Orlando, FL: Academic Press.

Crisp, R. J. & Turner, R. N. (2011). Cognitive adaptation to the experience of social and cultural diversity. *Psychological Bulletin, 137*(2), 242–266.

Crotty, S. K. & Brett, J. M. (2012). Fusing creativity: Cultural metacognition and teamwork in multicultural teams. *Negotiation and Conflict Management Research, 5*(2), 210–234.

Cummings, J. N. & Kiesler, S. (2008). Who collaborates successfully? Prior experience reduces collaboration barriers in distributed interdisciplinary research. *Proceedings of the ACM conference on Computer-Supported Cooperative Work*, (November 10–12), San Diego, CA.

De Dreu, C. K. W. & West, M. A. (2001). Minority dissent and team innovation: The importance of participation in decision making. *Journal of Applied Psychology*, *86*(6), 1191–1201.

De Dreu, C. K. W., Nijstad, B. A., Bechtoldt, M. N., & Baas, M. (2011). Group creativity and innovation: A motivated information processing perspective. *Psychology of Aesthetics, Creativity, and the Arts*, *5*, 81–89.

Diehl, M. & Stroebe, W. (1987). Productivity loss in brainstorming groups: Toward the solution of riddle. *Journal of Personality and Social Psychology*, *53*, 497–509.

DiPrete, T. A., Gelman, A., Teitler, J., Zheng, T., & McCormick, T. (2011). Segregation in social networks based on acquaintanceship and trust. *American Journal of Sociology*, *116*, 1234–1283.

Dovidio, J. F., Gaertner, S. L., & Thomas, E. L. (2013). Intergroup relations. In J. M. Levine (Ed.), *Group processes* (pp. 323–349). New York: Psychology Press.

Dugosh, K. L., Paulus, P. B., Roland, E. J., & Yang, H. (2000). Cognitive stimulation in brainstorming. *Journal of Personality and Social Psychology*, *79*, 722–735.

Dzindolet, M. T., Paulus, P. B., & Glazer, C. (2012). Brainstorming in virtual teams. In C. N. Silva (Ed.), *Online research methods in urban and planning studies: Design and outcome* (pp. 138–156). Hershey, PA; IGI Global.

Edmondson, A. C. & Mogelof, J. P. (2006). Explaining psychological safety in innovation teams: Organizational culture, team dynamics, or personality? In L. Thompson & H. S. Choi (Eds.), *Creativity and innovation in organizational teams* (pp. 109–136). Mahwah, NJ: Lawrence Erlbaum.

Egan, T. M. (2005). Creativity in the context of team diversity: Team leader perspectives. *Advances in Developing Human Resources*, *7*(2), 207–225.

Eisenberger, R. & Aselage, J. (2009). Incremental effects of reward on experienced performance pressure: Positive outcomes for intrinsic interest and creativity. *Journal of Organizational Behavior*, *30*(1), 95–117.

Fiske, S. T. & Neuberg, S. L. (1990). A continuum of impression formation, from category based to individuation processes: Influences of information and motivation on attention and interpretation. In M. Zanna (Ed.), *Advances in experimental social psychology* (pp. 1–74). New York: Academic Press.

Giambatista, R. C. & Bhappu, A. D. (2010). Diversity's harvest: Interactions of diversity sources and communication technology on creative group performance. *Organizational Behavior and Human Decision Processes*, *111*(2), 116–126.

Gibson, C. B. & Gibbs, J. L. (2006). Unpacking the concept of virtuality: The effects of geographic dispersion, electronic dependence, dynamic structure, and national diversity on team innovation. *Administrative Science Quarterly*, *51*(3), 451–495.

Greve, A. (2009). Social networks and creativity: Combining expertise in complex innovation. In T. Rickards, M. Runco, & S. Moger (Eds.), *The Routledge companion to creativity* (pp. 132–145). London: Routledge.

Han, J., Peng, S., Chiu, C-Y., & Leung, A. K.-Y. (2011). Workforce diversity and creativity: A multilevel analysis. In A. K.-Y, Leung, C-Y. Chiu & Y-Y. Hong (Eds.), *Cultural processes: A social psychological perspective* (pp. 286–311). New York: Cambridge University Press.

Harrison, D. A. & Klein, K. J. (2007). What's the difference: Diversity constructs as separation, variety, or disparity in organizations. *Academy of Management Review*, *32*, 1199–1228.

Harrison, D. A., Price, K. H., Gavin, J. H., & Florey, A. T. (2002). Time, teams, and task performance: Changing effects of surface- and deep-level diversity on group functioning. *Academy of Management Journal*, *45*, 1029–1045.

Hoever, I. J., Van Knippenberg, D., Van Ginkel, W. P., & Barkema, H. G. (2012). Fostering team creativity. Perspective taking as key to unlocking diversity's potential. *Journal of Applied Psychology*, *97*(5), 982–996.

Hofhuis, J., Van der Zee, K. I. & Otten, S. (2012). Social identity patterns in culturally diverse organizations: The role of diversity climate. *Journal of Applied Social Psychology*, *42*(4), 964–989.

Hogg, M. A. (2006). Social identity theory. In P. J. Burke (Ed.), *Contemporary social psychological theories* (pp. 111–136). Palo Alto, CA: Stanford University Press.

Holtzman, Y. & Anderberg, J. (2011). Diversify your teams and collaborate: Because great minds don't think alike. *Journal of Management Development*, *30*(1), 75–92.

Homan, A. C., Van Knippenberg, D., Van Kleef, G. A., & De Dreu, C. K. W. (2007). Bridging faultlines by valuing diversity: Diversity beliefs, information elaboration, and performance in diverse work groups. *Journal of Applied Psychology*, *92*, 1189–1199.

Homan, A. C., Greer, L. L., Jehn, K. A., & Koning, L. (2010). Believing shapes seeing: The impact of diversity beliefs on the construal of group composition. *Group Processes & Intergroup Relations*, *13*, 477–493.

Homan, A. C., Hollenbeck, J. R., Humphrey, S. E., Van Knippenberg, D., Ilgen, D. R., & Van Kleef, G. A. (2008). Facing differences with an open mind: Openness to experience, salience of intragroup differences, and performance of diverse work groups. *Academy of Management Journal*, *51*(6), 1204–1222.

Hülsheger, U. R., Anderson, N., & Salgado, J. F. (2009). Team-level predictors of innovation at work: A comprehensive meta-analysis spanning three decades of research. *Journal of Applied Psychology*, *94*, 1128–1145.

Jans, L., Postmes, T., & Van der Zee, K. I. (2011). The induction of shared identity: The positive role of individual distinctiveness for groups. *Personality and Social Psychology Bulletin*, *37*, 1130–1141.

Jans, L., Postmes, T., & Van der Zee, K. I. (2012). Sharing differences: The inductive route to social identity formation. *Journal of Experimental Social Psychology*, *48*(5), 1145–1149.

Janssens, M. & Brett, J. M. (2006). Cultural intelligence in global teams: A fusion model of collaboration. *Group and Organization Management*, *31*(1), 124–153.

Ji, L-J., Zhang, Z., & Nisbett, R. E. (2004). Is it culture or is it language? Examination of language effects in cross-cultural research on categorization. *Journal of Personality and Social Psychology*, *87*(1), 57–65.

Kearney, E., Gebert, D., & Voelpel, S. C. (2009). When and how diversity benefits teams: The importance of team members' need for cognition. *Academy of Management Journal*, *52*, 581–598.

Kohn, N. W., Paulus, P. B., Choi, Y. (2011). Building on the ideas of others: An examination of the idea combination process. *Journal of Experimental Social Psychology*, *47*, 554–561.

Kooij-de Bode, Hanneke J. M., Van Knippenberg, D., & Van Ginkel, W. P. (2008). Ethnic diversity and distributed information in group decision making: The importance of information elaboration. *Group Dynamics: Theory, Research, and Practice, 12*(4), 307–320.

Leung, K. Y. & Chiu, C.-Y. (2008). Interactive effects of multicultural experiences and openness to experience on creative potential. *Creativity Research Journal, 20,* 376–382.

Leung, K. Y., Maddux, W. M., Galinsky, A. D., & Chiu, C. Y. (2008). Multicultural experience enhances creativity: The when and how. *American Psychologist, 63,* 169–181.

Lubart, T. (2010). Cross-cultural perspectives on creativity. In J. C. Kaufman & R. J. Sternberg (Eds.), *The Cambridge handbook of creativity* (pp. 265–278). New York: Cambridge University Press.

Luijters, K., Van der Zee, K. I., & Otten, S. (2008). Cultural diversity in organizations: Enhancing identification by valuing differences. *International Journal of Intercultural Relations, 32*(2), 154–163.

McLeod, P. L., Lobel, S. A., & Cox, T. H. (1996). Ethnic diversity and creativity in small groups. *Small Group Research, 27,* 248–264.

Maddux, W. W., Adam, H., & Galinsky, A. D. (2010). When in Rome . . . Learn why the Romans do what they do: How multicultural learning experiences facilitate creativity. *Personality and Social Psychology Bulletin, 36*(6), 731–741.

Mannix, E. A. & Neale, M. A. (2005). What difference makes a difference: The promise and reality of diverse groups in organizations. *Psychological Science in the Public Interest, 6,* 31–55.

Milliken, F. J., Bartel, C. A., & Kurtzberg, T. R. (2003). Diversity and creativity in work groups: A dynamic perspective on the affective and cognitive processes that link diversity and performance. In P. B. Paulus & B. A. Nijstad (Eds.), *Group creativity: Innovation through collaboration* (pp. 32–62). New York: Oxford University Press.

Mok, A. & Morris, M. W. (2010). Asian-Americans' creative styles in Asian and American situations: Assimilative and contrastive responses as a function of bicultural identity integration. *Management and Organization Review, 6*(3), 371–390.

Mullen, B., Johnson, C., & Salas, E. (1991). Productivity loss in brainstorming groups: A meta-analytic integration. *Basic and Applied Social Psychology, 12,* 3–24.

Nakui, T. (2006). The effects of attitude toward diverse workgroups on diverse brainstorming groups. *Dissertation Abstracts International: Section B: The Sciences and Engineering, 67*(6-B), 3495.

Nakui, T., Paulus, P. B. & Van der Zee, K. I. (2011). The role of attitudes in reactions to diversity in work groups. *Journal of Applied Social Psychology, 41,* 2327–2351.

Nemeth, C. J. & Kwan, J. L. (1985). Originality of word associations as a function of majority vs. minority influence. *Social Psychology Quarterly, 48,* 277–282.

Nemeth, C. J. & Nemeth-Brown, B. (2003). Better than individuals? The potential benefits of dissent and diversity for group creativity. In P. B. Paulus & B. A. Nijstad (Eds.), *Group creativity: Innovation through collaboration* (pp. 63–84). New York: Oxford University Press.

Nijstad, B. A. & Stroebe, W. (2006). How the group affects the mind: A cognitive model of idea generation in groups. *Personality and Social Psychology Review, 10,* 186–213.

O'Reilly, C. A. III, Williams, K. Y., & Barsade, S. (1998). Group demography and innovation: Does diversity help? In D. H. Gruenfeld (Ed.), *Composition* (pp. 183–207). US: Elsevier Science/JAI Press.

Parnes, S. J. (1975). CPSI: A program for balanced growth. *Journal of Creative Behavior*, *9*(1), 23–29.

Paulus, P. B. & Yang, H. (2000). Idea generation in groups: A basis for creativity in organizations. *Organizational Behavior and Human Decision Processes*, *82*, 76–87.

Paulus, P. B. & Brown, V. R. (2003). Enhancing ideational creativity in groups: Lessons from research on brainstorming. In P. B. Paulus & B. A. Nijstad (Eds.), *Group creativity: Innovation through collaboration* (pp. 110–136). New York: Oxford University Press.

Paulus, P. B. & Brown, V. R. (2007). Toward more creative and innovative group idea generation: A cognitive-social-motivational perspective of group brainstorming. *Social and Personality Psychology Compass*, *1*, 248–265.

Paulus, P. B. & Dzindolet, M. T. (2008). Social influence, creativity and innovation. *Social Influence*, *3*, 228–247.

Paulus, P. B., Larey, T. S., Ortega, A. H. (1995). Performance and perception of brainstormers in an organizational setting. *Basic and Applied Social Psychology*, *17*, 249–265.

Paulus, P. B., Dzindolet, M. T., & Kohn, N. (2011). Collaborative creativity—group creativity and team innovation. In M. D. Mumford (Ed.), *Handbook of organizational creativity* (pp. 327–357). New York: Elsevier.

Paulus, P. B., Kohn, N. W., & Arditti, L. E. (2011). Effects of quantity and quality instructions on brainstorming. *Journal of Creative Behavior*, *45*, 38–46.

Paulus, P. B., Dzindolet, M. T., Poletes, G., & Camacho, L. M. (1993). Perception of performance in group brainstorming: The illusion of group productivity. *Personality and Social Psychology Bulletin*, *19*, 78–89.

Paulus, P. B., Nakui, T., Putman, V. L., & Brown, V. R. (2006). Effects of task instructions and brief breaks on brainstorming. *Group Dynamics: Theory, Research, and Practice*, *10*(3), 206–219.

Paulus, P. B., Kohn, N. W., Arditti, L. E., & Korde, R. M. (2013). Understanding the group size effect in electronic brainstorming. *Small Group Research*, *44*(3), 332–352.

Paulus, P. B., Dugosh, K. L., Dzindolet, M. T., Coskun, H., & Putman, V. L. (2002). Social and cognitive influences in group brainstorming: Predicting production gains and losses. *European Review of Social Psychology*, *12*, 299–325.

Phillips, K. W., Northcraft, G. B., & Neale, M. A. (2006). Surface-level diversity and decision-making in groups: When does deep-level similarity help? *Group Processes & Intergroup Relations*, *9*(4), 467–482.

Polzer, J. T., Milton, L. P., & Swann, W. B., Jr. (2002). Capitalizing on diversity: Interpersonal congruence in small work groups. *Administrative Science Quarterly*, *47*, 296–324.

Postmes, T., Spears, R., Lee, A. T., & Novak, R. J. (2005). Individuality and social influence in groups: Inductive and deductive routes to group identity. *Journal of Personality and Social Psychology*, *89*(5), 747–763.

Puccio, G. J. & Cabra, J. F. (2012). Idea generation and evaluation: Cognitive skills and deliberate practices. In M. D. Mumford (Ed.), *Handbook of organizational creativity* (pp. 189–215). Amsterdam: Elsevier.

Putman, V. L. & Paulus, P. B. (2009). Brainstorming, brainstorming rules and decision making. *Journal of Creative Behavior*, *43*, 23–39.

Reinig, B. A., Briggs, R. O., & Nunamaker, J. F. (2007). On the measurement of ideation quality. *Journal of Management Information Systems*, *23*, 143–161.

Reiter-Palmon, R., Wigert, B., De Vreede, T. (2012). Team creativity and innovation: The effect of group composition, social processes, and cognition. In M. D. Mumford (Ed.), *Handbook of organizational creativity* (pp. 295–326). Amsterdam: Elsevier.

Richard, O. C., Barnett, T., Dwyer, S., & Chadwick, K. (2004). Cultural diversity in management, firm performance, and the moderating role of entrepreneurial orientation dimensions. *Academy of Management Journal, 47*(2), 255–266.

Rietzschel, E. F., Nijstad, B. A., & Stroebe, W. (2006). Productivity is not enough: A comparison of interactive and nominal brainstorming groups on idea generation and selection. *Journal of Experimental Social Psychology, 42*, 244–251.

Rietzschel, E. F., Nijstad, B. A., Stroebe, W. (2010). The selection of creative ideas after individual idea generation: Choosing between creativity and impact. *British Journal of Psychology, 101*(1), 47–68.

Roberge, M. & Van Dick, R. (2010). Recognizing the benefits of diversity: When and how does diversity increase group performance? *Human Resource Management Review, 20*(4), 295–308.

Salas, E., Rosen, M. A., Burke, C. S., & Goodwin, G. F. (Eds.) (2009). The wisdom of collectivities in organizations: An update of teamwork competencies. In E. Salas, G. F. Goodwin, and C. S. Burke (Eds.), *In team effectiveness in complex organizations: Cross-disciplinary perspectives and approaches* (pp. 39–79). New York: Routledge.

Schulz-Hardt, S., Mojzisch, A., & Vogelgesang, F. (2008). Dissent as a facilitator: Individual- and group-level effects on creativity and performance. In C. K. W. De Dreu & M. J. Gelfand (Eds.), *The psychology of conflict and conflict management in organizations* (pp. 149–177). New York: Taylor & Francis Group/Lawrence Erlbaum Associates.

Stangor, C., Lynch, L., Duan, C., & Glas, B. (1992). Categorization of individuals on the basis of multiple social features. *Journal of Personality and Social Psychology, 62*(2), 207–218.

Swann, W. B. Jr., Kwan, V. S. Y., Polzer, J. T., & Milton, L. P. (2003). Fostering group identification and creativity in diverse groups: The role of individuation and self-verification. *Personality and Social Psychology Bulletin, 29*(11), 1396–1406.

Swann, W. B. Jr., Polzer, J. T., Seyle, D. C., & Ko, S. J. (2004). Finding value in diversity: Verification of personal and social self-views in diverse groups. *The Academy of Management Review, 29*(1), 9–27.

Tadmor, C. T., Galinksy, A. D., Maddux, W. W. (2012). Getting the most out of living abroad: Biculturalism and integrative complexity as key drivers of creative and professional success. *Journal of Personality and Social Psychology, 103*(3), 520–542.

Tadmor, C. T., Satterstrom, P., Jang, S., & Polzer, J. T. (2012). Beyond individual creativity: The superadditive benefits of multicultural experience for collective creativity in culturally diverse teams. *Journal of Cross-Cultural Psychology, 43*(3), 384–392.

Tindale, R. S. & Kameda, T. (2000). Social sharedness as a unifying theme for information processing in groups. *Group Processes & Intergroup Relations, 3*(2), 123–140.

Van der Zee, K. I. & Paulus, P. B. (2008). Social psychology and modern organizations: Balancing between innovativeness and comfort. In L. Steg, A. P. Buunk, & T. Rothengatter (Eds.), *Applied social psychology: Understanding and managing social problems* (pp. 271–290). New York: Cambridge University Press.

Van der Zee, K. I., Zaal, J. N., & Piekstra, J. (2003). Validation of the Multicultural Personality Questionnaire in the context of personnel selection. *European Journal of Personality*, *17*, S77–S100.

Van der Zee, K., Atsma, N., & Brodbeck, F. (2004). The influence of social identity and personality on outcomes of cultural diversity in teams. *Journal of Cross-Cultural Psychology*, *35*(3), 283–303.

Van der Zee, K., Paulus, P., Vos, M., & Parthasarathy, N. (2009). The impact of group composition and attitudes towards diversity on anticipated outcomes of diversity in groups. *Group Processes & Intergroup Relations*, *12*(2), 257–280.

Van Dick, R., Van Knippenberg, D., Hägele, S., Guillaume, Y. R. F., & Brodbeck, F. C. (2008). Group diversity and group identification: The moderating role of diversity beliefs. *Human Relations*, *61*(10), 1463–1492.

Van Dijk, H., Van Engen, M. L., & Van Knippenberg, D. (2012). Defying conventional wisdom: A meta-analytical examination of the differences between demographic and job-related diversity relationships with performance. *Organizational Behavior and Human Decision Processes*, *119*(1), 38–53.

Van Knippenberg, D. & Schippers, M. C. (2007). Work group diversity. *Annual Review of Psychology*, *58*, 515–541.

Van Knippenberg, D., De Dreu, C. K. W., & Homan, A. C. (2004). Work group diversity and group performance: An integrative model and research agenda. *Journal of Applied Psychology*, *89*, 1008–1022.

Van Knippenberg, D., Haslam, S. A., Platow, M. J. (2007). Unity through diversity: Value-in-diversity beliefs, work group diversity, and group identification. *Group Dynamics: Theory, Research, and Practice*, *11*(3), 207–222.

Van Veelen, R., Otten, S., & Hansen, N. (2013). A personal touch to diversity: Self-anchoring increases minority members' identification in a diverse group. *Group Processes & Intergroup Relations*, *16*(6), 671–683.

Watson, W. E., Kumar, K., & Michaelson, L. K. (1993). Cultural diversity's impact on interaction process and performance: Comparing homogeneous and diverse task groups. *Academy of Management Journal*, *36*, 590–602.

West, M. A. & Richter, A. W. (2008). Climates and cultures for innovation and creativity at work. In J. Zhou & C. E. Shalley (Eds.), *Handbook of organizational creativity* (pp. 211–236). New York: Psychology Press.

Williams, K. Y. & O'Reilly, C. A. (1998). Demography and diversity in organizations: A review of 40 years of research. *Research in Organizational Behavior*, *20*, 77–140.

8 Faultlines in diverse teams

Astrid C. Homan and Daan van Knippenberg

Due to increasing globalization, immigration, and other forms of demographic change, organizations have to deal with an increasingly diverse workforce. People of, for instance, different nationalities, ages, races, educational backgrounds, and cultures have to find a way to efficiently work together. In the last decades, therefore, examining diversity effects in teams has been of core interest for research into organizational behavior (e.g. Van Knippenberg et al., 2004; Van Knippenberg & Schippers, 2007; Williams & O'Reilly, 1998). Interestingly, this work has shown that the effects of diversity are inconsistent (e.g. Bell et al., 2011). That is, (demographic) differences have been found to be sometimes positively related (e.g. Cox et al., 1991), sometimes negatively related (e.g. Gruenfeld et al., 1996), and sometimes unrelated (e.g. Jehn et al., 1999) to group performance. In a comprehensive review of the literature, Williams and O'Reilly (1998) discussed two streams of theoretical viewpoints regarding these potential positive (information/decision-making perspective) and negative (social categorization perspective and similarity/attraction paradigm) effects of diversity.

According to the information/decision-making perspective, diversity can enhance the elaboration of task-relevant information and perspectives within the group—that is, the exchange, discussion, and integration of ideas, knowledge, and insights relevant to the group's task—which is in turn related to enhanced team functioning (e.g. Kooij-de Bode et al., 2008; see also Paulus and Van der Zee, this volume). However, from a social categorization perspective (Brewer & Brown, 1998) it can be expected that, within demographically diverse teams, subgroup categorization creates "we–they" distinctions that may in turn lead to intergroup bias, such as in-group favoritism or prejudice. These subgroup categorizations and concomitant intergroup biases have been found to lead to decreased group performance (e.g. Gruenfeld et al., 1996; Harrison et al., 2002).

Although the two competing theoretical perspectives described above can explain *why* diversity may lead to positive or negative effects, they cannot explain *when* diversity benefits or hurts team functioning. To address this issue, Van Knippenberg et al. (2004) integrated the two perspectives and proposed that diverse team functioning is determined by the interplay between categorization processes and information elaboration. They argue that, when subgroup categorization gives rise to intergroup bias, information elaboration is hindered and group performance harmed. However, subgroup categorization and concomitant intergroup bias do not always occur within diverse groups. Whether diverse groups indeed experience subgroup categorization is determined by the salience of social categories within the group.

The significance of category salience has been stressed in classical social psychological work on the importance and effects of group membership (e.g. Doise, 1978). The most salient social category will, within a certain context, most significantly influence someone's self-perceptions, perceptions by others, and resulting attitudes and behaviors (Oakes & Turner, 1986). Based on previous work, we know that a salient social categorization becomes more probable to the degree that (1) it is often used, (2) the situation makes the categorization likely, and (3) there are minimal differences within categories and maximal differences between categories (Turner et al., 1987). The third factor has been labeled "comparative fit," and we will first zoom in on how category salience is related to this higher perceived homogeneity within categories than between categories.

The idea of comparative fit has recently received attention in diversity research when people started to examine more complex compositional patterns of diversity in teams (Mathieu et al., 2008; Thatcher & Patel, 2011, 2012). Teams are almost never diverse on just one diversity dimension, but are composed of people from different cultures, personality types, ages, gender, and educational expertise. The specific combination of these different diversity dimensions is predictive of category salience. To the degree that different diversity dimensions are more strongly correlated within the team, that is, creating relatively high uniformity within subgroups and high differentiation between subgroups, the categorization becomes more salient. This concept of diversity faultlines (Lau & Murnighan, 1998), which refers to the distribution of multiple diversity attributes simultaneously (Thatcher & Patel, 2011), explains how diverse teams can split up into subgroups and as a result experience negative effects of their diversity (e.g. Choi & Sy, 2010; Molleman, 2005).

Diversity faultlines

Diversity faultlines refer to the alignment of demographic attributes that lead to hypothetical dividing lines (Lau & Murnighan, 1998). These hypothetical lines increase the fit of a potential categorization and are therefore one of the prerequisites for high category salience. For instance, when an eight-person team consists of four Asian females and four Caucasian males, the team is objectively characterized by a strong dividing line creating two subgroups that have high intrasubgroup homogeneity and high intersubgroup heterogeneity on race and sex. The higher the homogeneity within the subgroups, the higher the faultline strength (Thatcher & Patel, 2011), and the stronger the comparative fit. Because people prefer to interact with people who are similar rather than dissimilar to them, these categorizations or subgroup formations can lead people to make "us–them" distinctions (Byrne, 1971). Going back to our example, this could mean that the Asian females evaluate their own subgroup as better and more positive than the Caucasian male subgroup (Hewstone et al., 2002; Turner et al., 1987). These "us–them" distinctions are likely to result in reduced levels of trust between subgroups (Brewer, 1979), reduced motivation to cooperate with members of other social categories (Wit & Kerr, 2002), less group cohesion (e.g. Flache & Mäs, 2008), lowered commitment to the full group (in favor of increased commitment to one's subgroup; Hewstone et al., 2002), increased interpersonal tension and conflict (Bezrukova et al., 2009; Thatcher et al., 2003), lower frequency and quality of communication, and lowered performance (e.g. Barkema & Shvyrkov, 2007; Earley & Mosakowski, 2000; Hambrick, 2005; Homan et al., 2007b; Lau & Murnighan, 2005; Polzer et al., 2006; Sawyer et al., 2006; Thatcher et al., 2003; for a review see Thatcher & Patel, 2012).

Corroborating these empirical findings, a recent meta-analysis on faultline effects (Thatcher & Patel, 2011) has illuminated that faultlines indeed instigate more conflicts in teams, and have a negative relationship with team performance, team satisfaction, and team cohesion. Interestingly enough, these findings seem to imply that diverse teams with a faultline (i.e. that have high comparative fit) will always experience negative effects of their diversity. However, this conclusion is inconsistent with the original ideas of Lau and Murnighan (1998) and theory regarding category salience. Additionally, some empirical findings show positive effects of faultlines (e.g. Gibson & Vermeulen, 2003).

Key here is the notion of category salience highlighted in self-categorization theory (SCT), which is determined by perceived fit as well as the relative accessibility of the categorization (Turner et al., 1987). SCT (Turner et al., 1987) proposes that category salience is a function of an interaction between the "relative accessibility" of that categorization and the perceived fit of the categorization (Oakes, 1987). In other words, SCT would propose that whether differences between people give rise to a categorization based on these differences is not only a function of comparative fit, but also determined by two other factors, namely normative fit and cognitive accessibility. *Normative fit* is the extent to which the categorization makes sense within individuals' subjective frame of reference. For instance, revisiting our earlier example, a categorization capturing a subgrouping distinguishing Asian women and Caucasian men is more likely to be salient to individuals to which sex and/or cultural differences are more meaningful. For instance, the normative fit of the categorization would increase to the degree that the Asian women within the team adhere to the stereotype of being modest and submissive, whereas the Caucasian men behave arrogantly and are dominant. The final factor governing salience is *cognitive accessibility*, the ease with which the categorization is retrieved. For instance, a gender categorization may come to mind much more readily than a categorization based on, say, car brand preferences, and thus is more likely to be salient. Organizations may increase cognitive accessibility by, for instance, frequently mentioning the existence of certain social categories.

Thus, although an objective existing faultline is potentially highly salient because of *comparative fit* of the categorization, the *normative fit* and *accessibility* of the categorization might be low, limiting the category salience. In line with this reasoning, previous work has distinguished between dormant and active faultlines. Jehn and Bezrukova (2010) define dormant faultlines as potential faultlines that exist based on objectively measured demographic characteristics. Active faultlines exist when the members of the team actually perceive subgroups based on the demographic characteristics. This distinction automatically implies that dormant (or objectively existent faultlines) are not automatically perceived by the group members (see Meyer et al., 2011). Whether or not the dormant faultline is activated within the team may be determined by the group task or context (Lau & Murnighan, 1998; see also Pearsall et al., 2008). This idea of faultline "activators" or "triggers" constitutes the basis of the second part of this chapter.

Faultline (de)activators

We propose that the cues that increase the normative fit and/or accessibility of the categorization can act as faultline triggers (e.g. Rink & Jehn, 2010; see also Van der Kamp et al., 2012). In this respect, we would argue that a diversity faultline matters for groups only to the extent that it is perceived by the team members (e.g. Ashfort & Mael, 1989; Homan & Jehn, 2010; see e.g. Van der Vegt & Van de Vliert, 2005; Williams et al., 2007). If team members do not experience the faultline, it will also not affect their attitudes, cognitions, and behaviors (c.f. Harrison et al., 2002; Homan et al., 2010; Riordan, 2000; Williams et al., 2007; Zellmer-Bruhn et al., 2008). Chrobot-Mason et al. (2009) distinguished five types of faultline triggers, that all deal with negative interactions between the subgroups, such as insults or humiliation, differential treatment, and differences in values. The qualitative research reported in their paper showed, for instance, that faultlines were activated or triggered when the employees experienced that members of certain groups were treated differently than members from other groups, when employees experienced that others expected them to completely adhere to the majorities' norms of behavior, and when insulting remarks or comments were made (see Otten and Jansen, this volume, and Verkuyten and De Vroome, this volume, for illustrations on how to avoid these triggers).

Although it is important to examine which situational aspects influence the activation of faultlines in teams, it might be even more interesting to examine factors that can decrease the, often strong, positive relationship between dormant and active faultlines (Zanutto et al., 2011). We will discuss variables that can act as such "deactivators" and facilitate the decrease of salience of dormant faultlines by lowering the normative fit and/or accessibility of the categorization, and thereby limit the negative effects of subgroup

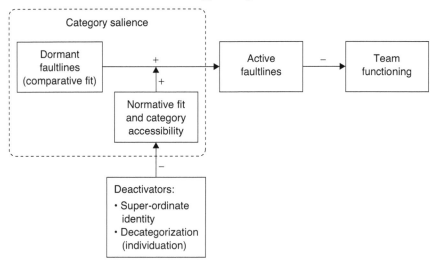

Figure 8.1 A category salience model of deactivators of faultline effects.

formation on team processes and performance. More specifically, we focus in on factors that either stress a super-ordinate identity or instigate decategorization (i.e. individuation of the team members), such as shared goals, leadership behaviors, and diversity beliefs (see Figure 8.1).

Super-ordinate identity

Stressing the salience of a super-ordinate categorization (instead of the salience of subgroupings) has been found to be a powerful tool in decreasing the normative fit and/or accessibility of a subgroup categorization (Gaertner & Dovidio, 2000; Gaertner et al., 1993; Roberge & Van Dick, 2010; Van Knippenberg, 2003). Importantly, Wenzel et al. (2007) stress that, in order for a super-ordinate identity to work, the overarching team should be defined as consisting of complementary, equal, and indispensable subgroups that are valued for their input in obtaining the team's goals. Evidence for the importance of a collective identity in influencing faultline effects comes from a study by Jehn and Bezrukova (2010). They found that, when the team members identified more with the team, the faultline was less strongly related to conflicts than when team members identified less with the team. There are a number of potential contextual variables that can influence the degree to which the super-ordinate identity is salient to the team members (see Van der Kamp et al., 2012).

Shared goals

Van Knippenberg et al. (2011) examined shared objectives as such a variable. There may be important differences between teams in the extent to which their objectives are clear and shared among team members. Such "shared objectives" (Anderson & West, 1998) offer a shared focus that guides team process and provides reference points for team self-regulation (Kozlowski & Bell, 2003). Van Knippenberg et al. (2011) proposed that shared objectives are related to the existence of super-ordinate goals, and thereby counteract the salience of subgroupings by rendering the super-ordinate categorization more salient (Van Knippenberg, 2003). Moreover, by providing clear focal points, shared objectives may also structure and guide team communication rather than communication between subgroups. In short, shared objectives may render the accessibility of the category less salient, and therefore attenuate the relationship between faultlines and team outcomes. Results from their study indeed show that faultlines were no longer negatively related to organizational productivity and profitability when shared objectives were high rather than low (see also Rico et al., 2012).

Interdependence

Another concept that can influence the strength of the super-ordinate goals within a team, is the degree of interdependence within the team. Both task and outcome interdependence have been studied in this respect. Regarding outcome interdependence, there is a very large research stream on the effects of reward structures on team functioning. When people are more dependent on each other for their outcomes, they tend to perceive the group as more important and more cooperative because everyone is working toward the same goal (e.g. Sherif, 1958). When outcomes are based more on individual performance within the team, within-team competition can increase, because everyone wants to maximize their own performance (De Dreu, 2007). In sum, team rewards have been found to promote trust, cohesiveness, and mutually supportive behavior (e.g. Beersma et al., 2003; Wageman & Baker, 1999) and thereby positively influence processes and outcomes of diverse teams (e.g. Schippers et al., 2003). Within research on faultlines, the few studies that have examined outcome interdependence have reported similar positive effects. For instance, Homan and colleagues (2008) have shown that objective faultline groups that were rewarded based on team performance performed better than faultline groups that were rewarded based on subgroup performance (cf. Van der Vegt & Janssen, 2003).

The reasoning regarding task interdependency is quite similar: To the degree that team members are more interdependent for task progress, they experience stronger cooperation, rely on each other, and feel collectively responsible (Wageman, 1995). Again, this makes the collective identity more salient to the team members relative to subgroup identities. Indeed, multiple studies have found support for the positive moderating effect of task inter-dependence on the relationship between diversity and team outcomes (e.g. Jehn et al., 1999; Timmerman, 2000; Van der Vegt et al., 2003). Similarly, research has found that higher task interdependence makes faultlines less negatively related to social integration, innovation, and decision-making quality (e.g. Nishii & Goncalo, 2008; Rico et al., 2007). Interestingly, there is some evidence that task interdependence can strengthen the effects of shared goals (high goal interdependence) by making free riding less likely. In this respect, Van der Vegt and Janssen (2003) showed that diverse teams with high goal interdependence and high task interdependence were more innovative than teams in which one or both interdependencies were low.

Leadership

Leaders may play a crucial role in influencing the effects of faultlines (Homan & Jehn, 2010; Gratton et al., 2007; Zander & Butler, 2010) by affected subgroup salience. In this respect, transformational leadership has been linked to increasing the salience of a super-ordinate identity, by creating strong group norms and building identification and group cohesion. Transformational leaders are characterized by showing behaviors that inspire their team members (Shamir et al., 1993; but see Greer et al., 2012; Van Knippenberg & Sitkin, 2013). They are able to reconcile the personal goals of followers with the goals of the collective (i.e. the team; Haslam, 2001). The subgroup identity will be less accessible to the team members, because everyone is seen as a member of the same in-group and everyone identifies with the collective (Shin & Zhou, 2007; Yukl, 2010). This super-ordinate identification will increase the salience of the collective (De Poel, 2011) and will in turn be related to better team functioning (Kearney & Gebert, 2009). Supporting this reasoning, Kunze and Bruch (2010) showed that transformational leaders mitigated the negative effects of age-based faultlines.

Individual and organizational diversity beliefs

It has been argued that people may differ in their beliefs about and attitudes toward diversity (e.g. Strauss et al., 2003; Van der Zee & Van Oudenhoven, 2000; Van Knippenberg & Haslam, 2003; also see Van Oudenhoven, Van der Zee and Paulus, this volume) and that organizational climates and cultures may differ in the extent to which they value diversity (e.g. Ely & Thomas, 2001; Kossek & Zonia, 1993; also see Van Knippenberg et al., 2013; Van der Zee and Otten, this volume). Diversity beliefs can be defined as beliefs about the value of diversity to work group functioning (Van Knippenberg & Haslam, 2003). Contingent on such beliefs, diversity may affect the extent to which one's own work group is perceived as being a good group—where good may refer to (expectations of) task performance as well as to other aspects of group functioning.

Diversity beliefs may lead people to respond more favorably to work group diversity the more they believe in the value of diversity for work group functioning (Van Knippenberg et al., 2007). We propose that diversity beliefs can have positive effects on faultline teams being able to instigate a strong super-ordinate team identity. In this respect, Van Knippenberg et al. (2007) showed that the relationship between diversity and group members' identification with their work group was moderated by diversity beliefs (see also Van Dick et al., 2008). When individuals believed that diversity was beneficial, diversity was positively related to group identification, whereas diversity tended to be negatively related to identification when individuals believed in the value of similarity. In a similar vein, Ely and Thomas (2001) observed that, when an organization's perspective on diversity emphasized cultural diversity as a valuable resource for the organization, members felt more valued and respected, reported a higher quality of intergroup relations, and felt that they were more successful than when the organization's perspective was not focused on the potential value of diversity. A number of studies have shown that diversity beliefs can indeed positively influence the processes and performance of faultline teams (e.g. Homan et al., 2007a, 2008; Van der Zee et al., 2009). Importantly, Meyer and Schermuly (2012) found that task motivation qualified the moderating role of diversity beliefs. Teams that were characterized by a strong faultline only benefitted from positive beliefs about diversity when they were motivated to work on the task. The degree to which teams are motivated and need their diversity to do well thus seem to be important predictors of the effects of diversity beliefs. In sum, these studies showed that both instigated diversity beliefs (by means of instructions) and personality-related diversity beliefs (e.g. openness to experience; Flynn, 2005) can make faultline teams elaborate more upon information and in turn perform better.

Individual traits

Finally, individual characteristics can also make the team goals more salient (and subgroup categorization less likely). Mohammed and Angell (2004) proposed that the degree to which individuals are focused on teamwork (i.e. teamwork orientation) affects their response to diversity in teams. They found that, when team orientation was high, the negative effects of categorization and demographic distinctiveness were less likely to occur. People with high teamwork orientation find the collective more important and are committed to the team as a whole, making it less likely that they experience subgroup formations.

Decategorization

Another way to influence the accessibility and/or normative fit of the subgroupings is by means of decategorization (Brewer & Miller, 1984; Wilder, 1981). The decategorization perspective proposes that, if team members conceive of their fellow team members as separate individuals (i.e. individuation; Wilder, 1978), subgroup formation and intergroup bias are reduced (Brewer & Miller, 1984). Interestingly, whereas stressing a super-ordinate identity may limit the occurrence of category-based biases, it may also discourage individuals from thinking and acting in ways associated with their unique category memberships (Gaertner et al., 1989; Janssens & Brett, 2006; Polzer et al., 2002). That is, to obtain the potential benefits of differences between team members, it might even be more fruitful to individuate the team members than to stress a super-ordinate identity. In this respect, Swann et al. (2003) showed that diverse groups who perceived their group members as unique individuals were better able to make use of each other's unique characteristics and were more creative as a result. Again, there are a number of potential contextual variables that can influence the degree to which decategorization occurs.

Personalized interactions

Decategorization can occur by instigating personalized interactions between the members of the respective subgroups. Although most empirical support for this type of decategorization was obtained in experimental studies in social psychology (e.g. Bettencourt et al., 1992; Marcus-Newhall et al., 1993), these findings are insightful for organizational teams as well (Cunningham, 2004). For instance, Bettencourt et al. (1992) showed that personalized interactions (as compared to task-focused interactions) reduced bias against out-group members who were physically present, as well as those who were not present. Along similar lines, Ensari and Miller (2006) proposed that organizational meetings with members from different work groups would lead to a greater understanding of individual differences and better cross-functional communication (see also Ensari, 2001).

Cross-categorization

Another method to instigate decategorization is cross-categorization (e.g. Ensari & Miller, 2001; Crisp & Hewstone, 2000), which implies that the groups to which a person belongs cut across rather than nest in another. Cross-cutting categories makes social categorization more complex and decreases the distinction between in-group and out-group (Doise, 1978). In other words, by means of cross-categorization one can lower the comparative fit of the categorization, making the objective faultline less obvious to team members (Brewer & Pierce, 2005) and creating a more personalized and individuated perception of the team members (Brewer & Miller, 1984). The effects of cross-categorization on diminishing inter-group bias have been shown in a meta-analysis by Migdal et al. (1998), as well as in research pertaining to the effects of diversity in groups (see e.g. Homan et al., 2007b; Sawyer et al., 2006). One can create cross-categorization by, for instance, crossing existing subgroups with role expectancies, reward structures, or informational background (Homan et al., 2007b, 2008; Marcus–Newhall et al., 1993).

Leadership

Researchers have proposed that relationship-oriented leadership can be a fruitful tool to instigate decategorization. Relationship-focused leaders show personalized attention for their subordinates and heal relationships, increase trust, and manage frictions (Burke et al., 2006). Next to limiting subgroup formation, this individuation will also result in transferring perceptions that the team consists of unique individuals (Yukl, 2010; cf. Homan et al., 2010). This, in turn, creates the opportunity for teams to make adequate use of their diversity and function effectively. A study by Homan and Greer (2013) indeed showed that relationship-focused leaders tended to decategorize their team members and in turn perceived their teams to perform better. Leaders can thus also lower subgroup salience by stressing individual identities rather than the super-ordinate identity.

Diversity beliefs

Next to creating a strong super-ordinate identity, recent theorizing has also proposed that diversity beliefs can lead to decategorization. Being open to diversity makes detrimental "us–them" distinctions less likely to occur (Flynn, 2005), even though differences may still be visible. In this respect, Swann and colleagues (2003) showed that more favorable impressions of group members resulted in more individuation in diverse groups. Based on these findings, Homan and colleagues (2010) proposed that objective diversity is likely to be perceived in terms of subgroups when individuals have negative diversity beliefs and in terms of differences (i.e. decategorization) when individuals have positive diversity beliefs. In two studies, they indeed showed that diversity beliefs were related to a decrease in subgroup perceptions and an increase in individual differences perceptions. These results were qualified by an interaction with task type, showing that only when the task required diversity, diversity beliefs moderated the dormant faultline–active faultline link.

Conclusions

In this chapter we gave an overview of faultline effects in teams and proposed that the specific constellation of diversity in teams is potentially highly predictive of diversity effects. The stronger the correlation or comparative fit between the different diversity dimensions, the more likely the group will split up into homogeneous subgroups. These subgroupings can potentially be very detrimental for team functioning, provided that they are noticed by the team members and influence their attitudes, cognitions, and behaviors. Whether these subgroups will actually be perceived by team members, depends, we argued, on the accessibility and/or normative fit of the subgroup categorization.

We discussed some important organizational and contextual factors that can be used by organizations to deactivate faultlines. More specifically, we focused on factors that stimulate either a stronger super-ordinate identity or individuation. By making other identities salient within teams, it is possible to make the subgroup identities less salient. A super-ordinate identity can be stressed by means of organizational factors such as shared objectives, interdependence, and leadership. Additionally, individual differences between people, such as the need for team work or positive diversity beliefs, can help to promote identifying with the super-ordinate team rather than the sub-groups. As a second deactivating mechanism, we focused on decategorization. Previous work has indeed shown that creating personalized interactions between team members results in individuation in teams and as a result better team functioning. Interestingly, some of the strategies that could be used to instigate a super-ordinate identity could also be used to make team members perceive each other as unique individuals. For instance, leaders can obtain both, depending on their specific leadership behaviors (e.g. transformational leadership results in a stronger super-ordinate identity, whereas considerate leadership results in individuation). Similarly, recent research has shown that diversity beliefs can lead to a stronger identification as well as individuation within diverse teams. Depending upon the goals of the organization, department, or team, installing a super-ordinate identity or decategorization might be more desired. For instance, if one wants to utilize differences and increase the creative potential of a team, decategorization might be the most fruitful approach (e.g. Homan et al., 2010). On the other hand, if one is interested in creating a team that is effective on more convergent tasks, stressing a strong super-ordinate identity might be more required (e.g. Harrison & Humphrey, 2010).

The overview of faultltine deactivators we presented here is by no means complete. Some other interesting tools might be available that can help to limit the activation of faultlines. For instance, research has shown that a richer communication medium, lower informality of communication, a stronger error management culture, smaller team size, a more collectively focused organizational culture, and longer team tenure also deactivate fault-line effects in teams (e.g. Barkema & Shvyrkov, 2007; Chatman et al., 1998; Rockmann et al., 2007; Rupert et al., 2013; Tuggle et al., 2010), which opens up the road for many more studies on faultline deactivators. We believe that it is crucial in this respect to understand how these and other contextual factors can help to make the objectively present subgroups in faultline teams less salient.

Although outside of the scope of the present chapter, we would also propose that the negative relationship between activated faultlines and team outcomes might be contingent upon (contextual) factors that influence how teams deal with their active faultline. For instance, an activated faultline might be less problematic to the degree that team members do not feel threatened by the subgroupings (e.g. Van Knippenberg et al., 2004). In this respect, future research might set out to also examine ways to deactivate already active faultlines, and we believe that the notion of category salience could again provide direction in distinguishing potentially effective moderators.

Dormant faultlines do not necessarily have to be activated, but once they are, negative effects of diversity—in terms of intersubgroup bias and deteriorated performance—are likely to occur. It is therefore crucial to understand when and how dormant faultlines are deactivated in order to be able to avoid negative effects of diversity, and make faultlines teams benefit from their potentially extremely valuable differences, which can result in better communication and concomitant group performance and creativity.

References

Anderson, N. R. & West, M. A. (1998). Measuring climate for work group innovation: Development and validation of the team climate inventory. *Journal of Organizational Behavior, 19*, 235–258.

Ashfort, B. E. & Mael, F. (1989). Social identity theory and the organization. *Academy of Management Review, 14*, 20–39.

Barkema, H. G. & Shvyrkov, O. (2007). Does top management team diversity promote or hamper foreign expansion? *Strategic Management Journal, 28*, 663–680.

Beersma, B., Hollenbeck, J. R., Humphrey, S. E., Moon, H., Conlon, D. E., & Ilgen, D. R. (2003). Cooperation, competition and group performance: Towards a contingency approach. *Academy of Management Journal, 46*, 572–590.

Bell, S. T., Villado, A. J., Lukasik, M. A., Belau, L., & Briggs, A. L. (2011). Getting specific about demographic diversity variable and team performance relationships: A meta-analysis. *Journal of Management, 37*, 709–743.

Bettencourt, B. A., Brewer, M. B., Croak, M. R., & Miller, N. (1992). Cooperation and the reduction of intergroup bias: The role of reward structure and social orientation. *Journal of Experimental Social Psychology, 28*, 301–319.

Bezrukova, K., Jehn, K. A., Zanutto, E. L., & Thatcher, S. M. (2009). Do workgroup faultlines help or hurt? A moderated model of faultlines, team identification, and group performance. *Organization Science, 20*, 35–50.

Brewer, M. B. (1979). In-group bias in the minimal intergroup situation: A cognitive motivational analysis. *Psychological Bulletin, 86*, 307–324.

Brewer, M. B. & Miller, N. (1984). Beyond the contact hypothesis: Theoretical perspectives on desegregation. In N. Miller & M. B. Brewer (Eds.), *Groups in contact: The psychology of desegregation* (pp. 281–302). Orlando, FL: Academic Press.

Brewer, M. B. & Brown, R. J. (1998). Intergroup relations. In D. T. Gilbert & S. T. Fiske (Eds.), *The handbook of social psychology* (4th ed., Vol. 2, pp. 554–594). New York: McGraw-Hill.

Brewer, M. B. & Pierce, K. P. (2005). Social identity complexity and outgroup tolerance. *Personality and Social Psychology Bulletin, 31*, 428–437.

Burke, C. S., Stagl, K. C., Klein, C., Goodwin, G. F., Salas, E., & Halpin, S. M. (2006). What type of leadership behaviors are functional in teams? A meta-analysis. *The Leadership Quarterly, 17*, 288–307.

Byrne, D. (1971). *The attraction paradigm.* New York: Academic Press.

Chatman, J. A., Polzer, J. T., Barsade, S. G., & Neale, M. A. (1998). Being different yet feeling similar: The influence of demographic composition and organizational culture on work processes and outcomes. *Administrative Science Quarterly*, 749–780.

Choi, J. N. & Sy, T. (2010). Group-level organizational citizenship behavior: Effects of demographic faultlines and conflict in small work groups. *Journal of Organizational Behavior*, *31*, 1032–1054.

Chrobot-Mason, D., Ruderman, M. N., Weber, T. J., & Ernst, C. (2009). The challenge of leading on unstable ground: Triggers that activate social identity faultlines. *Human Relations*, *62*, 1763–1794.

Cox, T. H., Lobel, S. A., & Mcleod, P. L. (1991). Effects of ethnic group cultural differences on cooperative and competitive behavior on a group task. *Academy of Management Journal*, *34*, 827–847.

Crisp, R. J. & Hewstone, M. (2000). Crossed categorization and intergroup bias: The moderating roles of intergroup and affective context. *Journal of Experimental Social Psychology*, *36*, 357–383.

Cunningham, G. B. (2004). Strategies for transforming the possible negative effects of group diversity. *Quest*, *56*, 421–438.

De Dreu, C. K. W. (2007). Cooperative outcome interdependence, task reflexivity, and group effectiveness: A motivated information processing perspective. *Journal of Applied Psychology*, *92*, 628–638.

De Poel, F. (2011). *Making a difference: About the underlying mechanisms of effective leadership in a change-oriented organizational context* (doctoral dissertation). Retrieved from http://irs.ub.rug.nl/ppn/335091563.

Doise, W. (1978). *Groups and individuals*. Cambridge: Cambridge University Press.

Earley, P. C. & Mosakowski, E. (2000). Creating hybrid team cultures: An empirical test of transnational team functioning. *Academy of Management Journal*, *43*, 26–49.

Ely, R. J. & Thomas, D. A. (2001). Cultural diversity at work: The effects of diversity perspectives on work group processes and outcomes. *Administrative Science Quarterly*, *46*, 229–273.

Ensari, N. (2001). How can managers reduce intergroup conflict at a workplace? Social-psychological approach to prejudice in organizations. *The Psychologist-Manager Journal*, *5*, 83–93.

Ensari, N. & Miller, N. (2001). Decategorization and the reduction of bias in the crossed categorization paradigm. *European Journal of Social Psychology*, *31*, 193–216.

Ensari, N. K. & Miller, N. (2006). The application of the personalization model in diversity management. *Group Processes & Intergroup Relations*, *9*, 589–607.

Flache, A. & Mäs, M. (2008). Why do faultlines matter? A computational model of how strong demographic faultlines undermine team cohesion. *Simulation Modelling Practice and Theory*, *16*, 175–191.

Flynn, F. J. (2005). Having an open mind: The impact of openness to experience on interracial attitudes and impression formation. *Journal of Personality and Social Psychology*, *88*, 816–826.

Gaertner, S. L. & Dovidio, J. F. (2000). *Reducing intergroup bias: The Common Ingroup Identity Model*. Philadelphia, PA: Psychology Press.

Gaertner, S. L., Mann, J. A., Murrell, A. J., & Dovidio, J. F. (1989). Reduction of intergroup bias: The benefits of recategorization. *Journal of Personality and Social Psychology*, *57*, 239–249.

Gaertner, S. L., Dovidio, J. F., Anastasio, P. A., Bachman, B. A., & Rust, M. C. (1993). The common ingroup identity model: Recategorization and the reduction of intergroup bias. In W. Stroebe & M. Hewstone (Eds.), *European Review of Social Psychology* (Vol. 4, pp. 1–26). London, UK: Wiley.

Gibson, C. & Vermeulen, F. (2003). A healthy divide: Subgroups as a stimulus for team learning behavior. *Administrative Science Quarterly, 48*, 202–239.

Gratton, L., Voigt, A., & Erickson, T. (2007). Bridging faultlines. *MIT Sloan Management Review*.

Greer, L. L., Homan, A. C., De Hoogh, A. H. B., & Den Hartog, D. N. (2012). Tainted visions: The effect of visionary leader behaviors and leader categorization tendencies on the financial performance of ethnically diverse teams. *Journal of Applied Psychology, 97*, 203–213.

Gruenfeld, D. H., Mannix, E. A., Williams, K. Y., & Neale, M. A. (1996). Group composition and decision making: How member familiarity and information distribution affect process and performance. *Organizational Behavior and Human Decision Processes, 67*, 1–15.

Hambrick, D. C. (2005). Factional groups: A new vantage on demographic faultlines, conflict, and disintegration in work teams. *Academy of Management Journal, 48*, 794–813.

Harrison, D. A. & Humphrey, S. E. (2010). Designing for diversity or diversity for design? Tasks, interdependence, and within-unit differences at work. *Journal of Organizational Behavior, 31*, 328–337.

Harrison, D. A., Price, K. H., Gavin, J. H., & Florey, A. T. (2002). Time, teams, and task performance: Changing effects of surface- and deep-level diversity on group functioning. *Academy of Management Journal, 45*, 1029–1045.

Haslam, S. A. (2001). *Psychology in organizations: The social identity approach*. London: Sage.

Hewstone, M., Rubin, M., & Willis, H. (2002). Intergroup bias. *Annual Review of Psychology, 53*, 575–604.

Homan, A. C. & Jehn, K. A. (2010). How leaders can make diverse groups less difficult: The role of attitudes and perceptions of diversity. In S. Schuman (Ed.), *Handbook for working with difficult groups* (pp. 311–322). Hoboken, NJ: Jossey-Bass.

Homan, A. C. & Greer, L. L. (2013). Considering diversity: The positive effects of considerate leadership in diverse teams. *Group Processes & Intergroup Relations, 16*, 105–125.

Homan, A. C., Van Knippenberg, D., Van Kleef, G. A., & De Dreu, C. K. (2007a). Bridging faultlines by valuing diversity: Diversity beliefs, information elaboration, and performance in diverse work groups. *Journal of Applied Psychology, 92*, 1189–1199.

Homan, A. C., Van Knippenberg, D., Van Kleef, G. A., & De Dreu, C. K. (2007b). Interacting dimensions of diversity: Cross-categorization and the functioning of diverse work groups. *Group Dynamics: Theory, Research, and Practice, 11*, 79–94.

Homan, A. C., Greer, L. L., Jehn, K. A., & Koning, L. (2010). Believing shapes seeing: The impact of diversity beliefs on the construal of group composition. *Group Processes & Intergroup Relations, 13*, 477–493.

Homan, A. C., Hollenbeck, J. R., Humphrey, S. E., Van Knippenberg, D., Ilgen, D. R., & Van Kleef, G. A. (2008). Facing differences with an open mind: Openness to experience, salience of intragroup differences, and performance of diverse work groups. *Academy of Management Journal, 51*, 1204–1222.

Janssens, M. & Brett, J. M. (2006). Cultural intelligence in global teams: A fusion model of collaboration. *Group and Organization Management, 31*, 124–153.

Jehn, K. A. & Bezrukova, K. (2010). The faultline activation process and the effects of activated faultlines on coalition formation, conflict, and group outcomes. *Organizational Behavior and Human Decision Processes, 112*, 24–42.

Jehn, K. A., Northcraft, G. B., & Neale, M. A. (1999). Why differences make a difference: A field study of diversity, conflict, and performance in workgroups. *Administrative Science Quarterly, 44*, 741–763.

Kearney, E. & Gebert, D. (2009). Managing diversity and enhancing team outcomes: The promise of transformational leadership. *Journal of Applied Psychology, 94*, 77–89.

Kooij-de Bode, H. J., Van Knippenberg, D., & Van Ginkel, W. P. (2008). Ethnic diversity and distributed information in group decision making: The importance of information elaboration. *Group Dynamics: Theory, Research, and Practice, 12*, 307.

Kossek, E. E. & Zonia, S. C. (1993). Assessing diversity climate: A field study of reactions to employer efforts to promote diversity. *Journal of Organizational Behavior, 14*, 61–81.

Kozlowski, S. W. J. & Bell, B. S. (2003). Work groups and teams in organizations. In W. C. Borman & D. R. Ilgen (Eds.), *Handbook of psychology: Industrial and organizational psychology* (Vol. 12, pp. 333–375). New York: Wiley.

Kunze, F. & Bruch, H. (2010). Age-based faultlines and perceived productive energy: The moderation of transformational leadership. *Small Group Research, 41*, 593–620.

Lau, D. C. & Murnighan, J. K. (1998). Demographic diversity and faultlines: The compositional dynamics of organizational groups. *Academy of Management Review, 23*, 325–340.

Lau, D. C. & Murnighan, J. K. (2005). Interactions within groups and subgroups: The effects of demographic faultlines. *Academy of Management Journal, 48*, 645–659.

Marcus-Newhall, A., Miller, N., Holtz, R., & Brewer, M. B. (1993). Cross-cutting category membership with role assignment: A means of reducing intergroup bias. *British Journal of Social Psychology, 32*, 125–146.

Mathieu, J., Maynard, M. T., Rapp, T., & Gilson, L. (2008). Team effectiveness 1997–2007: A review of recent advancements and a glimpse into the future. *Journal of Management, 34*, 410–476.

Meyer, B. & Schermuly, C. C. (2012). When beliefs are not enough: Examining the interaction of diversity faultlines, task motivation, and diversity beliefs on team performance. *European Journal of Work and Organizational Psychology, 21*, 456–487.

Meyer, B., Shemla, M., & Schermuly, C. C. (2011). Social category salience moderates the effect of diversity faultlines on information elaboration. *Small Group Research, 42*, 257–282.

Migdal, M. J., Hewstone, M., & Mullen, B. (1998). The effects of crossed categorization on intergroup evaluations: A meta-analysis. *British Journal of Social Psychology, 37*, 303–324.

Mohammed, S. & Angell, L. C. (2004). Surface- and deep-level diversity in workgroups: Examining the moderating effects of team orientation and team process on relationship conflict. *Journal of Organizational Behavior, 25*, 1015–1039.

Molleman, E. (2005). Diversity in demographic characteristics, abilities and personality traits: Do faultlines affect team functioning?. *Group Decision and Negotiation*, *14*, 173–193.

Nishii, L. H. & Goncalo, J. A. (2008). Demographic faultlines and creativity in diverse groups. *Research on Managing Groups and Teams*, *11*, 1–26.

Oakes, P. J. (1987). The salience of social categories. In J. C. Turner, M. A. Hogg, P. J. Oakes, S. D. Reicher, & M. S. Wetherell (Eds.), *Rediscovering the social group: A self-categorization theory*. Oxford: Basil Blackwell.

Oakes, P. & Turner, J. C. (1986). Distinctiveness and the salience of social category memberships: Is there an automatic perceptual bias towards novelty?. *European Journal of Social Psychology*, *16*, 325–344.

Pearsall, M. J., Ellis, A. P., & Evans, J. M. (2008). Unlocking the effects of gender faultlines on team creativity: Is activation the key? *Journal of Applied Psychology*, *93*, 225.

Polzer, J. T., Milton, L. P. & Swann, W. B., Jr. (2002). Capitalizing on diversity: Interpersonal congruence in small work groups. *Administrative Science Quarterly*, *47*, 296–324.

Polzer, J. T., Crisp, C. B., Jarvenpaa, S. L., & Kim, J. W. (2006). Extending the faultline model to geographically dispersed teams: How colocated subgroups can impair group functioning. *Academy of Management Journal*, *49*, 679–692.

Rico, R., Molleman, E., Sánchez-Manzanares, M., & Van der Vegt, G. S. (2007). The effects of diversity faultlines and team task autonomy on decision quality and social integration. *Journal of Management*, *33*, 111–132.

Rico, R., Sánchez-Manzanares, M., Antino, M., & Lau, D. (2012). Bridging team faultlines by combining task role assignment and goal structure strategies. *Journal of Applied Psychology*, *97*, 407.

Rink, F. A. & Jehn, K. A. (2010). How identity processes affect faultline perceptions and the functioning of diverse teams. In R. Crisp (Ed.), *Psychology of social and cultural diversity*: 281–296. Malden, MA: Wiley-Blackwell.

Riordan, C. M. (2000). Relational demography within groups: Past developments, contradictions, and new directions. In G. R. Ferris (Ed.), *Research in personnel and human resources management* (Vol. 19, pp. 131–173). Greenwich, CT: JAI Press.

Roberge, M. É. & Van Dick, R. (2010). Recognizing the benefits of diversity: When and how does diversity increase group performance? *Human Resource Management Review*, *20*, 295–308.

Rockmann, K. W., Pratt, M. G., & Northcraft, G. B. (2007). Divided loyalties— Determinants of identification in interorganizational teams. *Small Group Research*, *38*, 727–751.

Rupert, J., Jehn, K. A., & Homan, A. C. (2013). *Error culture in diverse teams: Do faultline teams benefit more?* Manuscript under review.

Sawyer, J. E., Houlette, M. A., & Yeagley, E. L. (2006). Decision performance and diversity structure: Comparing faultlines in convergent, crosscut, and racially homogeneous groups. *Organizational Behavior and Human Decision Processes*, *99*(1), 1–15.

Schippers, M. C., Den Hartog, D. N., Koopman, P. L., & Wienk, J. A. (2003). Diversity and team outcomes: The moderating effects of outcome interdependence and group longevity and the mediating effect of reflexivity. *Journal of Organizational Behavior*, *24*, 779–802.

Shamir, B., House, R. J., & Arthur, M. B. (1993). The motivational effects of charismatic leadership: A self-concept based theory. *Organization Science, 4,* 577–594.

Sherif, M. (1958). Superordinate goals in the reduction of intergroup conflict. *American Journal of Sociology, 63,* 349–356.

Shin, A. J. & Zhou, J. (2007). When is educational specialization heterogeneity related to creativity in research and development teams? Transformational leadership as a moderator. *Journal of Applied Psychology, 92,* 1709–1721.

Strauss, J. P., Connerley, M. L., & Ammermann, P. A. (2003). The "Threat Hypothesis," personality, and attitudes toward diversity. *Journal of Applied Behavioral Science, 39,* 32–52.

Swann, W. B., Jr., Kwan, V. S. Y., Polzer, J. T., & Milton, L. P. (2003). Fostering group identification and creativity in diverse groups: The role of individuation and self-verification. *Personality and Social Psychology Bulletin, 29,* 1396–1406.

Thatcher, S. & Patel, P. C. (2011). Demographic faultlines: A meta-analysis of the literature. *Journal of Applied Psychology, 96,* 1119–1139.

Thatcher, S. & Patel, P. C. (2012). Group faultlines: A review, integration, and guide to future research. *Journal of Management, 38,* 969–1009.

Thatcher, S. M., Jehn, K. A., & Zanutto, E. (2003). Cracks in diversity research: The effects of diversity faultlines on conflict and performance. *Group Decision and Negotiation, 12,* 217–241.

Timmerman, T. A. (2000). Racial diversity, age diversity, interdependence, and team performance. *Small Group Research, 31,* 592–606.

Tuggle, C. S., Schnatterly, K., & Johnson, R. A. (2010). Attention patterns in the boardroom: How board composition and processes affect discussion on entrepreneurial issues. *Academy of Management Journal, 53,* 550–571.

Turner, J. C., Hogg, M. A., Oakes, P. J., Reicher, S. D., & Wetherell, M. S. (1987). *Rediscovering the social group: A self-categorization theory.* Oxford, UK: Blackwell.

Van der Kamp, M., Tjemkes, B., & Jehn, K. (2012, June). *The rise and fall of subgroups and conflict in teams: Faultline activation and deactivation.* Paper presented at the 25th Annual Conference International Association for Conflict Management (IACM), Spier, South-Africa (Available at SSRN: http://ssrn.com/abstract=2084738 or http://dx.doi.org/10.2139/ssrn.2084738).

Van der Vegt, G. S. & Janssen, O. (2003). Joint impact of interdependence and group diversity on innovation. *Journal of Management, 29,* 729–751.

Van der Vegt, G. S. & Van de Vliert, E. (2005). Effects of perceived skill dissimilarity and task interdependence on helping in work teams. *Journal of Management, 31,* 73–89.

Van der Vegt, G. S., Van de Vliert, E., & Oosterhof, A. (2003). Informational dissimilarity and organizational citizenship behavior: The role of intrateam interdependence and team identification. *Academy of Management Journal, 46,* 715–727.

Van der Zee, K. I. & Van Oudenhoven, J. P. (2000). Psychometric qualities of the Multicultural Personality Questionnaire: A multidimensional instrument of multicultural effectiveness. *European Journal of Personality, 14,* 291–309.

Van der Zee, K. I., Paulus, P., Vos, M., & Parthasarathy, N. (2009). The impact of group composition and attitudes towards diversity on anticipated outcomes of diversity in groups. *Group Processes & Intergroup Relations, 12,* 257–280.

Van Dick, R., Van Knippenberg, D., Hagele, S., Guillaume, Y., & Brodbeck, F. (2008). Group diversity and group identification: The moderating role of diversity beliefs. *Human Relations, 61,* 1463–1492.

Van Knippenberg, D. (2003). Intergroup relations in organizations. In M. West, D. Tjosvold, & K. G. Smith (Eds.), *International handbook of organizational teamwork and cooperative working* (pp. 381–399). Chichester, UK: Wiley.

Van Knippenberg, D. & Haslam, S. A. (2003). Realizing the diversity dividend: Exploring the subtle interplay between identity, ideology, and reality. In S. A. Haslam, D. van Knippenberg, M. J. Platow, & N. Ellemers (Eds.), *Social identity at work: Developing theory for organizational practice* (pp. 61–77). New York: Psychology Press.

Van Knippenberg, D. & Schippers, M. C. (2007). Work group diversity. *Annual Review of Psychology, 58*, 515–541.

Van Knippenberg, D. & Sitkin, S. B. (2013). A critical assessment of charismatic-transformational leadership research: Back to the drawing board? *Academy of Management Annals.*

Van Knippenberg, D., De Dreu, C. K. W., & Homan, A. C. (2004). Work group diversity and group performance: An integrative model and research agenda. *Journal of Applied Psychology, 89*, 1008.

Van Knippenberg, D., Haslam, S. A., & Platow, M. J. (2007). Unity through diversity: Value-in-diversity beliefs as moderator of the relationship between work group diversity and group identification. *Group Dynamics, 11*, 207–222.

Van Knippenberg, D., Van Ginkel, W. P., & Homan, A. C. (2013). Diversity mindsets and the performance of diverse teams. *Organizational Behavior and Human Decision Processes, 121*, 183–193.

Van Knippenberg, D., Dawson, J. F., West, M. A., & Homan, A. C. (2011). Diversity faultlines, shared objectives, and top management team performance. *Human Relations, 64*, 307–336.

Wageman, R. (1995). Interdependence and Group Effectiveness. *Administrative Science Quarterly, 40*, 145–180.

Wageman, R. & Baker, G. (1999). Incentives and cooperation: The joint effects of task and reward interdependence on group performance. *Journal of Organizational Behavior, 18*, 139–158.

Wenzel, M., Mummendey, A., & Waldzus, S. (2007). Superordinate identities and intergroup conflict: The ingroup projection model. *European Review of Social Psychology, 18*, 331–372.

Wilder, D. A. (1978). Reduction of intergroup discrimination through individuation of the outgroup. *Journal of Personality and Social Psychology, 36*, 1361–1374.

Wilder, D. A. (1981). Perceiving persons as a group: Categorization and intergroup relations. In D. L. Hamilton (Ed.), *Cognitive processes in stereotyping and intergroup behavior*. Hillsdale, NJ: Erlbaum.

Williams, K. Y. & O'Reilly, C. A. (1998). Demography and diversity in organizations. *Research in Organizational Behavior, 20*, 77–140.

Williams, H. M., Parker, S. K., & Turner, N. (2007). Perceived dissimilarity and perspective taking in work teams. *Group and Organization Management, 32*, 569–597.

Wit, A. P. & Kerr, N. L. (2002). "Me versus just us versus us all" categorization and cooperation in nested social dilemmas. *Journal of Personality and Social Psychology, 83*, 616–637.

Yukl, G. A. (2010). *Leadership in organizations* (7th ed.). Upper Saddle River, NJ: Pearson.

Zander, L. & Butler, C. L. (2010). Leadership modes: Success strategies for multi-cultural teams. *Scandinavian Journal of Management, 26,* 258–267.

Zanutto, E. L., Bezrukova, K., & Jehn, K. A. (2011). Revisiting faultline conceptualization: Measuring faultline strength and distance. *Quality and Quantity, 45,* 701–714.

Zellmer-Bruhn, M. E., Maloney, M. M., Bhappu, A. D., & Salvador, R. B. (2008). When and how do differences matter? An exploration of perceived similarity in teams. *Organizational Behavior and Human Decision Processes, 107,* 41–59.

9 Individuals in the diverse workplace

The role of personality[1]

Jan Pieter van Oudenhoven, Karen van der Zee, and Paul B. Paulus

Nations across the world are increasingly interconnected. The world is becoming our homeland. As a result, at work, at school, and in their private lives, individuals have to be able to deal effectively with cultural differences. Dealing effectively with cultural differences will also be referred to as "intercultural success" in this chapter. Individual differences seem to be an important predictor of how successful individuals are in actually dealing with intercultural situations (e.g. Huang et al., 2005; Shaffer et al., 2006). Personality not only determines the perception of intercultural situations as threatening or not, but it also influences whether individuals are capable of constructive behavioral reactions to such situations (Connor-Smith & Flachsbart, 2007). In this chapter we discuss the role of individual differences for effectiveness in intercultural encounters at work. We will focus on three categories of individual difference variables, namely intercultural traits, attachment styles, and attitudes towards diversity. The three categories represent different theoretical and empirical paradigms (see also Van der Zee & Van Oudenhoven, in press). Intercultural traits are connected to personality psychology and the Big Five area of research, in particular. Attachment styles refer to a robust concept from developmental psychology, which also promises to be an interesting predictor of adults' well-being in intercultural situations. Finally, attitudes towards diversity at work are obviously related to organizational psychology.

In contemporary cross-cultural research, different terms are used to define the concept of intercultural effectiveness or intercultural success, although considerable overlap exists in such definitions. Vulpe et al. (2001) define an interculturally effective person as someone who is able to live contentedly and to work successfully in another country. A disadvantage of their definition is that it restricts the definition of success to individuals moving from one country to another. Hammer et al. (2003) define intercultural effectiveness more broadly in terms of the ability to communicate effectively in intercultural situations and to perform appropriately in a variety of cultural contexts. Taking a comparable approach, Van der Zee and Van Oudenhoven (2000) define intercultural success as effectiveness in the fields of professional performance, personal adjustment, and intercultural interactions. This definition is derived from the three-dimensional view of expatriate adjustment proposed by Black et al. (1991) and will be the guiding principle of intercultural success in this chapter. Individuals may have stable characteristics that enable them to deal effectively with cultural differences. We call these characteristics "intercultural traits."

Intercultural traits and intercultural success

The relevance of personality to intercultural success in a work context has widely been documented in research on expatriate success (Caligiuri, 2000; Huang et al., 2005; Shaffer et al., 1999; Ward et al., 2004). A majority of this work relies on the Big Five general personality traits: Extraversion, Agreeableness, Conscientiousness, Emotional Stability, and Intellect/Autonomy/ Openness to Experience. For example, Caligiuri (2000) showed that expatriates with high scores on extraversion, agreeableness, and emotional stability were less likely to terminate their assignment, and conscientiousness predicted supervisor-rated success of performance. Openness to experience appeared to be an important predictor of professional effectiveness, and extraversion and agreeableness were related to constructive intercultural relations.

The Big Five Model is a general model of personality. In our own work we distinguish five dimensions that are specifically defined in relation to intercultural situations: cultural empathy, open-mindedness, social initiative, emotional stability, and flexibility (Van der Zee & Van Oudenhoven, 2000, 2001). *Cultural empathy* is the ability to empathize with the thoughts, behaviors, and feelings of culturally different individuals. It includes an affective component, referring to the expression of warmth in interpersonal relations, as well as a cognitive component, indicating the ability to read the meaning behind another person's verbal and nonverbal expressions. *Open-mindedness* refers to an open and unprejudiced attitude towards culturally different individuals and towards different cultural norms and values. *Social initiative* is related to approaching social situations in an active manner and taking initiatives. *Emotional stability* is the tendency to remain calm versus a tendency to show strong emotional reactions under stressful circumstances. *Flexibility* is the tendency to approach unknown situations as a challenge and the ability to adapt one's behavior to the expectations of novel and ambiguous situations. Three of these five dimensions are substantially related to Big Five traits: Open-mindedness to Intellect/Autonomy/ Openness to Experience; Social Initiative to Extraversion; and both models include Emotional Stability.

Empirical evidence suggests that these intercultural traits indeed predict successful intercultural adjustment of employees (Brinkmann & Van der Zee, 1999; Van der Zee, Atsma et al., 2004; Van der Zee et al., 2003), expatriates (Peltokorpi, 2008; Van Oudenhoven et al., 2003), and international students (Leong, 2007; Van Oudenhoven & Van der Zee, 2002), and that they are better predictors of intercultural adjustment than the Big Five (Van der Zee et al., 2003) and self-efficacy (Van Oudenhoven & Van der Zee, 2002). For example, Peltokorpi (2008) investigated expatriates in Japan and found that emotional stability and cultural empathy were related to psychological adjustment, intercultural interactions and professional effectiveness. A longitudinal study of Leong (2007), who investigated undergraduate international exchange students, reported that social initiative was related to social-cultural and psychological adjustment. This is in line with research of Van Oudenhoven et al. (2003) who found social initiative to be a strong predictor of psychological well-being among Western expatriates in Taiwan.

Intercultural traits and acculturation

Intercultural traits have also been linked to acculturation strategies. On a society level, four acculturation strategies have been distinguished that reflect the orientation of migrants towards the majority group: integration, assimilation, separation, and marginalization (Berry, 1997). Integrating migrants maintain their own culture and at the same time engage in contacts with the majority group. Assimilating migrants also regard contact with the dominant group as important but do not stick to their original culture. Separating migrants stick to their own culture, but do not value contact with the majority group. Marginalizing migrants, finally, neither try to maintain their original culture nor to adopt the dominant culture. Interestingly, high scores on intercultural traits seem to be related to a preference for integration among immigrants (e.g. Bakker et al., 2006). Research on immigrants shows that integration is most consistently associated with immigrants' well-being (Berry, 1997). Specifically relevant to the topic of this volume, the link between intercultural traits and acculturation preferences has also been studied in a work context: A study by Luijters et al. (2006) suggests that employees high in emotional stability show a preference for integration. Apparently, emotionally stable individuals are more capable of dealing with the conflicting demands of two cultures.

Stress-buffering versus social-perceptual intercultural traits

Van der Zee and Van Oudenhoven (in press) provide a theoretical explanation as to why the five intercultural traits may contribute to intercultural effectiveness (see also Van der Zee, Van Oudenhoven et al., 2004; Van der Zee & Van der Gang, 2007). They argue that intercultural traits can be divided into two higher-order factors consisting of stress-buffering traits and social-perceptual traits. These two factors seem to correspond to two higher-order factors of Big Five traits (Stability and Plasticity) distinguished by De Young (2006). On the one hand, stress-buffering traits protect against loss of control, uncertainty, and adversity in intercultural settings. Imagine, for example, the Asian-American supervisor in the United States who is confronted with employees who openly criticize him. Their behavior will evoke strong feelings of uncertainty and discomfort. Stress-buffering traits such as emotional stability and flexibility may promote intercultural effectiveness because they protect against such negative feelings. Social-perceptual traits on the other hand, make individuals feel challenged by the social and cognitive opportunities of intercultural situations. Consider a group of employees in an intercultural team. The literature has repeatedly stressed the potential of such diverse groups to be more creative and to generate better decisions (e.g. Mannix & Neale, 2005; Nemeth & Nemeth-Brown, 2003; Van Knippenberg et al., 2004). With more available perspectives on a situation, there is a greater potential for finding the "right solution" or for generating unconventional approaches. However, such outcomes are not inevitably reached in diverse workgroups. It requires careful listening to the various points of view that are present and opening oneself up to different perspectives and contacts with those group members who do not share the same norms and values. The intercultural traits of cultural empathy, open-mindedness, and social initiative seem to predispose individuals to approach and benefit from differences.

The novelty of input that is present in an intercultural work environment may provide opportunities for learning (e.g. Austin, 1997). Confrontation with new and different perspectives seems to evoke more thorough and active modes of information processing. This is reminiscent of the minority influence literature which suggests that exposure to minority perspectives can under some conditions lead to changes in opinions. Again, social-perceptual traits, and in particular open-mindedness, may predispose individuals to use novelty of input for learning rather than avoid or disregard such input.

The implication of the differential function of stress-buffering traits and social-perceptual traits is that these traits may be beneficial under different circumstances. In two laboratory studies on responses to diversity Van der Zee, Van Oudenhoven et al. (2004) and Van der Zee and Van der Gang (2007) found that, in the presence of threat, stress-buffering traits protected individuals from negative responses to diversity, but social-perceptual traits did not provide this protection. When no threat was present, the social-perceptual trait of social initiative facilitated positive responses to a diverse work setting, whereas the stress-buffering trait of emotional stability did not affect the responses (Van der Zee & Van der Gang, 2007).

Intercultural traits and stages of adjustment

The distinction between stress-buffering versus social-perceptual functions of traits also points to the potential *relevance of time*. The relevance of time for intercultural adjustment has largely been neglected in the organizational diversity literature (see for exceptions, for example, Watson et al., 1993) but received considerable attention in work on adjustment of sojourners. The adjustment of sojourners has been described as a U-shaped curve. Following a short 'honeymoon' period of high adjustment characterized by excitement about the new experience, feelings of frustration, anxiety and loneliness take over (Black et al., 1991; Oberg, 1960). This phase is usually referred to as culture shock, which is assumed to end approximately eight months after arrival in a new cultural environment. In the period that follows, sojourners gradually learn to cope with the new circumstances and their well-being increases. Hofstede and Hofstede (2005) refer to this phase as 'acculturation'. They describe this phase as one in which the sojourner has gradually learned to function under the new conditions, has adopted some of the local values, finds increased self-confidence and becomes integrated in a new social network. The phase lasts approximately one to two years and ends in a period of mastery in which a stable state of mind is reached (Black et al., 1991; Hofstede & Hofstede, 2005).

In an intercultural work context, however, the honeymoon phase does not really apply, because one is confronted with daily contacts and practical demands from the very first day. Besides this work-related point, the honeymoon phase has been a topic of debate in general (e.g. Ward et al., 1998). Nowadays traveling has become much less expensive, and the internet has created many forms of direct and cheap communication with the country of origin (Van Oudenhoven & Ward, 2013). However, it does make sense to assume that in an intercultural work setting an initial period of culture shock is followed by cultural learning, ending in a sense of mastery both at the level of individual employees and at the team level. Consistent with the idea that "culture shock" is characteristic of the first phase of adjustment, in a study among international students we found that emotional stability appeared to be particularly helpful in the first phase of adjustment and social-perceptual traits in later phases of adjustment (Van Oudenhoven & Van der Zee, 2002). As we have argued, the latter traits may particularly facilitate cultural learning.

Intercultural traits and coping with identity threat

Intercultural traits may also protect individuals against the challenge that intercultural settings pose to one's identity (Van der Zee & Van Oudenhoven, 2014). The five intercultural traits differ in the extent to which they are helpful in identifying with a foreign culture or in switching between one's original and the host culture identity. With respect to the ability to switch between identities, Brewer and Miller and colleagues introduced the construct of identity complexity (e.g. Miller et al., 2009; Roccas & Brewer, 2002). Individuals with complex identities define themselves in terms of multiple group memberships (e.g. being Chinese, a liberal, and a dentist) rather than in terms of one dominant identity (e.g. primarily being Chinese). Individuals with complex identities are better able to connect with others regardless of background and tend to be tolerant towards different cultures. The five intercultural traits may help in the development of more complex identities in which elements of the old and the new culture are integrated (e.g. Miller et al. 2009).

As an expression of a complex identity, Benet-Martinez and colleagues introduced the term *biculturalism*. Their research suggests that *biculturalism* is relevant for indicators of intercultural competence such as developing cross-group social networks, well-being, and achievement (Benet-Martinez, in press). Biculturals are individuals whose self-label reflects their cultural dualism and who are able to move easily between both cultural orientations (Benet-Martinez et al., 2002). Research has supported the role of general traits like neuroticism and openness to experience as antecedents of biculturalism (Nguyen & Benet-Martinez, 2007). Individuals high on neuroticism are more inclined to perceive a clash between their native and host culture, and individuals high in openness tend to perceive a smaller distance between native and host culture (Benet-Martinez & Haritatos, 2005; Nguyen & Benet-Martinez, 2007). The concept of biculturalism is somehow related to that of *dual identity* (Gaertner et al., 2000). Having a dual identity, consisting of identifying with the own ethnic or cultural group (e.g. Mexican-Americans) in combination with developing a common in-group (e.g. Americans), has a positive effect of reducing intergroup biases.

Stress-buffering traits may also be helpful for immigrants integrating and defining their identity in a work setting. They may help to protect themselves against identity threat by refraining from making their cultural identity salient. Living with different identities can be stressful as the tension between norms linked to each identity may give rise to role conflict (Gaertner et al., 1994). Individuals who seek contacts with the new culture but also clearly define and present themselves as members of their cultural background probably encounter more diversity-related stress (Van Oudenhoven & Eisses, 1998). Emotionally stable individuals seem better equipped to deal with this kind of stress. Social-perceptual traits primarily seem to reinforce identification with the new culture (Van der Zee, Van Oudenhoven et al., 2004; Van der Zee & Van der Gang, 2007), which may foster the emergence of a complex identity. So far, empirical evidence to support this claim is scarce. An exception is a study by Swagler and LaRae (2005) showing that emotional stability is related to better psychological adjustment and extraversion is positively related to socio-cultural adjustment. Further support comes from the study by Luijters et al. (2006) in a work setting. They confronted culturally different employees with a description of a fellow employee from a minority group who was either assimilating or integrating. This study showed that employees scoring low on emotional stability preferred assimilation over integration. Future studies are needed to shed further light on this relationship.

Attachment styles

Attachment theory has been related to a host of psychological phenomena but, strangely enough, only very rarely to intercultural adjustment. That is remarkable because attachment theory refers to interaction with unknown others and exploration of new social environments. Therefore attachment styles seem obvious candidates as predictors of intercultural effectiveness. Attachment theory deals with the way individuals have been taught to approach others, and attachment styles influence the way people approach unknown individuals in new situations (Cassidy & Shaver, 1999). Four adult attachment styles can be distinguished. The *secure* attachment style is characterized by a positive model of self and a positive model of others. The *preoccupied* attachment style indicates a feeling of unworthiness of oneself, combined with a positive evaluation of others. The *dismissive* attachment style is characterized by a positive model of self and a negative one of others. Lastly, the *fearful* attachment style is characterized by a negative model of the self and of the other (Bartholomew & Horowitz, 1991). In general, research suggests that a secure attachment style is related to more cognitive openness (Mikulincer, 1997) and a less negative reaction towards out-group targets (Mikulincer & Shaver, 2001).

A few studies have explicitly investigated the relation between attachment styles and adjustment in a new culture. They show that differences in attachment styles may facilitate adaptation to new cultures. For example, a study by Handojo (2000) revealed that securely attached Chinese-Indonesian immigrants in the USA had fewer problems relating to American culture as compared to insecurely attached immigrants. Research by De Pater et al. (2003) among expatriates found a secure attachment style to be positively related to the number of close contacts with locals. In a large study among Dutch immigrants in Canada, the USA, Europe, Australia, New Zealand, and some other countries, Bakker et al. (2004) also reported a positive relation between secure attachment and social relationships, and a negative relationship between insecure styles and social relationships in the host culture. Finally, in a study among Chinese, Surinamese, and Turkish immigrants, and among majority members in the Netherlands, Van Oudenhoven and Hofstra (2006) found that both immigrants and majority members preferred integration as acculturation strategy. Immigrants with a dismissive attachment style had a preference for separation.

We are currently exploring in culturally diverse organizational contexts how attachment styles, intercultural traits, and self-esteem affect the trust that employees have in their colleagues, their supervisor, and their organization. In general, data suggest that a positive self-esteem, a secure attachment style, and open-mindedness help employees to develop trust in their colleagues, supervisor, and organization (Wöhrle et al., 2014). However, there are some subtle differences between first-generation immigrants on the one hand and majority members and second-generation immigrants on the other hand. For majority members and second-generation immigrants, who have lived their whole life in the Netherlands, a secure attachment style seems to be most important for interpersonal trust. In contrast, for first-generation immigrants self-esteem may be most helpful for interpersonal trust. Possibly, first-generation immigrants experience more stress in daily interactions with colleagues than those who have lived their whole life in the country of settlement. Self-esteem may thus have a stress-buffering function for the first-generation immigrants. For majority members and second-generation immigrants, daily interactions in a cultural context that is highly familiar may evoke less feelings of uncertainty, as they have well-developed schemas for such situations. For this group of employees who more easily 'feel at home', a secure attachment makes them open up to all parties involved. It is tempting to further test this speculation. In sum, it is clear that attachment styles play a relevant role in the effects on intercultural effectiveness, but the precise mechanisms have to be more thoroughly examined.

Attitudes towards diverse work groups

Despite the growing interest in individual differences in reactions to diversity, research on individual differences in *attitudes* towards diversity in workgroups is still scarce (Van Knippenberg & Schippers, 2007). Yet, it is very plausible that attitudes towards diversity in the workplace will have an influence on the performance and affective reactions of employees. Attitudes towards diversity refer to the degree to which an individual likes working or interacting with those from different backgrounds in work contexts (e.g. Nakui et al., 2011; Van der Zee et al., 2009). In this section we discuss the role of attitudes towards diversity outcomes in a work setting.

Compared to intercultural traits and attachment styles, attitudes towards diverse workgroups probably refer to individual differences that are most strongly related to intercultural success in culturally diverse workgroups. General attitudes towards diversity at the society level also apply to the organizational level. However, because in organizations daily contacts between individuals from different cultures are inevitable, the effects of attitudes towards diversity may even be stronger than at the society level. The literature on the effects of cultural diversity on affective and productivity factors in organizations is vast and typically reports both positive and negative effects (e.g. Mannix & Neale, 2005; see also several contributions in this book). What is happening at the workplace does not remain unnoticed by employees in diverse organizations and consequently influences people's attitudes.

Once attitudes towards diversity are formed, they may be resistant to change. For example, Harrison and colleagues (2006) provide a meta-analysis showing how affirmative action programs, some of the most widely used diversity interventions, may even have an adverse impact on majority members' acceptance of diversity. However, they also mention that these negative effects may be reduced by the way in which diversity policies are communicated and justified within the organization. In this vein, we believe that, in order to create a sense of inclusion among minority employees, overcoming resistance and fostering positive attitudes towards diversity among majority members may be of crucial importance (Hofhuis et al., 2013).

Several scales have been developed to measure attitudes towards diversity in the workplace. We will explain three different scales to measure attitudes towards diversity, because diversity in organizations can have many forms and aspects. The first scale is a broad evaluative instrument; the second distinguishes the two crucial aspects (affective reactions and performance) of diversity in the workplace; and the third one tries to assess both positive and negative characteristics of the diverse organization.

De Meuse and Hostager (2001) were among the first to focus research on attitudes towards diversity. They developed the *Reaction-to-Diversity Inventory*. They wanted to develop an instrument which may be used to evaluate the effect of time and money spent on diversity programs on employees. The instrument should also be used to adapt Human Resource Development efforts to the specific needs of the participants. The instrument distinguishes five categories: Emotional reactions, judgments, behavioral reactions (corresponding with the three theoretically distinct aspects of attitudes), and personal and organizational outcomes. These categories are helpful to diagnose the effects of diversity programs in organizations. Moreover, in order to have a quick and easy measure of individual attitudes they categorized respondents into diversity optimists, diversity realists, or diversity pessimists (De Meuse & Hostager, 2001). The inventory provides a reliable and valid assessment of majority attitudes on diversity.

A decade later Van der Zee et al. (2009) and Nakui et al. (2011) developed the *Attitude toward Diverse Workgroups Scale* (ADWS) to measure two components of attitudes towards diverse workgroups, namely attitudes towards productivity and social/affective aspects of diverse workgroups. Both studies showed evidence for the existence of these two distinct components of attitudes towards diversity. Importantly, the scale shows no relation with social desirability, but is related in predictable ways to constructs such as prejudice and with the Big Five traits of agreeableness, extraversion, and openness to experience (Nakui et al., 2011). This is in line with the results of the Bouncken et al. (2008) study which also showed that being high on personality factors such as agreeableness, openness to experience, and extraversion leads to positive attitudes towards diversity within teams. Van der Zee et al. (2009) found that high scorers on the ADWS more strongly favored preferences for culturally diverse over homogeneous teams compared to low scorers who did not display a preference for diversity. Most importantly, in a study of the outcomes for actual brainstorming groups, Nakui et al. (2011) also found that high-productivity ADWS scores were related to higher quality of generated ideas in heterogeneous groups but not in homogeneous groups.

The third type of instrument is the *Benefit and Trust Diversity Scale* (BTDS; Hofhuis et al., 2013). This scale has been developed to take into account the fact that employees may be positive and negative at the same time. The BTDS enables researchers to compile a ranking of different types of threats or benefits as perceived by employees, thus providing more detailed information to its users. The BTDS can be used as an instrument to measure where in the organization resistance to diversity is likely to originate. By analyzing employees' perceptions in more detail, organizations may be able to communicate more effectively about diversity and target those employees who feel most threatened by the process of diversification. An example of a negative point may be the perception of the out-group's beliefs, values and symbols as a threat to the in-group's beliefs, values and symbols. On the positive side, the increase of *creative potential* within organizations (as discussed by Paulus and Van der Zee, this volume) may be seen as a way in which diversity can favorably influence the attitudes towards diversity.

There is not yet much empirical evidence for the BTDS, but it seems to be a promising diagnostic instrument for interventions at the individual and organizational level. Research by Hofhuis et al. (2013) provides some evidence for its construct validity because two multicultural personality traits, particularly the traits *Cultural Empathy* and *Emotional Stability*, appear to be related to perceiving benefits and threats. Cultural empathy is related to the perception of benefits, and emotional stability may serve as a buffer reducing the negative impact of diversity-related threats. As might be expected, the study also showed higher scores on diversity-related attitudes in organizations that are *open* and *appreciative* of diversity (Harquail & Cox, 1993; Luijters et al. 2007). In organizations with an *open* climate, differences are not only allowed but also discussed openly. In addition, a climate that is *appreciative* of diversity is characterized not only by a general attitude that positively values diversity but also by a willingness to exploit this diversity rather than perceiving it as a problem. Also, at the individual level, attitudes may reflect an acceptance dimension, which may in part be rooted in stress-related personality dimensions (e.g. uncertainty tolerance indicative of high emotional stability) and in an appreciation dimension related to the social perceptual traits (e.g. curiosity and positive inspiration indicative of open-mindedness). As in the case of the climate measure that Hofhuis et al. (2013) used in their study, current attitude measures may not be sensitive enough to differentiate between those two aspects. Future studies may shed further light on this hypothesis.

Conclusions and discussions

During the last decade a number of researchers have focused on the relationship between personality factors and intercultural effectiveness. In this chapter we focused on individual factors that appear to have a specific theoretical, empirical, or instrumental relation with success in intercultural settings, and in the work context, in particular. First, five intercultural traits tailored to intercultural situations have proved to be predictive for success in intercultural encounters beyond the predictive power of more general factors such as the Big Five (Van der Zee et al., 2003). Moreover, the five traits differ in their predictive value depending on the kind of situation and the phase of the intercultural contact. The distinction between stress-buffering and social-perceptual traits is of special theoretical interest here, because these traits seem to correspond to the higher-order factors, stability and plasticity, of Big Five traits. Stress-buffering traits may for instance be extra helpful for immigrant workers who are confronted with a work setting that is unfriendly to immigrants. On the other hand, social-perceptual traits may be very functional for employees who start their career in an international company. In general, intercultural traits are predictive of adjustment in diverse organizations, but to a lesser degree in culturally homogenous organizations.

Second, attachment styles, originally examined in relation to the exploration behavior of infants in the presence of their caretakers, can also be seen as personal tendencies of adult employees to approach unknown persons in unfamiliar situations. In diverse organizations employees are confronted with unknown persons and unfamiliar situations. Research shows that secure attachment, in particular, is a promising concept for the cultural diversity literature. Whereas intercultural traits may be trained to some extent, an effective strategy to enhance secure attachment is to create a secure work climate in which cultural differences are not seen as threatening (see the chapters by Huo, Binning, and Begeny, by Van der Zee and Otten, and by Otten and Jansen, in this volume).

Third, attitudes towards diversity in work groups are important predictors for performance and emotional satisfaction within culturally diverse organizations. We discussed three different instruments. The Reaction-to-Diversity Inventory offers a diagnostic evaluation of the diversity effects on employees and a simple evaluation of employees as diversity pessimists, realists, or optimists. More informative about the diversity climate of an organization is the Attitude towards Diverse Workgroups Scale, which measures attitudes towards productivity and social/affective aspects of diverse workgroups. The most recent attitude measure is the Benefit and Trust Diversity Scale (Hofhuis et al., 2013). This scale offers diagnostic information about the positive and negative aspects of diverse organizations as perceived by their employees. That information can be used to help individual employees and provide a way of improving the diversity policies of organizations. All three attitude scales appeared to be related to personality factors, which suggest that they too are stable factors to some degree.

Altogether this chapter shows that the literature on cultural diversity in organizations, and on the role of individual differences herein, has matured. We all know that individuals differ. So do organizations. Some individuals thrive in one type of organization or team, but not in other types. This chapter has made clear that it is a matter of interaction between personality-related factors and type of organization or team that makes an organization successful. Not only do we know what are the important positive and negative antecedents and consequences of a diverse workplace, but we are increasingly able to predict the effectiveness of individuals to deal with *culturally diverse work environments*. Training or selection of employees may help to get the right person with the right personality to fit into a team. On the other hand, culturally diverse organizations may be flexible enough to host different personalities.

Note

1 This chapter and related efforts were supported by a collaborative grant BCS
0729305 to the third author from the National Science Foundation, which included
support from the Deputy Director of National Intelligence for Analysis and a
collaborative CreativeIT grant 0855825 from the National Science Foundation.
Any opinions, findings, and conclusions or recommendations expressed in this
material are those of the authors and do not necessarily reflect the views of the
National Science Foundation. Runa Korde assisted in the preparation of this chapter.

References

Austin, J. R. (1997). A cognitive framework for understanding demographic influences
in groups. *International Journal of Organizational Analysis*, *5*, 342–360.

Bakker, W., Van Oudenhoven, J. P., & Van der Zee, K. I. (2004). Attachment
and emigrants' intercultural adjustment. *European Journal of Personality*, *18*,
387–404.

Bakker, W., Van der Zee, K. I., & Van Oudenhoven, J. P. (2006). Personality and
Dutch emigrants' reactions to acculturation strategies. *Journal of Applied Social
Psychology*, *12*, 2864–2891.

Bartholomew, K. & Horowitz, L. M. (1991). Attachment styles among young adults:
A test of a four category model. *Journal of Personality and Social Psychology*, *61*,
226–244.

Benet-Martínez, V. (in press). Multiculturalism: Cultural, social, and personality
processes. In K. Deaux & M. Snyder (Eds.). *Handbook of personality and social
psychology*. Oxford: Oxford University Press.

Benet-Martínez, V. & Haritatos, J. (2005). Bicultural identity integration (BII): Components and psychosocial antecedents. *Journal of Personality*, *73*, 1015–1050.

Benet-Martínez, V., Leu, J., Lee, F., & Morris, M. (2002). Negotiating biculturalism:
Cultural frame-switching in biculturals with oppositional vs. compatible cultural
identities. *Journal of Cross-Cultural Psychology*, *33*, 492–516.

Berry, J. W. (1997). Immigration, acculturation, and adaptation. *Applied Psychology:
An International Review*, *46*, 5–34.

Black, J. S., Mendenhall, M., & Oddou, G. (1991). Toward a comprehensive model
of international adjustment: An integration of multiple theoretical perspectives.
Academy of Management Review, *16*, 291–317.

Bouncken, R. B., Ratzmann, M., & Winkler, V. A. (2008). Cross-cultural innovation
teams: Effects of four types of attitudes towards diversity. *International Journal of
Business Strategy*, *8*, 26–36.

Brinkmann, U. & Van der Zee, K. I. (1999). Benchmarking intercultural training:
Is experience its biggest competitor? *Language and intercultural training*, *17*(32),
9–11.

Caligiuri, P. (2000). The big five personality characteristics as predictors of expatriates'
desire to terminate the assignment and supervisor-rated performance. *Personnel
Psychology*, *53*, 67–88.

Cassidy, J. & Shaver, P. R. (1999). *Handbook of attachment: Theory, research, and
clinical applications*. New York: Guilford Press.

Connor-Smith, J. K. & Flachsbart, C. (2007) Relations between personality and
coping: A meta-analysis. *Journal of Personality and Social Psychology*, *93*, 1080–1107.

De Meuse, K. P. & Hostager, J. T. (2001). Developing an instrument for measuring attitudes towards and perceptions of workplace diversity. An initial report. *Human Resource Development Quarterly, 12*, 33–51.

De Pater, I. E., Van Vianen, A. E. M., & Derksen, M. (2003). Het aangaan van hechte relaties en de cross-culturele aanpassing van expatriates: De rol van persoonlijkheid en hechtingsstijl [Close relationships and cross-cultural adaptation of expatriates: the role of personality and attachment style]. *Gedrag in organisaties, 16*, 89–107.

De Young, C. G. (2006). Higher-order factors of the Big Five in a multi-informant sample. *Journal of Personality and Social Psychology, 91*, 1138–1151.

Gaertner, S. L., Rust, M. C., Dovidio, J. F., Bachman, B. A., & Anastasio, P. A. (1994). The contact hypothesis: the role of a common ingroup identity on reducing intergroup bias. *Small Group Research, 25*, 224–249.

Gaertner, S. L., Dovidio, J. F., Nier, J. A., Banker, B. S., Ward, C. M., Houlette, M., & Loux, S. (2000). The common ingroup identity model for reducing intergroup bias: Progress and challenges. In Capozza, D. and Brown, R. (Eds.), *Social identity processes* (pp. 133–148). London: Sage.

Hammer, M. R., Bennett, M. J., & Wiseman, R. (2003). Measuring intercultural sensitivity: the intercultural development inventory. *International Journal of Intercultural Relations, 27*, 421–443.

Handojo,V. (2000). Attachment Styles, acculturation attitudes/behaviors, and stress among Chinese Indonesian immigrants in the United States. *Dissertation Abstracts International: Section B: The Sciences and Engineering, 61*(4B), 2271.

Harquail, C. V. & Cox, T. C. (1993). Organizational culture and acculturation. In T. Cox, Jr. *Cultural diversity in organizations. Theory, research and practice* (pp. 161–176). San Francisco: Berrett-Koehler Publishers.

Harrison, D. A., Kravitz, D. A., Mayor, D. M., Leslie, L. M., & Lev-Arey, D. (2006). Understanding attitudes towards affirmative action programs in employment: Summary and meta-analysis of 35 years of research. *Journal of Applied Psychology, 22*, 293–307.

Hofhuis, J., Van der Zee, K. I., & Otten, S. (2013). Measuring employee perception on the effects of diversification: Development of the benefits and threats of diversity scale. Manuscript under review.

Hofstede, G. J. & Hofstede, G. (2005). *Cultures in organizations. Culture's consequences.* London: McGraw-Hill.

Huang, T., Chi, S., & Lawler, J. J. (2005). The relationship between expatriates' personality traits and their adjustment to international assignments. *International Journal of Human Resource Management, 16*, 1656–1670.

Leong, C. (2007). Predictive validity of the Multicultural Personality Questionnaire: A longitudinal study on the socio-psychological adaptation of Asian undergraduates who took part in a study-abroad program. *International Journal of Intercultural Relations, 31*, 545–559.

Luijters, K., Van der Zee, K. I., & Otten, S. (2006). Acculturation strategies among ethnic minority workers and the role of intercultural personality traits. *Group Processes & Intergroup Relations, 9*, 561–575.

Luijters, K., Van der Zee, K. I., & Otten, S. (2007). Cultural diversity in organizations: Enhancing identification by valuing differences. *International Journal of Cross-cultural Relationships, 32*, 154–163.

Mannix, E. & Neale, M. A. (2005). What difference makes a difference: The promise and reality of diverse groups in organizations. *Psychological Science in the Public Interest, 6*, 31–55.

Mikulincer, M. (1997). Adult attachment style and information processing: Individual differences in curiosity and cognitive closure. *Journal of Personality and Social Psychology, 72*, 1217–1230.

Mikulincer, M. & Shaver, P. R. (2001). Attachment theory and intergroup bias: Evidence that priming the secure base schema attenuates negative reactions to out-groups. *Journal of Personality and Social Psychology, 81*, 97–115.

Miller, K. P., Brewer, M. B., & Arbuckle, N. L. (2009). Social identity complexity: Its correlates and antecedents. *Group Processes & Intergroup Relations, 12*, 79–94.

Nakui, T., Paulus, P. B., & Van der Zee, K. I. (2011). The role of attitudes in reactions to diversity in work groups. *Journal of Applied Social Psychology, 41*, 2327–2351.

Nemeth, C. J. & Nemeth-Brown, B. (2003). Better than individuals? The potential benefits of dissent and diversity for group creativity. In P. B. Paulus & B. A. Nijstad (Eds.), *Group creativity: Innovation and collaboration in groups* (pp. 63–84). New York: Oxford University Press.

Nguyen, A. D. & Benet-Martínez, V. (2007). Biculturalism unpacked: Components, measurement, individual differences, and outcomes. *Social and Personality Psychology Compass, 1*, 101–114.

Oberg, K. (1960) Culture shock: Adjustment to new culture environments. *Practical Anthropology, 7*, 177–182.

Peltokorpi, V. (2008). Cross-cultural adjustment of expatriates in Japan. *The International Journal of Human Resource Management, 19*, 1588–1606.

Roccas, S. & Brewer, M. (2002). Social identity complexity. *Personality and Social Psychology Review, 6*, 88–106.

Shaffer, M., Harrison, D., & Gilley, K. (1999). Dimensions, determinants, and differences in the expatriate adjustment process. *Journal of International Business Studies, 30*, 557–558.

Shaffer, M. A., Harrison, D. A., Gregersen, H., Black, J. S., & Ferzandi, L. A. (2006). You can take it with you: Individual differences and expatriate effectiveness. *Journal of Applied Psychology, 91*, 109–125.

Swagler, M. A. & La Rae, M. J. (2005). The effects of personality and acculturation on the adjustment of North American sojourners in Taiwan. *Journal of Counseling Psychology, 52*, 527–536.

Van der Zee, K. I. & Van Oudenhoven, J. P. (2000). Psychometric qualities of the Multicultural Personality Questionnaire: A multidimensional instrument of multicultural effectiveness. *European Journal of Personality, 14*, 291–309.

Van der Zee, K. I. & Van Oudenhoven, J. P. (2001). The Multicultural Personality Questionnaire: Reliability and validity of self- and other ratings of multicultural effectiveness. *Journal of Research in Personality, 35*, 278–288.

Van der Zee, K. I. & Van der Gang, I. (2007). Personality, threat and affective responses to cultural diversity. *European Journal of Personality, 21*, 453–470.

Van der Zee, K. I. & Van Oudenhoven, J. P. (2014). Personality and intercultural effectiveness. In V. Benet-Martinez & Y. Hong (Eds.), *Handbook of multicultural identity*. New York: Oxford University Press.

Van der Zee, K. I., Zaal, J. N., & Piekstra, J. (2003). Validation of the Multicultural Personality Questionnaire in the context of personnel selection. *European Journal of Personality, 117*, S77–S100.

Van der Zee, K., Atsma, N., Brodbeck, F. (2004). The influence of social identity and personality on outcomes of cultural diversity in teams. *Journal of Cross-Cultural Psychology, 35*, 283–303.

Van der Zee, K. I., Van Oudenhoven, J. P., & De Grijs, E. (2004). Personality, threat and cognitive and emotional reactions to intercultural situations. *Journal of Personality, 72*, 1069–1096.

Van der Zee, K. Paulus, P. B., Vos, M., & Parthasarathy, N. (2009). The impact of group composition and attitudes towards diversity on anticipated outcomes of diversity in groups. *Group Processes & Intergroup Relations, 12*, 257–280.

Van Knippenberg, D. & Schippers, M. C. (2007). Work group diversity. *Annual Review of Psychology, 58*, 515–545.

Van Knippenberg, D., De Dreu, C. K., & Homan, A. C. (2004). Work group diversity and group performance: An integrative model and research agenda. *Journal of Applied Psychology, 89*, 1008–1022.

Van Oudenhoven, J. P. & Eisses, A. M. (1998). Integration and assimilation of Moroccan immigrants in Israel and the Netherlands, *International Journal of Intercultural Relations, 22*, 293–307.

Van Oudenhoven, J. P. & Van der Zee, K. I. (2002). Predicting multicultural effectiveness of international students: The multicultural personality questionnaire. *International Journal of Intercultural Relations, 26*, 679–694.

Van Oudenhoven, J. P. & Hofstra, J. (2006). Personal reactions to "strange" situations: Attachment styles and acculturation attitudes of immigrants and majority members. *International Journal of Intercultural Relations, 30*, 783–798.

Van Oudenhoven, J. P. & Ward, C. (2013). Fading majority cultures: The implications of transnationalism and demographic changes for immigrant acculturation. *Journal of Community & Applied Social Psychology, 23*(2), 81–97.

Van Oudenhoven, J. P., Mol, S., & Van der Zee, K. I. (2003). Study of the adjustment of Western expatriates in Taiwan ROC with the multicultural personality questionnaire. *Asian Journal of Social Psychology, 6*, 159–170.

Vulpe, T., Kealey, D. J., Protheroe, D., & Macdonald, D. (2001). A profile of the interculturally effective person. Hull, Canada: Centre for Intercultural Learning, Canadian Foreign Service Institute.

Ward, C., Leong, C., & Low, M. (2004). Personality and sojourner adjustment: An exploration of the Big Five and the cultural fit proposition. *Journal of Cross-Cultural Psychology, 35*, 137–151.

Ward, C., Okura, Y., Kennedy, A., & Kojima T. (1998). The U-Curve on trial: A longitudinal study of psychological and sociocultural adjustment during cross-cultural transition. *International Journal of Intercultural Relations, 22*, 277–291.

Watson, W. E., Kumar, K., & Michaelsen, L. K. (1993). Cultural diversity's impact on interaction process and performance: Comparing homogeneous and diverse task groups. *Academy of Management Journal, 36*, 590–602.

Wöhrle, J., Van Oudenhoven, J. P., Otten, S., & Van der Zee, K. I. (2014). Personality characteristics and workplace trust of majority and minority employees in the Netherlands. *European Journal of Work and Organizational Psychology.*

Index

Note: "n" after a page number indicates a note; "f" indicates a figure; "t" indicates a table.

DATE DUE

PRINTED IN U.S.A.

Printed by PGSTL